# Victorian Literature

The CONTEMPORARY ESSAYS Series

GENERAL EDITOR: LEONARD W. LEVY

# Victorian Literature

## Selected Essays

—◄●►—

Edited by

# ROBERT O. PREYER

HARPER TORCHBOOKS ⚑ *The Academy Library*
*Harper & Row, Publishers*
*New York, Evanston, and London*

## VICTORIAN LITERATURE

Introduction, compilation and editorial notes
© 1966 by Robert O. Preyer.

Printed in the United States of America.

First edition: HARPER TORCHBOOKS, 1967,
Harper & Row, Publishers, Incorporated,
49 East 33rd Street,
New York, N.Y. 10016.

Library of Congress Catalog Card Number:
67–11605.

*Designed by Darlene Starr Carbone*

# CONTENTS

# *Introduction*

———◄●►———

## Robert O. Preyer

### I

The essays reprinted here will indicate, if nothing else, how varied are the responses we make today to the literature of the Victorian period. There is no single approach to this body of writing and, for that matter, there is no clear-cut agreement as to what sorts of works should be included in the canon. Macaulay is read today as an essayist and historian; does an account of his style really belong here? Walter Bagehot, founder of *The Economist,* wrote a few literary essays and a number of books on technical subjects—the British Constitution, banking, politics, and the like. A representative Victorian intellectual to be sure—but a figure in literature? "The Issue Between Huxley and Newman" would hardly seem to be a matter of urgent concern to students of Victorian literature—if one believes that writing somehow goes on in a void, that it has no connections with non-literary areas of experience. Essays on the work and thought of these writers are nevertheless included, and not simply for historical background or as a gesture towards the "history of ideas" in the period. The immense readability of Macaulay is a stylistic achievement that deserves close attention. As A. L. Rowse remarked (in 1946), "... the *Essays* have survived a hundred years. Few works have been so

severely criticized, or shown to have more serious errors; and yet
there is no doubt that they will go gaily on to their second century." [1]
In 1960, G. S. Fraser, better known as a critic of contemporary poets,
was still trying to account for the success of this style and its lasting
influence "in the field of high popularization, in the prose of opinion,
information, political persuasion." It is, he noted, ". . . of all the great
Victorian English styles, the most strikingly and lastingly imitable."
The present collection begins with Fraser's account of a great popular style, one which sets a norm from which other Victorian prose
styles depart. There are other reasons for placing Macaulay's name
at the beginning of this collection. In terms of chronology he is an
early Victorian, born in the first year of the new century and a lad
of fifteen when the battle of Waterloo was fought. Much of the posi-
tiveness and assurance of the eighteenth century is in his outlook.
He was rational, a tough debater, and a man who preferred a vivid
and definitive statement to a complicated and subtle analysis. He delighted in the novels of Walter Scott and Jane Austen; romantic
poets like Wordsworth and Coleridge, or romantic prose writers like
Thomas Carlyle, annoyed and puzzled him. He shared these cultural preferences and antipathies with other representatives of the
rising middle class that was coming to dominate England in the
1830s. As A. L. Rowse puts it, "He was a deeply conventional man,
a Philistine of genius; his work appealed to, was the very expression
of, the conventionalism, the Philistinism, of the Victorian age." [2]
For all these reasons it is useful to begin with Macaulay.

    In the second essay, "The Issue Between Kingsley and Newman,"
Walter Houghton reminds us that "we read Kingsley to understand
the liberal mind in its concrete, living temper." If Macaulay can be
considered a representative early Victorian Whig then perhaps
Charles Kingsley, a disciple of Coleridge and Carlyle, may be taken
as a representative middle-Victorian liberal—a man of action, earnest, assertive, zealous for the good, muddle-headed, above all rash
and enthusiastic. Ranged against him in one of the great feuds of
the mid-century was John Henry Newman, the conservative de-

---

[1] A. L. Rowse, *The English Spirit: Essays in History and Literature* (New York, 1946), 228.
[2] *Ibid.*, p. 230.

fender of dogma and authority, who abandoned Kingsley's Anglican Church for the Church of Rome where he rose to the rank of Cardinal. In the opinion of William E. Buckler, Newman remains "the greatest Victorian prose stylist." [3] Walter Houghton has referred to Newman as "the most highly gifted of all the Victorians . . . at once a thinker and an artist." [4] Newman was the great antagonist of Victorian liberalism, the expounder of an unpopular and seemingly irrelevant view of man and history, who sought in his writings to persuade readers of the sincerity, as well as the correctness, of his views. His method was often that of a true artist—he used language to record dramatically the feelings and circumstances which accompanied and modified his actions and responses at a given time and place.

> I write, I write again: I write a third time in the course of six months. Then I take the third: I literally fill the paper with corrections, so that another person could not read it. I then write it out fair for the printer. I put it by; I take it up; I begin to correct again: it will not do. Alterations multiply, pages are rewritten, little lines sneak in and crawl about. The whole page is disfigured; I write again; I cannot count how many times this process is repeated.[5]

This is a far cry from the impetuous, rough and ready "spontaneity" of Kingsley's writing. The result is a richly personal style which strikes the reader as transparently sincere, a style which rendered vividly the motions of a subtle and sensitive consciousness feeling its way to religious certainties amidst the conflicts of an age of rapid change and unprecedented dislocations. As Professor Houghton demonstrates, the issue between Kingsley and Newman far transcends its immediate occasion in 1864. It is concerned with the way in which ideas are held and the depth at which they are held, with, in short, the *experience* of the life of the mind, at a given moment in time and in a particular social and cultural situation.

With the third essay, "Trollope, Bagehot, and the English Con-

[3] William E. Buckler, *Prose of the Victorian Period* (New York, 1958), xxvi.
[4] Walter E. Houghton, "John Henry Newman" in H. Spencer, W. E. Houghton, H. Barrows, *British Literature from Blake to the Present Day* (Boston, 1952), 489.
[5] William E. Buckler, *op. cit.*, xxvi–xxvii.

stitution" by Asa Briggs, we leave the religious and ideological bat-
tles of the 1840s and 1850s and ascend (or descend) to the level at
which Victorian social and political arrangements were made in the
middle decades of the century. It is the age of Palmerston, an age of
compromise, or, as it has more recently been called, an age of equipoise. Asa Briggs reminds us that it has also been called "the age of
Bagehot" and "the age of Trollope." In them the intensity and soul-
searching of the early Victorian world are put by, and we stroll in a
pleasant, unstrident region inhabited by ladies and gentlemen who
trouble themselves about quite other matters. There is nothing
heroic about Trollope and Bagehot unless it be their strenuous and
determined efforts to hold a balance in the social and political life
of the country. They were the enemies of ideologues and enthusiasts:

> On fire with flame that burned intense
> They turned the hose of common-sense.

They were worldly, and they were also pragmatic humanists, men
with a passion for both justice and continuity. They saw the need
for change but were in no great hurry to disrupt traditional institutions and the structures of feeling, valuation and conduct which
had grown up. Their vision was ironic. Admitting the necessity for
reforms, they continued to observe the good that can flower in the
midst of "old corruption." (They frequently called attention to the
unexpectedly trivial results which might be obtained when rational
reforms had been instituted.) In a time of rapid and accelerating
change they were concerned to adjudicate between the forces of
change and the forces of inertia in the nation's institutions. Trollope
especially was alarmed by the ease of individual advancement in a
fluid society, and by the gradual erosion of conventional values that
this mobility frequently entailed. His only nightmare—vividly con-
veyed in *The Way We Live Now*, a novel of the 1870s—was the possibility that gentlemen would be pushed aside by vulgar men.
Changes in the distribution of wealth were making it impossible to
"keep people in their place" and the normal workings of a class system were being undermined. Bagehot was a liberal—even a radical—who often found himself arguing the conservative case, but for
different reasons. His concern was with a political problem: how

could individual mobility in society be reconciled with the maintenance of the system of checks and balances between groups and classes? He was capable of arguing that the best defense against the tyranny of brute financial power and ideological intransigence was, paradoxically, the antiquated "deferential view" of society epitomized in the expression "every Englishman loves a lord." This irrational affection for a feudal class system inhibited what might have been a singleminded worship of the power of money. Stupidity, Bagehot remarked, was the saving grace of the English—here was an example.

In his remarkable volume *Culture and Society 1780–1950,* Raymond Williams takes another look at the workings of this "stupid" conservatism in the English, their slowness in perceiving exactly where they were in a process of change. He notes, for example, that the phrase "Industrial Revolution" was a French import of the 1820s; that "industrialism" was first used in the 1830s as a collective term referring to a new system created by the rapid growth in importance of manufacturing and productive institutions—and this, of course, was long after the situation it described had begun to exist. (Before then "industry" designated a particular human attribute and nothing else.) Similarly, it was only after the French Revolution that Englishmen came to speak of the "lower classes," instead of the lower orders, while the "upper classes" did not come into the language until the 1820s. It was not until the 1890s that the "upper middle classes" made their appearance—supplanting Trollope's sacred rank of gentleman.

It is important that the student of literature understand the appeal and the strength of this native conservatism of the British, their preference for continuity especially in eras of rapid transition. Otherwise he will have but a dim notion of the point and relevance of the satirical literature of the period, or will frequently misconstrue its tone. Literature is a reflection of life, to be sure, but it is also a distortion and criticism of it. Dickens was frequently infuriated by the same stupidity that delighted Bagehot. Asa Briggs reminds us of a part of the Victorian scene which is less dramatic, less problematic than others, and therefore more apt to be ignored—at peril to our understanding. The novels of Trollope and the good-humored

political and cultural analysis of Bagehot remind us of the sort of
reality admired by the great Dutch *genre* painters. It is a far cry from
the existential literature we associate with the names of Emily Brontë
and Thomas Carlyle.

The remaining essays may be left to speak for themselves. They
deal with some of the ways in which contemporary critics and
scholars respond to the poems and the novels of this period. The
essays were chosen for a number of reasons, not the least of which
was their intrinsic interest. They illustrate the great variety of critical
approaches today and thus provide an opportunity to estimate the
craftsmanship of the critic as well as the artist. The editor has left
out several essays that are easily available in order to include offer-
ings from journals which are not widely represented even in fairly
good college libraries. Walter Houghton's "The Issue Between
Kingsley and Newman" is the antiquity of the collection, having
appeared in *Theology Today* in 1947. Most students of Victorian letters are unaware of the existence of this journal. Asa Briggs' "Trollope, Bagehot and the English Constitution" was taken from the
now defunct *Cambridge Journal*; Gabriel Pearson's "Dickens and His
Readers" was printed in the *Universities and Left Review* (now issued
under the name *The Left Review*), also an unfamiliar source for essays
on the Victorian period. There are, of course, essays from respected
and even respectable scholarly journals like *PMLA, English Literary
History, Essays in Criticism* and *Victorian Studies*. But an effort has been
made to include work from new and relatively unknown British and
American journals such as *Victorian Poetry, The Critical Quarterly*, and
the *Review of English Literature* (not to be confused with *The Review of
English Studies*). One of the richest sources of stimulating essays on
Victorian literature is not represented here—the *University of Toronto
Quarterly*. It has already been thoroughly mined. Eight of the essays
were published in the 1960s, four in the 1950s and one in the 1940s.
It is a contemporary collection. The scholarly reader who wishes for
a fuller account of the bibliography for the period is urged to consult
two volumes sponsored by the Modern Language Association, *The
Victorian Poets: A Guide to Research* (1956) and *Victorian Fiction: A Guide
to Research* (1964) in addition to *The Cambridge Bibliography of English
Literature*. He will find useful a carefully annotated scholarly edition

of *Victorian Poetry and Poetics* (1959), edited by Walter Houghton and
Robert Stange, and the bulkier third edition of *Poetry of the Victorian
Period* (1965), edited by Jerome Buckley and the late Benjamin
Woods. William Buckler's paperback *Prose of the Victorian Period*
(1958) is a useful period anthology. E. D. H. Johnson's *The World
of the Victorians* (1964) is a well edited paperback anthology of prose
and poetry. Walter Houghton's *The Victorian Frame of Mind* (1957)
offers the best general account of the ideas and attitudes of the period. There exists a *Guide to Doctoral Dissertations in Victorian Literature,
1886–1958* compiled by Richard D. Altick and William R. Matthews
in 1960, volumes on *The Dickens Critics* (1961, edited by George Ford
and Lauriat Lane) and *The Browning Critics* (1965, edited by Boyd
Litzinger and K. L. Knickerbocker). One can also consult the an-
nual bibliographies in *Victorian Studies,* quarterly bibliographies in
the *Victorian News Letter,* or look through the files of *Victorian Poetry,
Nineteenth-Century Fiction,* or *English Fiction in Transition* (which covers
the period 1880–1920). For the history of the period G. M. Trevelyan's *British History in the Nineteenth Century* (1922, revised 1938) is
still useful and for intellectual background one can recommend
especially the following works: J. H. Randall, *The Making of the
Modern Mind* (1940), D. C. Somervill, *English Thought in the Nineteenth Century* (1929), H. V. Routh, *Towards the Twentieth Century*
(1937), G. M. Young, *Victorian England: Portrait of an Age* (1936),
Basil Willey, *Nineteenth Century Studies* (1949 and 1966) and *More
Nineteenth Century Studies* (1955 and 1966), Raymond Williams, *Culture and Society 1780–1950* (1958 and 1966), and Jerome Buckley, *The
Victorian Temper* (1951).

# II

A word should be added about the omissions from this collection.
There are no essays here on Thomas Carlyle (1795–1881), John
Stuart Mill (1806–1873), and John Ruskin (1819–1900), nor on the
Pre-Raphaelites. It has proved very difficult to locate individual
essays on these writers suitable for such a volume as this. The first-
rate essays are too specialized; others are mediocre. There is also a
dearth of serious critical commentary in recent periodical literature

on the Rossettis, Meredith, and Swinburne. The older analyses and
encomiums no longer satisfy—and no one has yet replied convincingly in a short space to the objections raised against their work by
twentieth century critics. The bibliography of these writers contains
no equivalent for, say, Kenneth Allott's superb "placing" of the
poetry of Matthew Arnold. Good books exist of course. Emery Neff's
*Carlyle and Mill* (revised edition, 1926) holds up very well, as does
Louis Cazamian's *Thomas Carlyle* (translated by E. K. Brown, 1932).
There is a good recent life of Ruskin by John Rosenberg. *Mill on
Bentham and Coleridge* (introduction by F. R. Leavis, 1950) is very
useful, as are the individual chapters in John Holloway's *The Victorian Sage* (1953). Graham Hough's *The Last Romantics* (1949) offers
a pleasant and shrewd introduction to the Pre-Raphaelites.

The influence of Carlyle and his followers cannot, however, be
passed over in this summary fashion. Carlyle's passionate concern
for the quality of life being lived in his time, his reverence and deep
seriousness, left their mark on the age. He was the passionate ad-
versary of every sort of lassitude of spirit, indifference, blandness and
half-belief. But more important than this—after all the earnest are
always with us—was his power of direct responsiveness, his ability
to reach down into the experience of life in the first true industrial
system and see what it did to men. The following passage is taken
from the chapter entitled "Democracy" in *Past and Present*:

Life was never a May-game for men: in all times the lot of the
dumb millions born to toil was defaced with manifold sufferings,
injustices, heavy burdens, avoidable and unavoidable; not play
at all, but hard work that made the sinews sore and the heart
sore. As bond-slaves, *villani, bordarii, sochemanni,* nay indeed as
dukes, earls and kings, men were often-times made weary of their
life; and had to say, in the sweat of their brow and of their soul,
Behold, it is not sport, it is grim earnest, and our back can bear
no more! Who knows not what massacrings and harryings there
have been; grinding, long-continuing, unbearable injustices,—till
the heart had to rise in madness, and some *"Eu Sachsen, nimith
euer sachses,* You Saxons, out with your gully-knives, then!" You
Saxons, some "arrestment," partial "arrestment of the Knaves
and Dastards" has become indispensable!—The page of Dryas-
dust is heavy with such details.

And yet I will venture to believe that in no time, since the beginnings of Society, was the lot of those same dumb millions of toilers so entirely unbearable as it is even in the days now passing over us. It is not to die, or even to die of hunger, that makes a man wretched; many men have died; all men must die,—the last exit of us all is in a Fire-Chariot of Pain. But it is to live miserable we know not why; to work sore and yet gain nothing; to be heart-worn, weary, yet isolated, unrelated, girt-in with a cold universal Laissez-faire: it is to die slowly all our life long, imprisoned in a deaf, dead, Infinite Injustice, as in the accursed iron belly of a Phalaris' Bull! This is and remains for ever intolerable to all men whom God has made. Do we wonder at French Revolutions, Chartisms, Revolts of Three Days? The times, if we will consider them, are really unexampled.

A passage like this is worth volumes of theory on the plight of post-industrial man. Carlyle has named the trouble; he has gone to the heart of the difficulty and has answered, in the only way they could be answered, the arguments of men like Macaulay who could quote statistics which "proved" that the poor were better off in the Vic-torian period than ever before in history. To have penetrated so deeply into the heart of the matter was and is a great achievement and it is no wonder that Carlyle's influence was pervasive, even in the minds of men who strongly objected to his mode of thinking. "Few men," wrote Thomas Huxley after hearing of the death of Carlyle in 1881, "can have dissented more strongly from his way of looking at things than I; but I should not yield to the most devoted of his followers in gratitude for the bracing wholesome influence of his writings when, as a very young man, I was essaying without rudder or compass to strike out a course for myself." [6] It is a testi-mony which could be repeated from many quarters. Carlyle was a revered master as well as a friend for most of the great novelists and poets of his day—Tennyson, Browning, Dickens, Meredith and Thackeray among them. Nor did his influence stop with his own generation: the writer of our times who owes most to Carlyle—and most nearly resembles him in his passionate concern for the quality of life—is D. H. Lawrence.

Since Carlyle's *Collected Works* run to thirty volumes, it may be

[6] Leonard Huxley, *Life and Letters of Thomas Henry Huxley* (New York, 1900), II, pp. 36–37.

useful here to propose a short reading list. Two early essays exhibit him at the top of his bent: "Signs of the Times" (1829) and "Characteristics" (1831). They can be followed by *Sartor Resartus* (1833), *The History of the French Revolution* (1837), and *Past and Present* (1843). One of his best known works, *Heroes and Hero-Worship* (1841), is a collection of biographies ranging from Odin to Mohammed and Napoleon. His later works, today largely unread, *Letters and Speeches of Cromwell* (1845) and *The History of Frederick the Great* (1858–1865) offer a mixture of history, biography and political theory.

John Ruskin and William Morris were important continuators of the Carlylean tradition of cultural criticism. Both men began as artists and critics of the arts and both came to see that there existed a necessary and close relationship between the quality of the life being lived in a society and the quality of its artistic productions. Stated thus baldly, this "discovery" sounds rather commonplace, which it is not. As Sir Kenneth Clark pointed out in *The Gothic Revival*,

> Standard writers of art criticism—Aristotle, Longinus, and Horace—all described art as something imposed, so to speak, from without. The idea of style as something organically connected with society, something which springs inevitably from a way of life, does not occur, as far as I know, in the Eighteenth Century.[7]

This discovery came gradually and more or less by accident. Ruskin's first volume, *Modern Painters* (1843), was published when he was twenty-four. It offers primarily a passionate defense of the realism of contemporary landscape painters, notably Turner. A few years later we find Ruskin writing enormous illustrated volumes on architecture: *The Seven Lamps of Architecture* (1849) and *The Stones of Venice* (1851, 1853). Here the relationship between artifact and society is more obvious than it is with painting. He became more and more preoccupied, as the years went by, with the character of the age that built the buildings and decorated them. Eventually he abandoned art criticism altogether and wrote a series of political and economic tracts for the times, among them *Unto This Last* (1862), *The Crown of Wild Olives* (1866), and *Fors Clavigera* (1871–1884), a

[7] Quoted in Raymond Williams, *Culture and Society 1780–1950* (London, 1958), 130.

collection of letters addressed to workingmen. He had come to feel that the only way to improve the art of a period was to improve the society in which the work was done.

The standard edition of Ruskin's writings runs to thirty-nine volumes. It is easy to get lost in the maze of good and indifferent writing and it is also very difficult to provide a critical estimate of the production of such a prolific and many-sided writer. The interested reader might make a start by reading "The Nature of Gothic" (chapter six of the second volume of *The Stones of Venice*) and then the famous Lecture II from *The Crown of Wild Olives,* entitled "Traffic."

William Morris (1834–1896) was also a prolific writer in prose and verse (twenty-four volumes in his collected works) as well as a painter, a designer, and a craftsman, who made stained glass windows, tapestries, carpets, illuminated manuscripts, wall papers, and furniture. Perhaps the best way to approach this versatile master of the decorative arts is by quoting his own words from an address delivered before the Birmingham Society of Arts and School of Design in 1879. The address is entitled *The Art of the People*:

> That thing which I understand by real art is the expression by man of his pleasure in labour. I do not believe he can be happy in his labour without expressing that happiness; and especially is this so when he is at work at anything in which he specially excels. . . . If a man has work to do which he despises, which does not satisfy his natural and rightful desire for pleasure, the greater part of his life must pass unhappily and without self-respect. Consider, I beg of you, what that means, and what ruin must come of it in the end.
> . . . it is not possible to dissociate art from morality, politics, and religion. Truth in these great matters of principle is of one, and it is only in formal treatises that it can be split up diversely.

Morris was a passionate medievalist, a lover of Malory and Chaucer and a translator of Norse Sagas. He went on to become a socialist (and by his writings to make at least one remarkable convert, George Bernard Shaw). It is an instructive career and will remind us, perhaps, of the characteristic Victorian habit of ordering daily existence by a continual reference back to the past and forward into the future. We find it everywhere in Carlyle, even in his titles: *Past and Present,* for example. Never before had the study of the past interested such a wide popular audience; never before were so many members of a society proccupied with the legacy which they hoped to leave posterity. As John Stuart Mill pointed out in "The Spirit of the Age," a series of articles written in 1831, "The idea of comparing one's own age with former ages, or with our notion of those which are yet to come, had occurred to philosophers; but it never before was the dominant idea of any age."

> It is [he continued] an idea essentially belonging to an age of change. Before men begin to think much and long on the peculiarities of their own times, they must have begun to think that those times are, or are destined to be, distinguished in a remarkable manner from the times that preceded them. . . . The conviction is already not far from being universal, that the times are pregnant with change; and that the nineteenth century will be known to posterity as the era of one of the greatest revolutions of which history has preserved the remembrance, in the human mind, and in the whole constitution of human society. . . . The first of the leading peculiarities of the present age is, that it is an age of transition. Mankind have outgrown old institutions and old doctrines, and have not yet acquired new ones.

There speaks the true voice of the Victorian intellectual, self-conscious, excited, and eager to encounter whatever experience may bring, open to possibility and variety, yet seeking always to control and master his destiny. The literature produced in the Victorian period offers a superb response to a new sort of experience, that of life lived in the midst of a permanent revolution started by the manufacturing and productive institutions of the modern industrial state. There was nothing jaded in this response—it was freshly seen and evaluated by a group of writers who had themselves experienced life under an older dispensation and were in a position to judge what had been gained, what lost in the process. It is a literature crisscrossed with nostalgia and hope; with anger and humor. Above all it is the literature of an expansive age which knows it is going places but cannot name a specific destination, a literature of transition. Victorian authors were conscious of experiencing life in a new way and under novel conditions. We live today in the midst of this novelty without recognizing it as such—in this sense we are "post-Victorians." Yet their writing can speak directly to us for we live in what appears to be the middle of a dynamic process of change, first observed and named in the works of the Victorian writers. To read them is to renew in ourselves their sense of wonder, their pity and concern, above all their energy of response in the face of the contemporary human situation.

# 1

# *Macaulay's Style as an Essayist*

———◆———

## G. S. Fraser

EDITORIAL NOTE. *Thomas Babington Macaulay was born in 1800. As a schoolboy he memorized Sir Walter Scott's Lays; as a young man he developed a consuming interest in the gradually unfolding world of the* Waverley Novels *as they appeared. Scott's works projected a new view of history and a new view of the past and it was no wonder, perhaps, that a gifted youth who was, as we have seen, aged fifteen at the time of Waterloo, and whose imagination was dominated by Scott, should decide to write history. What is astonishing, however, is the magnitude of his success. As the historian G. M. Trevelyan noted,*

> *Gibbon had been read by an aristocratic class and its appendages, but Macaulay was read by an enormous public in both hemispheres, including almost everyone who read books at all, and this was true not only of his* Essays, *but to a scarcely less degree of his* History of England, *a very closely packed narrative of the last fifteen years of the seventeenth century, the only history of such length and detail that has ever been so widely read.*

1

*With Thomas Carlyle (born 1795), Macaulay was largely responsible for creating that vast popular interest in history which is such an astonishing feature of the Victorian age. G. S. Fraser, a distinguished literary critic especially known for his writings on contemporary poetry, has attempted, in the following essay, to explain some of the stylistic reasons for this popular success.*

Macaulay's style—the style of his essays even more than of his great history—was, of all the great Victorian English styles, the most strikingly and lastingly imitable. Nobody, today, attempts to write like Carlyle or Ruskin, or even like that master of an uneccentric pure conversational prose, Newman. To do so would be like dressing up in a dead man's clothes. But when I come upon a middle-page article in *The New Statesman*, say, by Professor Trevor-Roper or Mr. A. J. P. Taylor, I often fancy that I am reading a Macaulay who has had, drastically, to condense himself; the old machinery of allusion, point, and antithesis, of the periodic sentence coming down with a snap or a bang at the end, still works. And I remember, also, the excitement with which a young friend of mine, now a political commentator on one of our respectable daily papers, announced to me that he had discovered Macaulay's essays. No critic and no imaginative writer today at all resembles Macaulay. But he is still a useful model in the field of high popularisation, in the prose of opinion, information, political persuasion. His heirs are not only among the popular historians and the political journalists. There is more than a touch of Macaulay's manner, for instance, in the less technical writings of Bertrand Russell.

If the influence has been lasting, it was also immediate. Sir George Otto Trevelyan's fine biography of his uncle catches almost uncannily the structure and emphasis of Macaulay's sentences; the style of Trevelyan's *The Early History of Charles James Fox,* an even more vivacious and sparkling book, is just that of Macaulay, with the addition of a touch of genuine aristocratic insouciance which Macaulay, a middle-class convert to Whiggism, never quite caught. Matthew Arnold deplored the prevalence in the late 1860s and early 1870s of what he called "middle-class Macaulayese,' but in fact the student of history and politics can trace Macaulay's influence, more fruitfully, in aristocratic writers; in, for instance, Lord Rosebery's excellent short life of the younger Pitt, in Lord Curzon's speeches, in Sir Winston Churchill's impressive life of his father. It can be traced, in fact, in unexpected places. I do not know if anyone has ever closely examined the prose style of the greatest of Victorian historical scholars, Lord Acton. Opposing almost everything, except the passion for liberty, that Macaulay stood for, he seems to me often to be imitating, perhaps unconsciously and certainly rather ineptly, Macaulay's manner. His prose is full of antitheses, of summary allusions, of pointed sentences, which do not quite come off, because they carry too heavy a burden of thought and learning. The greatest of Victorian critics, Matthew Arnold, brought the whole weight of his own rhetoric, his own 'heightened and telling way of putting things' to the demolishment of Macaulay's rhetoric; but, it would seem, with surprisingly little practical effect. Our most widely read living English historian is Macaulay's great-nephew, George Macaulay Trevelyan; and his style is very much Macaulay's style, with a subtler rhythm and with finer lights and shades.

'Where did you get that style?' asked Lord Jeffrey, when Macaulay first exploded, like a Roman candle, in the *Edinburgh Review*. But his wonder was not the wonder, mixed with perturbation, which he felt about the style of the young Carlyle. Macaulay's taste in literature was a conservative one; if one wants to know what a good critic he might have been, one has to read not his published essays but his marginal notes on Livy or Ovid or Thucydides. Vernacular literature was still, for him, something to be judged by the standards of Greece and Rome in their classical periods. The most recent English writer for whom he had a quite whole-hearted admiration was Jane Austen. He disliked Ruskin, he disliked Carlyle, he was too sharply opposed to everything that Newman stood for to appreciate Newman (though he recognised, grudgingly, his gifts). He was in a real sense old-fashioned not only in his tastes but in his opinions; one of the last important contemporary books he read was John Stuart Mill's essay on liberty, and Mill seemed to him like a man crying out 'Fire!' in the middle of Noah's flood.

He thought Wordsworth's *Prelude* a poorer *Excursion*. He read, voraciously, sentimental novels with happy endings, as a public man today reads detective stories, he enjoyed Dickens rather condescendingly, as a public man today enjoys P. G. Wodehouse. He admired Byron and Shelley and Scott, he admired some things in Wordsworth but not what today we think his greatest things, but he felt that the early Victorian age was, on the whole, a day of small men both in literature and politics. He was, in his latter years, a whole-hearted Palmerstonian in politics. The strength of his style, its confidence, comes from the two facts that he accepted unquestioningly the surface forward flow of his age, and rejected, just as unquestioningly, its deeper undertow.

His style, in the essays, in its dependence on point, balance, an abundance of not too recondite literary and historical allusion, periodic order, sharp antithesis, is essentially the old *Edinburgh Review* style, the style of Jeffrey or Sidney Smith, handled, however, without Jeffrey's scrupulosity or Smith's bubbling fun, handled with a new breadth, a new, sometimes harsh vividness, perhaps a new coarseness. It is never slovenly or straggly; it has no obscurities, and no fine shades. Though it is a rapid style, with an effect of very forcible impetus, even of rush, it never leaves even the most obtuse reader struggling hopelessly in its wake. In its use of diverse exemplification and concealed repetition—many concrete instances of even the most obvious generalisation, and the generalisation itself clothed in a succession of different phrases—it is very much the style of an orator. It hammers its points home; it illustrates them to a degree, for the more quick-witted reader, almost of tedium. It can rise, it perhaps rises too often, to a peroration; but it can also make a joke. Its tone is rather difficult to define, or even to describe. It is perhaps not unlike the tone, today, of a good university extension lecturer with the knack of handling, or subduing, almost any kind of audience. There is no deep intimacy, but there is a confidence that one will be listened to. Macaulay keeps at a certain dignified distance from the reader, but he is extremely aware, at the same time, of the importance of holding the reader's attention. He is friendly, he is vivacious, at times he almost verges on familiarity. He is not completely at ease, he is stretching himself, but he has a reassuring awareness of how much—how much information, what sound and yet surprising ideas, what a fertile field of illustration—he has to stretch. He is quite at the opposite pole from those writers whom Mr. John Holloway calls the Victorian sages, Carlyle, Ruskin, Arnold, Newman. He does not speak out of any deep inner uneasiness; his purpose is neither self-exploration nor, crudely and obviously, self-expression. Rather he seems often to be exploiting the possibilities of a rhetorical medium almost for the medium's own sake. If we want to know something about his simple, pathetic, generous, and honourable inner life—a life almost entirely dependent for its happiness on books, on daydreams, and on intense family affection divorced from sex—we have to turn to his nephew's biography, and to the extracts from Macaulay's letters and journals included in that. His biographer was well aware of this vulnerable and touching privacy of the central man:

> It may . . . be taken for granted that a desire exists to hear something authentic about the life of a man who has produced works which are universally known, but which bear little or no indication of the private history and personal qualities of the author.[1]

The style, Trevelyan seems to be implying there, is in Macaulay's case *not* the man. It is, of course, a style with an unmistakable external individuality about it. Yet the critical reader has an uneasy sense that it is a machine; a machine that, once set in motion, will carry the writer on, almost without his own effort, almost without his own volition.

It carries on the biographer as well as his subject. Sir George Otto Trevelyan has, for instance, this to say about Zachary Macaulay's affection for West Africa:

> But for the absence of an Eve, he regarded the West Coast of Africa as a veritable Paradise, or, to use his own expression, as a more agreeable Montpelier. With a temper which in the intercourse of society was proof against being ruffled by any possible treatment of any conceivable subject, to the end of his life he

[1] George Otto Trevelyan, *The Life and Letters of Lord Macaulay*, 1887 edition, p. 1.

showed faint signs of irritation if anyone ventured in his presence to hint that Sierra Leone was unhealthy.[2]

There is the note of Macaulay, there, in the doubling of literary and familiar or *mondain* allusions ('a veritable Paradise' doubled with 'a more agreeable Montpelier'). It is like Macaulay not to be able to mention Paradise without mentioning Eve. It is mildly amusing that Zachary Macaulay, in the innocence of his emancipating enthusiasm, should have enjoyed a climate which nearly all Europeans found oppressive and exhausting, if not actively dangerous. In case anybody has not seen the little joke, it is rubbed in in the next sentence. Zachary Macaulay is presented as a fantastically urbane man, who would never lose his temper in any conceivable circumstances but who would show 'faint' irritation if there were even a 'hint' that the climate of Sierra Leone was, not deadly, but merely 'unhealthy.' The reader is left with a sense of good-natured superiority to a saintly simpleton with a crotchet, a modern equivalent of Dr. Primrose or Parson Adams. For a portrait of Zachary Macaulay, a caricature is substituted; and Trevelyan himself must, in his heart, know that it is a caricature. He has himself depicted Zachary Macaulay as a Tory Evangelical utterly obsessed with African emancipation. Would such a man have remained unruffled by a conversation which treated lightly either the Christian faith or the horrors of the slave trade? Trevelyan also describes Zachary Macaulay as a kind but difficult parent, who inflicted long sermons on his children, and who was considerably ruffled by Tom's absorption in profane literature and by Tom's switch-over, at Cambridge, from Evangelical Tory to Erastian Whig politics. This is almost a better example than any in Macaulay's own works of the difficulty, in Macaulayan rhetoric, of telling the plain truth. The plain truth would be something like this; that Zachary Macaulay, though a very polite, patient, and tolerant man in all discussions where his central faith and purpose were not engaged, had an almost irritable defensive affection for West Africa.

There are plenty of examples of this kind of distortion, the exigent simplifications of rhetoric ironing out the awkward complications

[2] *Ibid,* p. 17.

of fact, in Macaulay's own essays. Take these sentences on Byron:

> The young peer had great intellectual powers; yet there was an unsound part in his mind. He had naturally a generous and feeling heart; but his temper was wayward and irritable. He had a head which statuaries loved to copy, and *a foot the deformity of which the beggars in the street mimicked.*[3]

I have read many contemporary accounts of Byron and I recently visited Newstead Abbey and looked both at the testimony of his shoemaker and at a pair of his shoe-lasts. I cannot think that he was ever mocked in the streets, except just possibly in Aberdeen, in his schooldays. The lame foot seems to have been of the same size as the sound foot; the ankle could not support the lame leg, which was perhaps a little shorter than the sound one. Byron's clothes, his boots, his mode of walking and standing were all calculated to make his deformity, which in any case was of a weakening rather than a disfiguring kind, as inconspicuous as possible. Macaulay must have known all this; the rhetorical machine carried him away, he could not resist a coarsely effective antithesis. Or take the even more notorious sentences on Boswell:

> If he had not been *a great fool,* he would never have been a great writer. Without all the qualities which made him the *jest and torment* of those among whom he lived, without the officiousness, the inquisitiveness, the effrontery, the toadeating, the *insensibility to all reproof,* he would never have produced so excellent a book.[4]

The subtle psychological penetration which is everywhere evident in the life of Johnson ought to have made it obvious to Macaulay that Boswell was, at least, not a fool *qua* writer. Nobody lives so long as Boswell did at the centre of the best intellectual company of his day who is merely the 'jest and torment' of his friends, and Macaulay must have known Johnson's own lively and sincere tribute to Boswell's charm as a travelling companion. We know today more about Boswell than Macaulay did, but there is plenty of evidence of his extreme 'sensibility to reproof' in the great

[3] Thomas Babington Macaulay. *Critical and Historical Essays.* Vol. 2. Everyman's Library, p. 614.
[4] *Ibid,* p. 540.

biography itself. Again, the steam-roller rhetoric crushes the truth
flat.

It was this coarseness in the fibre, not of Macaulay's private and
intimate self, but of his public rhetoric that Matthew Arnold never
tired of attacking. The most vivacious attack comes in *Friendship's
Garland,* in a conversation with Arminius von Thunder-ten-Tronckh
reported by Adolescens Leo of the *Daily Telegraph:*

> Now I detest this German lecturer and his oracles, but I am above
> everything, a man of letters myself, I never refuse to listen to a
> remark upon style. 'Explain yourself,' said I; 'why do you call
> Mr. Hepworth Dixon's style middle-class Macaulayese?' 'I call it
> Macaulayese,' says the pedant, 'because it has the same internal
> and external characteristics as Macaulay's style; the external
> characteristics being a hard metallic movement with nothing of
> the soft play of life, and the internal characteristic being a per-
> petual semblance of hitting the right nail on the head without the
> reality. And I call it middle-class Macaulayese, because it has
> these faults without the compensation of great studies and of
> conversance with great affairs, by which Macaulay partly re-
> deemed them.'[5]

In the essay on Joubert, Arnold calls Macaulay 'the great apostle
of the Philistines,' and describes him as:

> a born rhetorician; a splendid rhetorician doubtless, and beyond
> that, an *English* rhetorician also, an *honest* rhetorician; still beyond
> the apparent rhetorical truth of things he could never penetrate;
> for their vital truth, for what the French call the *vraie vérité,* he
> had absolutely no organ . . .[6]

Elsewhere he speaks of:

> the confident shallowness which makes [Macaulay] so admired
> by public speakers and leading-article writers, and so intolerable
> to all searchers for truth . . .[7]

Arnold's most sustained attack, an attack a little qualified by a
tribute to Macaulay's attractiveness to the reader who is just begin-

[5] *Friendship's Garland; being the Conversations, Letters, and Opinions of the late Arminius, Baron
von Thunder-ten-Tronckh, etc.* (Second Editon), 1897. p. 71.
[6] M. Arnold, *Essays Literary and Critical,* (Everyman). p. 172.
[7] M. Arnold, *The Study of Celtic Literature, etc.* (Everyman). p. 134.

ning to 'awake to the intellectual life,' comes in the excellent essay,
*A French Critic on Milton*: I quote some key phrases and sentences
from a passage running over several pages (it will be noticed that
Arnold repeats the general characterisation of Macaulay's style,
especially the remarks on its mechanical and external quality, its
lack of inner life, already uttered by Arminius):

> A style to dazzle, to gain admirers everywhere, to attract imitators
> in multitude! A style brilliant, metallic, exterior, making strong
> points, alternating invective with eulogy, wrapping in a robe of
> rhetoric the thing it represents . . . [The] writer has not for his aim
> to see and utter the real truth about his object . . . Substantial
> meaning such lucubrations can have none. And in like manner, a
> distinct and substantial meaning can never be got out of the fine
> phrases about 'Milton's conception of life uniting all the voluptu-
> ousness of the Oriental haram, with all the pure and quiet affec-
> tion of the English fireside' . . . the phrases are mere rhetoric . . .
> The immense popularity of Macaulay is due to his being pre-
> eminently fitted to give pleasure to all who are *beginning* to feel
> enjoyment in the things of the mind . . . The Bible and Shake-
> speare may be said to be imposed upon an Englishman as objects
> of his admiration; but as soon as the common Englishman, desir-
> ing culture, begins to choose for himself, he chooses Macaulay.
> Macaulay's view of things is, on the whole, the view of them he
> feels to be his own also . . . But with the increasing number of
> those who awake to the intellectual life, the number of those also
> increases, who, having awoke to it, go on with it, follow where it
> leads them . . . To be satisfied with fine writing about the object
> of one's study, with having it praised or blamed in accordance
> with one's like and dislikes, with any conventional treatment of it
> whatever, is at this stage of growth seen to be futile. At this stage,
> rhetoric, even when it is so good as Macaulay's, dissatisfies.[8]

It would, I think, be a futile exercise in paradox to attempt to
refute Arnold's general judgement, especially on Macaulay as a
literary critic. The rhetoric is much less harmful to the controversial
pieces on political thought, like the attacks on Southey, on James
Mill, and on Gladstone. Of these, the Southey essay is the worst in
tone and temper; I find the Mill essay sane and sympathetic; and I
agree with Gladstone himself in finding the Gladstone piece, on
Gladstone's early book on the relations of Church and State, a

[8] Matthew Arnold, *Mixed Essays*. London, 1879. pp. 238–46, *passim*.

model of controversial courtesy. Perhaps the finest of all the political pieces for tone, however, is the shortish essay on Lord Holland; Macaulay wrote it rather reluctantly, egged or nagged into doing so by Lady Holland, and the style somehow catches something of the easy stateliness of the old Whig society. There are no occasions for violent and coarse antithesis; something of the serene harmony of Lord Holland's own temperament chastens Macaulay's style. The masterpieces, however, among the essays are those which are almost pure narrative; the Clive, the Warren Hastings, the two essays on Chatham, the political part of the essay on Horace Walpole, the Frederick the Great. In these, the great historian is learning his trade. The best defence of Macaulay against Arnold, I think, or the best palliation of Arnold's case for the prosecution, is Macaulay's own view of his achievement as an essayist; a view remarkably modest.

In 1838, Lord Brougham, politically powerless and morally isolated, had, after scamping his contributions to the *Edinburgh Review* for many years, determined to exert himself as if he were a young writer struggling into note. Macaulay, writing to the editor of the *Edinburgh Review,* MacVey Napier, commented:

> [Brougham's contributions] are, indeed, models of magazine writing, as distinguished from other sorts of writing. They are not, I think, made for duration. Everything about them is exaggerated, incorrect, sketchy. All the characters are either too black, or too fair. The passions of the writer do not suffer him to maintain even the decent appearance of impartiality. And the style, though striking and animated, will not bear examination through a single paragraph. But the effect of the first perusal is great; and few people read through an article in a review twice.[9]

Brougham hated Macaulay, who had all his own gifts, combined with two things that Brougham lacked, perfect honour and loyalty in political relations, and a self-knowledge that took in not only scope but limitations. Macaulay did not love Brougham; and in our enemies we have a particularly sharp eye for our own faults in an exaggerated form. All that Macaulay says of Brougham might be said, by a hostile critic, of Macaulay himself. But, unlike Brougham,

[9] *The Life and Letters of Lord Macaulay, by his nephew George Otto Trevelyan, M. P.* New Edition, 1881. London, p. 345.

Macaulay had the gift of self-criticism. Writing again to Napier, in 1842, he says:

"The public judges, and ought to judge, indulgently of periodical works. They are not expected to be highly finished. Their natural life is only six weeks. Sometimes their writer is at a distance from the books to which he wants to refer. Sometimes he is forced to hurry through his task in order to catch the post. He may blunder; he may contradict himself; he may give an immoderate extension to one part of his subject, and dismiss an equally important part in a few words. All this is readily forgiven if there be a certain spirit and vivacity in his style. But, as soon as he republishes, he challenges a comparison with all the most polished and symmetrical of human compositions . . . My reviews are generally thought to be better written, and they certainly live longer, than the reviews of most other people; and this ought to content me. The moment I come forward to demand a higher rank, I must expect to be judged by a higher standard." [10]

Macaulay, also, was as keenly aware as Matthew Arnold himself that his gifts were not those of a literary critic. He refused, for that reason, in 1838, to review Lockhart's life of Scott. He wrote to Napier:

"I have written several things on historical, political, and moral questions of which, on the fullest reconsideration, I am not ashamed, and by which I would be willing to be estimated; but I have never written a page of criticism on poetry, or the fine arts, which I would not burn if I had the power. Hazlitt used to say of himself, 'I am nothing if not critical.' The case with me is directly the reverse. I have a strong and acute enjoyment of works of the imagination; but I have never habituated myself to dissect them. Perhaps I enjoy them the more keenly, for that very reason. Such books as Lessing's Laocoon, such passages as the criticism on Hamlet in Wilhelm Meister, fill me with wonder and despair. Now, a review of Lockhart's book ought to be a review of Sir Walter's literary performances. I enjoy many of them;—nobody, I believe, more keenly;—but I am sure that there are hundreds who will criticise them far better. Trust to my knowledge of myself. I never in my life was more certain of anything than of what I tell you, and I am sure that Lord Jeffrey will tell you exactly the same." [11]

---

[10] *Ibid*, p. 418.
[11] *Ibid*, p. 343.

He had a very sound measure of himself. The essays are, like
Brougham's, exaggerated, incorrect, sketchy. But they have proved,
unlike Brougham's, to be made for duration. Macaulay lived, from
his childhood on, in books; a life of great affairs and intense affections never got him out of books; as an orator urging through the
great Reform Bill, as an administrator reshaping the system of law
and education in India, as a conversationalist at Holland House,
he remained an eager and confident and very intelligent schoolboy,
stepping out of his library, his mind full of everything that he had
read. His great, and not really unwholesome influence, on political
and popular historical writing, suggests odd reflections about how
little of the subtlety and maturity of the personal life, of great
imaginative literature, ever gets into the discussion of public affairs;
about how much we are always ruled by intelligent schoolboys. But
in our own age, even more than in Arnold's, there is a great public
that is just '*beginning* to feel enjoyment in the things of the mind.' And
that public might do much worse than turn to what Arnold rightly
called Macaulay's honest and English rhetoric; it might turn to
Mr. Colin Wilson.

# 2

## *The Issue Between Kingsley and Newman*

---

## Walter E. Houghton

EDITORIAL NOTE. *In the eight years between 1833 and 1841 it was taken for granted that John Henry Newman was the most gifted spokesman for the Oxford Movement, the name given to a spiritual and doctrinal revival within the Church of England. Then he faltered. In 1842 he withdrew from the scenes of his triumph in Oxford. In 1843 he resigned as vicar of St. Mary's. Two years later, he was received into the Roman Catholic Church. Indignation was great and for the next twenty years Newman was reviled as a traitor to his country, his university, and the church of his birth. It was not until 1864 that Newman, by now a distinguished Catholic prelate, began to answer these calumnies. The following words from a review appearing in* Macmillan's Magazine *led to his first real protest:*

> *Truth, for its own sake had never been a virtue with the Roman clergy. Father Newman informs us that it need not, and on the whole ought not to be; that cunning is the weapon which Heaven has given to the Saints wherewith to withstand the brute male force of the wicked world which*

*marries and is given in marriage. Whether his notion be doctrinally correct or not, it is at least historically so.*

*The author of these words was the Reverend Charles Kingsley, an Anglican clergyman and successful novelist, a writer in psychology, theology, and philosophy, the very opposite of John Henry Newman. A controversy followed, culminating in the publication of Newman's great spiritual autobiography,* Apologia Pro Vita Sua, *a crushing rejoinder to the charges of sophistry and dishonesty which had been leveled over the years. The high drama of this personal confrontation should not obscure the fact that there was, after all, a serious controversy. Professor Houghton, one of the three or four great Victorian scholars of our time, here makes it clear that "The Issue Between Kingsley and Newman" was a good deal more than "a duel between Protestant prejudice and Catholic subtlety." He provides here a remarkable account of that "Victorian Liberalism" which Kingsley gloried in and which Newman early recognized as his chief intellectual and spiritual antagonist.*

*All the Reviews are busy with Newman's* Apologia. . . . *There is something wonderfully typical in the passage of arms between the Apostle of the flesh and the last of the Ascetics. Can you not fancy some future Strauss sublimating it into an allegorical representation of the tendencies of the age.*—Julia Wedgwood, in a letter to Robert Browning, Sept. 22, 1864.

The phrase "Kingsley versus Newman" has always meant the controversy of 1864, and the controversy has commonly meant a duel between Protestant prejudice and Roman Catholic subtlety —which issued, by great good fortune, in the *Apologia pro Vita Sua.* But for any one who goes back of the occasion to read their books today, side by side, the phrase is suddenly packed with deeper significance. For the clash between Kingsley and Newman is the fundamental clash, both then and now, between Protestant Liberalism and Christian Orthodoxy, whether Roman Catholic or Evangelical.

With respect to Newman, that battle is the central and unifying strand of his life. "For fifty years," he said, on becoming a cardinal in 1879, "I have resisted . . . the spirit of Liberalism in religion." He chose to resist it from the Roman Catholic position, but that, I think, was an accident of the time. Certainly the main principle of the Oxford Movement was not Catholicism, not, at any rate, in Newman's mind. He recorded, in the *Apologia,* its three basic principles:

> First was the principle of dogma: my battle was with liberalism; by liberalism I mean the anti-dogmatic principle and its developments. . . . Here I have the satisfaction of feeling that I have nothing to retract, and nothing to repent of. The main principle of the Movement is as dear to me now, as it ever was. . . . Even when I was under Dr. Whately's influence, I had no temptation to be less zealous for the great dogmas of the faith, and at various times I used to resist such trains of thought on his part, as seemed to me (rightly or wrongly) to obscure them.

To Newman, therefore, Liberalism was the attempt, from various sides and in various degrees, to modify "the great dogmas of the faith": the Holy Trinity, the Creation, Original Sin, the Incarnation, the Atonement and the Redemption, with the consequent availableness and efficacy of grace for the regeneration and ultimate salvation of man, together with the four last things—death, judgment, heaven, and hell. Newman's crucial problem, as he faced the liberals, especially Whately, across the Oriel common room, was how to make a stand against what he felt would ultimately "make shipwreck of Christian faith," for Liberalism, he saw, was "the halfway house" to Atheism. Where was he to turn? Certainly not to "sound Church-of-Englandism or orthodox Protestantism" straddling every issue ("faith only justifies, yet it does not justify without works," etc.). To Evangelicalism, then, in which he had been brought up? Its eighteenth-century roots had been planted in the Reformation, but by 1830 its latent pietism had largely submerged the theological structure, until it had declined into "the religion of the heart." Newman's charge that it had "no internal idea, no principle of unity, no theology," if not quite fair, was the exaggeration of a truth. Nor was the condition of Dissent any more promising. Under such circumstances, is it surprising that he turned to Catholicism, Anglican and then Roman? I do not say that there were not other factors in his development. I only say that had a strong Protestant tradition been available, he would have started his battle from that position

and turned, not to Laud and Hammond and Bull, but to Luther and
Calvin. Viewed from this angle, the Oxford Movement should not
be described as a Roman Catholic movement. It was an anti-liberal
movement which, due to the exigencies of the time, adopted Catholicism as a fighting bulwark.

# I

From our perspective today, we can see that Liberalism was a desperate, and in the end fatal, attempt to save religion from the destructive forces of modernism by compromise and accommodation.
It was, in effect, a policy of appeasement, with precisely the results
we have, at long last, learned to expect from such a policy. By the
forces of modernism we may mean, of course, modern tendencies of
thought, such as scientific empiricism, historical investigation, and
German transcendentalism; and the study of liberalism may be the
examination of how such influences were assimilated, and what
modifications of Christian doctrine resulted. For a study of that kind
Kingsley would be unimportant. It would be to Arnold and
Whately, to Coleridge and Maurice, and to Carlyle (to mention
the founders of English Liberalism in its three schools—the Broad
Churchmen, the Platonists, and the Non-Christian Theists and
Pantheists) that we should turn to investigate the philosophical origins of liberal doctrine in England. Kingsley, on the contrary, was
not a thinker. All of his ideas as such are derivative, adopted from
the men just named, especially Maurice and Carlyle. His importance, therefore, is of another kind. What he shows us, far better
than the liberal philosophers, is the impact of Liberalism at the point
that really matters—in the frame of mind, in the outlook on life.
We read Coleridge or Maurice to understand liberal ideology; we
read Kingsley to understand the liberal mind in its concrete, living
temper. He shows us the compromise, not with modern thought, in
the realm of ideas, though that is reflected in his work, but with the
modern spirit in Victorian society.

It is scarcely necessary to argue that the Victorian atmosphere was
perhaps more heavily secular and naturalistic than that of any century since the fall of Rome. For this the immediate responsibility

lay with science and big business. The vast expansion of industry and commerce, made possible by technological advance, stimulated national pride and personal avarice, the latter extending more widely through society as democracy widened the opportunities. At the same time, the tremendous prestige of science, owing as much to its practical achievements as to its striking discoveries in geology and biology, made the scientific outlook more and more pervasive, so that a single order of nature, ruled by universal law, quietly took its place in the Victorian mind. Above all, the age was permeated by a booming optimism, confident of human nature, and dedicated to the pursuit of bigger and better civilizations—of the western kind.

In the face of these conditions, the liberals tried to make the best of both worlds. They welcomed the modern secular spirit, but at the same time they wanted to maintain a Christian or at least religious attitude. And how was this to be done? By a simple formula which on the face of it seemed a perfect solution. The natural order was sanctified. Marriage, business, science, progress, human nature—all were accepted as religious because all of them revealed the presence or the will of God. The old dichotomies of Christian thought—the natural and the supernatural, the human and the divine, the unconverted and the converted, the city of man and the city of God—all of them conveniently disappeared, merged together in what Carlyle called the natural-supernatural order. Such a merger might seem to extend religion through the whole of life, to take it out of the Church on Sunday, and make it coextensive with the entire nation during the entire week. So the liberals boasted, so most of them believed. But in actual fact, what happened (and what still happens under these circumstances) was just the reverse: religion was swallowed up in a secular religiosity which was, to all practical effect, hardly distinguishable from naturalism. For where everything is "religious," there is no religion.

Of this disastrous policy Kingsley is a magnificent illustration, and all the more significant and influential because, unlike such men as Carlyle or Jowett or Seeley, he was not only a conservative supporter of "all the doctrines of the Catholic and Apostolic Church of England, as embodied in her Liturgy or Articles," and a defender, in later life, of the Athanasian creed (a fact which misled Newman into thinking he was "nearing the Catholic view of things"), but he was also the public enemy of many a thinker who was directly or indirectly aiding the liberal cause. He attacked Comte and Mill, Strauss and the writers of *Essays and Reviews,* Emerson, Francis Newman, and the whole pack of what he called Neo-Platonists, Pantheists, and Spiritualists. And yet how thin his orthodoxy has become is but too apparent when on page after page Liberalism breaks out in its most blatant form. Could anything be plainer, for example, or more plainly incompatible with a genuine Christianity, than his incredible letter of 1846 outlining a militant policy to save the Church of England? "In the widest and divinest sense," he says, "we must make friends of the Mammon of unrighteousness. It is the new commercial aristocracy; it is the scientific go-a-head-ism of the day which must save us, and which we must save." And how? By showing that "all this progress of society in the present day is really of God, and God's work, and has potential and latent spiritual elements, which it is the duty and the glory of the clergy . . . to unfold and christen." No wonder that, as he looked forward "to a nobler state of humanity"—to which his own contribution should be sanitary reform—he saw "the City of God . . . for ever coming down among men, and actualizing itself more and more in every succeeding age." Does not the very phrasing show that to merge the human and the divine is not to raise man to God but to lower God to man? What could be more revealing than Kingsley's discovery not merely that the "every-day relations and duties of life" are most divine, but that they are most divine *"because they are most human"?* This is Newman's "halfway house" with a vengeance.

## II

It is partly because the liberal compromise was the solution of his own personal crisis that Kingsley affirmed it so confidently and so often. From childhood his personality was nervous, impulsive, full of what he called "animal excitability." This is first seen at Barnack and Clovelly, where his father held successive livings, in his ecstatic and physical response to natural beauty. "The vast and the sublime" would affect him "almost to madness," and he would weep "at the sight of the most luscious and sunny prospects." Later, in 1841, he spoke "of the dreamy days of boyhood, when I knew and worshipped nothing but the physical; when my enjoyment was drawn not . . . from the consciousness of good, . . . but from the semisensual delights of ear and eye, from sun and stars, wood and wave."

In close association with the beauty of nature, the beauty of art was an early attraction, and his own poetry dates from his fifth year. But greatest of all was his passion for science, inherited from his father, and stimulated then and all through his life by the double pleasure of collecting specimens while he was delighting in the beauties of sea and woods. He corresponded with eminent naturalists, wrote books of popular science, was enormously pleased by his elections to the Linnean and Geological Societies. Indeed, in the last analysis, he cared more for science than for anything else. A letter from Torquay in 1854 amounts almost to a confession of faith (the serious implications of the last sentence will be considered later):

> I am now very busy at two things. Working at the sea-animals of Torquay for my friend, Mr. Gosse, the naturalist, and thundering in behalf of sanitary reform. Those who fancy me a "sentimentalist" and a "fanatic" little know how thoroughly my own bent is for physical science; how I have been trained in it from earliest boyhood; how I am happier now in classifying a new polype, or solving a geognostic problem of strata, or any other bit of hard Baconian induction, than in writing all the novels in the world; or how, again, my theological creed has grown slowly and naturally out of my physical one, till I have seen, and do believe more and more utterly, that the peculiar doctrines of Christianity . . . coincide with the loftiest and severest science.

Blessed with the delights of nature and art and science, to which were added the pleasures of sport (fishing, riding, hunting), what boy could be unhappy? Charles Kingsley. His father, though possessed of exactly the same tastes, was an Evangelical clergyman who could only feel that such worldly interests in himself, and in his son, if not positively evil, were certainly not approved of God. The hero of *The Snake's Book,* a manuscript story partly taken over later into *Yeast,* stands at once, I think, for both father and boy:

> There was in him a genial love of the beautiful, a seeing eye for God's earth. He dared a love of poetry, music, scenery—art of all

kinds. And yet all hampered, choked, as being a thing apart, a tertium quid in his life. Carnal he dared not call it—his conscience forbade him. Spiritual he dared not call it—his religious system said nothing about it. . . .

And thus divorced from that which he knew to be his highest life, the beautiful was a subject for mere prurient dilettantism, scenery hunting, flower and fossil collecting, sketching and ballad-reading—not without secret novel debauches—and so lived in him, godless, meaningless, a life in death. . . .

so *festered* in him, he might have said, thinking of himself; for the resulting tension, which was greatly increased as he reached physical maturity by finding that love was "ground tabooed and 'carnal,' " was expressed in his stammering, his terrible nightmares, and a nervous breakdown at the age of sixteen. I suspect that the religious skepticism which swept over him at Cambridge, where he matriculated in 1838, was in good part a solution, however inadequate and impermanent, for his inner conflict. If there was no God and nothing was spiritual, then the natural was good and to be enjoyed. At any rate, on his own evidence, the "darkling tempests of scepticism" were accompanied by a period of "sensuality and dissipation." But such a state of things, as disturbing to Kingsley, given his inheritance, as the previous conflict over nature and art and love, was highly unstable.

At this juncture, on July 6, 1839, the crucial day of his life, he met Fanny Grenfell, loved her at first sight, and eventually married her, in January, 1844. I call it crucial because it was his love for her which not only saved him, as he says, from spiritual and moral collapse, and made possible that recovery of faith and character upon which he built his later life, but also because from this total experience he first reached the liberal synthesis of human and divine. For how could love, so natural and instinctive, yet so morally strengthening, so clearly the means through which he had returned to God, how could it be anything but holy? Surely, he said, speaking later from his own knowledge, "these desires, which men call carnal, are truly most spiritual, most beloved by Him." And in *Yeast,* where Lancelot and Argemone are thinly disguised pictures of himself and Fanny Grenfell, Lancelot insists that "my body, and brain, and faculties, and appetites must be His will. . . . Whatsoever I can do with them in accordance with the constitution of them and nature must be His will." Or more explicit still, "Even . . . merely animal human appetites," he says, are not only "God-given" but "God-like symbols." No wonder that when Argemone finds that she cannot "stand against the energy of his manly will," Lancelot assures her that "God, the Father of spirits, is leading you!"

And as for marriage, Kingsley calls it the most "spiritual," the most "paradisiac" state one can attain to, for it is the "state through and in which men can know most of God:"

> He [the married man] can know most of God, because it is through those family ties, and by those family names that God reveals Himself to man, and reveals man's relations to Him. Fully to understand the meaning of "a Father in Heaven" we must be fathers ourselves; to know how Christ loved the Church, we must have wives to love, and love them. . . . Forgive me if I have seemed too dogmatic. But God has showed me these things in an eventful and blissful marriage history.

As a result, he can describe the "offices of husband, wife, and parent" as "spiritual, sacramental, Divine, eternal." Once Kingsley could sanctify love and marriage in this way, the same solution was available throughout the whole area of the natural. Whatever he loved— scenery and art and science, war and material progress—all might be saved by finding them divine.

This insistence, that things in themselves are good or evil, is what may be called the liberal fallacy. It appears in such characteristic questions as, "Are the duties, the relations, the daily food of men, of earth or heaven? Is nature a holy type or a foul prison to our spirits?" and so on. One or the other! So stated, the choice is obvious. But to state the moral issue in that form is to obliterate the essential distinction between the object in itself and the object in the human context. Newman did not make that mistake. "The physical nature of man," he said, "is good; nor can there be anything sinful in itself in acting according to that nature. Every natural appetite or function is lawful, speaking abstractly." Exactly so, speaking abstractly; so that a moment later Newman adds, "So much in the abstract—but when we come to *fact,* it may easily happen that what is in itself innocent may not be innocent to this or that person, or in this or that mode or degree." That is the crucial point. Kingsley missed it completely, which was only to be expected, given the basic direction of his thinking. For if, however unconsciously, one wants to justify the human by a transformation which will make it divine, he cannot afford to admit a principle which will find the human sometimes holy and sometimes carnal, and which must therefore assume, to account for this difference (quoting Newman again), that "we have in us by nature a something more" than the natural feelings which in themselves are good, "viz. an evil principle which perverts them to a bad end." That basic insight Kingsley rejected; and once he rejected it, his way was clear to set up the type question—is nature holy or is it carnal?—confident that the answer was absolute. But before we trace the extension of this method from love and marriage to other secular activities, we may glance here at Kingsley's reaction to Anglicanism, since the previous paragraphs provide the right context for understanding it.

## III

It is sometimes forgotten that after his flight from Evangelicalism, when he was searching to find a fresh road out of skepticism, Kingsley came strongly under the influence of the Tractarians, especially Newman. He said later that he had "held, one by one, every doctrine of the extreme High Church party, and faced their consequences"; and of the Oxford Tracts, that his "heart strangely yearned towards them from the first." His reasons—that he liked their "gentlemanlike and gentle earnestness" and recognized their sense of "veneration, imagination, and perception of the beautiful"—show an appeal he found lacking in Evangelical writing. Presently, like so many others, he came under the spell of Newman's preaching, and it was mainly the sermons Kingsley was thinking of when he told Newman that not until 1844 did he finally shake off "the strong influence which your writings exerted on me." Newman's personal attraction, however, continued to be felt: witness the fine portrait in *Yeast*, chapter XIV (1851), the praise of his art and "his knowledge of human cravings" in *Alexandria and Her Schools* (1854); a paragraph in *Fraser's* (January, 1859) on "a great genius and a great orator," ending with the eloquent apostrophe, "Oh, thou great and terrible—sophist, shall I call thee? or prophet? . . . Why is thy once sweet voice all jarred?"; and even after the bitter clash of 1864, there was a sermon at Chester in which, Newman was told, Kingsley preached "about me kindly, though, of course, with criticisms."

The criticisms, first to last, were mainly two, over and above the Protestant-English hatred of all things Catholic. One is the charge of sophistry just mentioned. Kingsley's mind was blunt: he had no taste for qualifications, no perception of the color gray, or the deli cacy and complexity of truth. "Do not be solicitous," he wrote his future wife, "to find deep meanings in men's words. Most men do, and all men ought to mean only what is evident at first sight," which is to say that subtlety of expression is morally suspect. In 1841 Kingsley pounced on Tract 90, taking it for a key to the whole movement, and finding that "whether wilful or self-deceived, these men are Jesuits, taking the oath to the Articles with moral reservations which allow them to explain them away in senses utterly different from those of their authors." And Newman, though believing what he preaches, uses arguments, here and elsewhere, "which he knows to be false."

The other criticism is more important because it is fundamental. In the pronounced asceticism of the Oxford movement Kingsley saw the enemy of everything he valued most deeply and was fighting to save; for asceticism, in whatever form, affirmed that very dichotomy of the two kingdoms which he was so intent on dissolving. Here he seized at once, as we could predict, on the doctrine of celibacy. When the Oxford Tracts "struck at the root of wedded happiness," they stirred him to a fury of indignation which betrays his personal commitment; and so led him to counter with the claim that marriage was the highest spiritual condition. "It is now a recognized principle with the world," remarked Newman dryly in 1841, "that there can be no certainty of holiness except in married life; and that celibacy is all but a state of sin." Kingsley spent a lifetime spreading that gospel.

But over and beyond celibacy as such, the larger implications of asceticism provoked the same self-protective scorn. Kingsley was shocked by a serman of Newman's which suggested the expiation of sin by fasting, alms, and penance. "Is this the liberty," he asked, "with which Christ has made us free?" Is it not rather a return "to the terrors of the law?" That may seem, perhaps, a justifiable objection to Catholic mortification, but a moment later when he adds that if these doctrines are true, "we should be happier here, and safer hereafter, as Jews or heathens," we know that his real objection is to any theology which finds "an evil principle" in human nature or which would discipline the natural impulses.

Finally, the ultimate distinction between the spiritual and the temporal, the Church and the World, which is at the heart of asceticism, is rejected by Kingsley, and in a form which again reflects the liberal fallacy. He is writing to an Anglican:

> I want proof whether you really believe in God the Father, God the Son, and God the Holy Spirit. . . . If you believe that God used to guide the world, or one nation of it, in the Jews' time: if you believe that God takes care of Episcopal churches, and the devil has the rest of the world to himself: if you believe that God takes care of souls, and not of bodies also; of Churches, and not of States also; of ecclesiastical events, and not of political and scientific ones also; of saints, and not of sinners also; of spiritual matters, and not of crops and trades and handicrafts also: then I cannot, cannot say that you believe in the creeds or the sacraments, or Him of whose Eternal being, presence and power they witness.

If we compare that passage with one from Newman's sermon on "The Church and the World" (1837), we can see at once not only that this is an unfair description of Angelican beliefs, but that it falsifies the real nature and meaning of a genuinely religious asceticism:

> He [God] has spread and diffused abroad a spiritual and regenerate kingdom far and wide, and this has encroached in a blessed way upon the world. But it is only in proportion as things that be are brought into this kingdom, and made subservient to it; it is only as kings and princes, nobles and rulers, men of business and men of letters, the craftsman, and the trader, and the labourer, humble themselves to Christ's Church . . . that the world becomes living and spiritual, and a fit object of love and a resting-place to the Christian.

Thus, the dichotomy of the two cities is firmly preserved, and the advance of the kingdom of God made to depend, not on its facile extension over the kingdom of man, but on bringing the latter into the former. Consequently, when Newman uses the Kingsleyan phrase, "the world becomes living and spiritual," he means something very different. He means that the world becomes spiritual only so far forth as it is permeated with the Christian spirit; and the Christian spirit is only to be won by the moral and religious struggle necessary before men can humble themselves to Christ's Church. In Kingsley's passage, however, there are no such distinctions. He assumes that Catholic asceticism means a rigid separation of the Church and the World, which he can then attack in a form which plainly implies that the two are not separate but identical. And if they are identical, there is no need for the bitter choice and the long discipline which is the price of Christian character.

## IV

What Kingsley needed in 1840 was a rationale of the liberal attitude which had been born of his own experience—his strongly secular nature, his natural tastes, his Evangelical home, his love for Fanny Grenfell, and his subsequent recovery of faith and virtue. And the rationale was at hand, in the works of Carlyle, which "laid the foundation," according to Mrs. Kingsley, "to which Coleridge's 'Aids' and Maurice's works were the superstructure." In a letter to Carlyle himself, in 1849, Kingsley analyzed his indebtedness:

> At a time when I was drowned in sloth and wickedness, your works awoke in me the idea of Duty; the belief in a living righteous God, who is revealing Himself in the daily events of History; the knowledge that all strength and righteousness, under whatever creed it may appear, comes from Him alone; and last, but not least, the belief in the Perfect Harmony of the Physical with the Spiritual Universe.

There could hardly be a better statement of what Carlyle meant to the Victorians; and for them, too, I think the final item is "last but not least." It was his German philosophy of nature which made religious faith, after the ravages of eighteenth-century rationalism, again "possible and inevitable," in Carlyle's own words, "for the scientific mind." No need to believe in miracles, in divine interference, nor in such superstitious and irrational dogmas as the incarnation, the virgin birth, the atonement. No, believe only in the fixed order of nature, in which nothing happens, as Bacon had announced in 1605, "but by second causes"—and yet manage to avoid both the absentee God of deism and the no-God of scientific materialism. And how? By finding the natural order supernatural—that is to say, by finding nature, in one way or another, a witness or reflection of God, his "garment" or his "voice" or his "countenance." In this light, we can understand Kingsley's major tribute to Carlyle, that his writings are "instinct with the very spirit of science" because they teach men "to face facts boldly, while they confess the divineness of the facts; not to be afraid of Nature, and not to worship Nature," and so vindicate "at once the dignity of Nature and the dignity of spirit."

The vindication took various related forms. Sometimes Carlyle speaks of nature as a divine symbol ("the visible Universe is indeed but the symbol and sensible manifestation of the Divine Idea"); sometimes this metaphysical conception shades off into mysticism and nature is felt instinct with the Divine Spirit ("The Universe is not dead and demoniacal . . . but godlike, and my Father's! . . . It is in very deed the star-domed City of God; and through every star, through every grass-blade . . . the glory of a present God still beams."). One can imagine the thrill of joy with which Kingsley read such remarks in *Sartor Resartus* and the essays on German transcendentalism, especially that on "Novalis," which he praised by name. Many a passage in his letters of the 1840's speaks of nature as "the countenance of God," finds natural objects "types of some spiritual truth or existence," or natural beauty a "type of the kingdom of heaven." He was more leary of Carlyle's Pantheism, or to speak more accurately, his reduction of God to Divine Immanence. Warned by Coleridge, in a passage of the *Aids* which he must have read, that it meant the substitution of

A sense sublime
Of something far more deeply interfused

for "the heavenly *Father*, the *Living* God," and further cautioned by Maurice against the "wild pantheistic rant" in the lectures on *Heroes and Hero-Worship,* he denied in 1857 that he was "in any wise in theology a follower of Mr. Thomas Carlyle"; and he filled his writings with disparagement of pantheists, neo-Platonists, and "impersonal" spiritualists. Nevertheless, given the whole direction of his thinking, toward merging the divine in the human, let alone his profound admiration for Carlyle and Wordsworth and the Christian Platonists, and we are not surprised by the recurrent references to nature "instinct with The Spirit," to "a living, immanent, ever-working God," or to "the living soul of the universe," so wonderfully described, he said, by William Wordsworth, "preacher and prophet of God's new and divine philosophy," in the famous lines already quoted,

A sense sublime
Of something far more deeply interfused.

This attraction toward divine immanence was strengthened, indirectly, by another Carlylean reconciliation of science and religion, the fideism based on the ultimate mystery of the universe. It is the famous chapter on "Natural Supernaturalism" in *Sartor* which lies behind Kingsley's scorn for "those who see no miracles in every blade of grass, no unfathomable mysteries in every animalculae," or his religious use of this truth in replying to the question why the little diatomaceae split into separate cells:

> Everywhere, skin deep below our boasted science, we are brought up short by mystery impalpable, and by the adamantine gates of transcendental forces and incomprehensible laws—gates of which the Lord . . . alone holds the key.

If emphasis is placed on the "transcendental forces," as it will be where the mystery is the mystery of life, the tendency is to draw the life-force and the spirit of God uncomfortably close together. This is seen in Carlyle's first lecture on *Heroes,* and in Kingsley's sermon at Sion College on "The Natural Theology of the Future" (1871). There, after praising the work of modern scientists, he asks:

> But what are they finding, more and more, below their facts, below all phenomena which the scalpel and the microscope can show? A something nameless, invisible, imponderable, yet seemingly omnipresent and omnipotent, retreating before them deeper and deeper, the deeper they delve: namely, the life which shapes

and makes, . . . which they call vital force and what not—meta-
phors all, or rather counters to mark an unknown quantity, as if
they should call it $x$ or $y$. . . .

Ah that we clergy would summon up courage to . . . tell them
. . . that the unknown $x$ which lies below all phenomena, which is
for ever at work on all phenomena, on the whole and on every part
of the whole, down to the colouring of every leaf and the curdling
of every cell of protoplasm, is none other than that which the old
Hebrews called . . . The Breath of God; The Spirit who is The
Lord and Giver of Life.

On the other hand, if emphasis is placed on the "incomprehensible
laws" of nature, then Kingsley reaches God, not by finding the divine
spirit in phenomena, but by finding the divine will in natural law.
This, indeed, is his central solution to the conflict of "science" and
"religion." It is what he means by saying, in the important letter
from Torquay quoted earlier, that his theological creed has grown
out of his physical one; or by resolving henceforth, in 1859, "to teach
a sound theology through physics"; or by deciding, in 1868, to devote
the rest of his life "to showing that there is a living God in nature."
It is the theme of many a lecture and many a sermon; it is perhaps his
main contribution to Victorian thought, not because it was in the
least original with him, but because he kept repeating it with great
rhetorical force. Its appeal to the age, and to himself, lay in its
avoidance of the metaphysics or the mysticism required by Carlyle's
solution, while at the same time it seemed to make scientific discovery not simply *compatible* with a religious view of the universe, but
*identical* with it. God is found, causatively, in the physical facts
themselves, as they can be observed and measured, rather than "felt"
or "imagined," spiritually, through or behind them—a consumma-
tion devoutly to be wished by the essentially non-mystical and scientific Victorians, including Charles Kingsley. By 1857 he could repudiate the German mode of thought seen in Novalis as a "boy's
love"; admit that though a mystic in theory, he was "an ultra-mate-
rialist in practice"; confess that he was happiest classifying a new
polype or solving a "bit of hard Baconian induction." But with a
magic incantation—"Nature is the Word of God revealed in things"
(Bacon's remark, always on Kingsley's tongue)—he could sanctify
the secular study of science and again merge the human and divine.

The fullest statement is the sermon on "The Meteor Shower" in *The Water of Life;* its essence is in the preface to *Town Geology* (1872), where he felt called on to defend his scientific writings:

> First, as to meddling with secular matters. I grudge that epithet of "secular" to any matter whatsoever. But I do more; I deny it to anything which God has made, even to the tiniest of insects, the most insignificant atom of dust. To those who believe in God, and try to see all things in God, the most minute natural phenomenon cannot be secular. It must be divine; I say, deliberately, divine; and I can use no less lofty word. The grain of dust is a thought of God; God's power made it; God's wisdom gave it whatsoever properties or qualities it may possess; God's providence has put it in the place where it is now, and has ordained that it should be in that place at that moment, by a train of causes and effects which reaches back to the very creation of the universe. . . . It will be obeying physical laws which we term hastily laws of Nature, but which are really the laws of God. . . . Only look at all created things in this light—look at them as what they are, the expressions of God's mind and will concerning this universe in which we live —"the Word of God," as Bacon says, "revealed in facts"—and then you will not fear physical science; for you will be sure that, the more you know of physical science, the more you will know of the works and of the will of God.

Is that anything but the substitution of the word God for the word Nature? Or, if we put the question differently, and ask what Kingsley means by the word God, we can let Newman give the answer:

> What the physical creation presents to us in itself is a piece of machinery, and when men speak of a Divine Intelligence as its Author, this god of theirs is not the Living and True, unless the spring is the god of a watch, or steam the creator of the engine. Their idol . . . is the animating principle of a vast and complicated system; it is subjected to laws, and it is connatural and co-extensive with matter. Well does Lord Brougham call it "the great architect of nature"; it is an instinct, or a soul of the world, or a vital power; it is not the Almighty God.

That is why Newman thought that Physical Theology told us nothing about Christianity; and indeed that "this so-called science tends, if it occupies the mind, to dispose it against Christianity." We remember Kingsley's "I see more and more that we shall work no deliverance till we teach people a little more common physical knowledge; . . . and I shall try henceforth to teach a sound theology through physics." One has an uneasy feeling that the real goal is the physics, whose pursuit is justified by a theology which finds that the laws of nature are the laws of God.

## V

Certainly, the values of applied science, both humanitarian (sanitation, in particular) and commercial (wealth, comfort, and Empire) were very much in Kingsley's mind. In the same preface to *Town Geology*, he rejoiced in the progress of physics, not because of its religious value, but because it promised "more and more of health and wealth; of peaceful and comfortable . . . means of life." The young men of Chester were told that if they would study botany and emigrate to the Tropics, there they would find "precious timbers, gums, fruits, what not, enough to give employment and wealth to thousands and tens of thousands." But if we challenged Kingsley with a suspicious forgetfulness of spiritual values, he would have his answer ready. As the laws of Nature are the laws of God, so "the spirit of progress and improvement" is "the Spirit of God"—at any rate, English progress is, especially the mutual advance of technology and business reflected in Colonial expansion (hence the relevance of Kingsley's remarks on emigration and tropical development). In the following passage we have a beautiful *mélange* of Power and Nationalism and Empire, of Bacon and the Export-Import Trade—and of God. After begging his audience remember that England is "the nation which above all others has conquered nature by obeying her," he points out that "as it pleased God that . . . the father of inductive science, Bacon, Lord Verulam, should have been an Englishman, so it has pleased Him that we, Lord Bacon's countrymen, should improve that precious heirloom of science, inventing, producing, exporting, importing," and that we should carry out "the glorious work which God seems to have laid on the English race, to replenish the earth and subdue it." It follows that "man's scientific conquest of nature must be one phase of His Kingdom on Earth"—which can only lead Kingsley on to finding our new hospitals and railroads, and the Great Exhibition of 1851, "proofs of the kingdom of God," or to the appalling conclusion of a chapter in *Yeast,* where Lancelot is answering a letter from his Catholic cousin:

> When your party compare sneeringly Romish Sanctity, and English Civilisation, I say, "Take you the Sanctity, and give me the Civilisation!" . . . Give me the political economist, the sanitary reformer, the engineer; and take your saints and virgins, relics and miracles. The spinning-jenny and the railroad, Cunard's liners and the electric telegraph, are to me, if not to you, signs that we are, on some points at least, in harmony with the universe; that there is a mighty spirit working among us, who cannot be your anarchic and destroying Devil, and therefore may be the Ordering and Creating God.

But not, we might add, in Newman's words, "not the Almighty God." Here, in the identification of religion with technology and business, we see more clearly than ever the dubious character of the liberal compromise; for here religion is scarcely more than a garment to clothe, and so render respectable, the Victorian passion for industrial and empirial power. In this light, how natural, and how significant, that Kingsley thought "the finest type of civilized man" to be "a combination of the truly military with the truly scientific man"; that he looked forward to the passing of political power "into the hands of scientific men, . . . an aristocracy of sound and rational science"; and that he confessed that for twenty-five years, from 1844–1869 (almost the entire period of his ministry in the Church), his "ruling idea" had been "that which my friend Huxley has lately set forth as common to him and Comte; . . . 'the reconstruction of society on a scientific basis.' "

## VI

Of Kingsley's Christian theology it is not necessary to do more than show how consonant it was with the liberal compromise we have been examining; for he himself was not a theologian, and all of his characteristic doctrines are derived from Maurice, his personal friend and "Master," as he called him, and the blessed means of bringing "me on *the* step beyond Carlyle," that is, to Christianity. But, as James Rigg has so ably shown in his *Modern Anglican Theology,* Kingsley's Christianity was strongly redefined under Neo-Platonic

influence; in fact, Rigg calls it a "variation of the Neo-Platonic
theosophy, baptized with a Christian nomenclature." Certainly
Neo-Platonism was precisely what was wanted to break down and
bring together the great dichotomies of Christian orthodoxy.

The determining factor is a "Platonising" of the Holy Trinity, so
that as God the Father is the One or the Absolute, the Son of God is
identified with Reason or the Logos; and then, because the individual Reason is but a ray or spark of the Universal Reason, Christ
becomes "the very archetype of men" and his Spirit is "infused" into
the whole of humanity. As early as 1843, Kingsley spoke of Christ
as "the One infinite divine Reason . . . a pure influence flowing from
the glory of the Almighty; and into this Spirit we are baptized. This
glorious Reason has been infused into even us!" And he significantly
added that this was the unifying truth that underlay the philosophies
of Coleridge and Maurice and Carlyle. As a result, man is not
thought of as separate from God, suffering from original sin, desper-
ately needing repentance and grace before he may be reborn again
in Christ. On the contrary, all men are born children of God, and
baptism is simply the sign of a fact existing from the beginning:

> You have a right to believe that, as human beings, you are
> dead with Christ to the old Adam, the old, sinful, brutal, pattern
> of man. Baptism is the sign of it to you. . . . And the Lord's Supper
> also is a sign to us that, as human beings, we are risen with
> Christ to a new life, . . . that we all have a share in the likeness of
> Christ.

No wonder that Kingsley thought the "essential idea of Protestantism" was "the dignity and divinity of man as God made him"—a
theory which would have surprised Luther and Calvin. It follows
that the purpose of the incarnation was not the redemption of man
by supernatural means, but the making known to him his divine
position and divine privileges that he might realize that eternal
union with God which self-will alone may break asunder. "Evil, as
such, has no existence; but men can and do resist God's will, . . .
and so punish themselves by getting into disharmony with their own
constitution and that of the universe." But only temporarily. For
God is "baffling all the lawlessness and self-will of the spirits whom
He has made," so that ultimately all men are "inheritors of the

kingdom of heaven." Like Maurice, therefore, Kingsley was a universalist; and like Maurice too he repudiated the doctrine of hell.

Needless to say, the Redemption and the Atonement are ignored or but lightly mentioned. In sermon after sermon one looks in vain for almost any recognition of human weakness or spiritual poverty, of the emptiness and wretchedness of life, or the profound need of divine grace. On the contrary, Kingsley's temper and his Platonic theology turned his whole focus upon the "bright side" of Christianity:

> There are two ways at looking at every occurrence—a bright and a dark side. Two modes of action—Which is most worthy of a rational being, a Christian and a friend? It is absurd, as a rational being, to torture one's self unnecessarily. It is inconsistent in a Christian to see God's wrath, rather than His mercy in everything. . . . All the deep things of God are bright—for God is light. The religion of terror is the most superficial of all religions. . . . Remember that His essence is love;—and the thundercloud will blaze with dewy gold, full of soft rain, and pure light!

Finally, there is Kingsley's heaven, which strictly speaking should not be different from his earth, because there is only one realm, there and here, and one life, the same divine-human life. Or, to speak more accurately, the only difference should be, that as earth is sanctified, heaven should be secularized. That is precisely what we find, and on the Victorian model. The landscape of heaven is beautiful ("gayer meadows and bluer skies await thee in the *world to come*"). The heavenly day is filled with "incident and action" because the "reward for having wrought well already, is to have more to do," and those who look for idleness, there or here, are base cowards, however they may call themselves saints. And love, so central in Kingsley's life and thought, which on earth is but the type of a divine archetype (and therefore holy), that too, of course, goes blessedly on: angels "may be united in pairs by some marriage bond," and as for husbands and wives, all earthly expressions of their love are "but dim shadows of a union which shall be perfect." The Kingsley tombstone bears the inscription "Amavimus, Amamus, Amabimus."

## VII

The best critique of Kingsley and Liberal Protestantism is to be found in two sermons by Newman, though neither was written, I imagine, with Kingsley in mind. The first, preached in 1832, is called "The Religion of the Day." Its theme is that in every age there is a religion of the world "which so far imitates the one true religion, as to deceive the unstable and unwary." The deception springs from accepting certain facts of holy doctrine while neglecting others; but the neglect, as Newman shrewdly observes, may well distort and corrupt even that portion of the Gospel which has been put forward. "What is the world's religion now?" he asks. "It has taken the brighter side of the Gospel,—its tidings of comfort, its precepts of love; all darker, deeper views of man's condition and prospects being comparatively forgotten. This is the religion *natural* to a civilized age." It includes no true fear of God, no deep hatred of sin, no jealous adherence to doctrinal truth, no sense of the authority of religion as external to the mind; "in a word, no serious-ness,—and therefore is neither hot nor cold, but (in Scripture lan-guage) *lukewarm*." And what men are attracted to this cheerful religion of the day? First, those who identify "their vision of Christ's kingdom with the elegance and refinement of mere human civiliza-tion," and have hailed every evidence of progress "as signs of their coming Lord." Second, men of skeptical minds who want a *"rational* form of religion." "They lay much stress on works of *Natural Theol-ogy*," which, besides being rational, reveal the beauty and the mercy of God. But such works are not, says Newman, religious at all in any true sense; for sun and moon and stars " 'declare the glory of God' but not His will." They show his brightness and benevolence, but not his wrath. They do not speak to sinners at all. They reveal only the God who made the heavens, not the God of justice and holiness. And so, by utterly ignoring the "dark side of religion," they tend not only to mutilate Christianity, but even to distort, by isolation, the real meaning of those very aspects of God which they emphasize.

The other sermon of Newman's which should be brought to bear on Kingsley's Liberalism is "Nature and Grace," published in 1849 among the *Discourses Addressed to Mixed Congregations*. It opens with the clearest and most devastating picture I know of what may be called the dead-end of Liberal Protestantism; and as such, the passage must be quoted at length.

> There are no special doctrines, necessary to be believed in order to salvation; it is not very difficult to be saved; and most men may take it for granted that they shall be saved. All men are in God's favour, except so far as, and while, they commit acts of sin; but when the sin is over, they get back into His favour again, naturally and as a thing of course, no one knows how, owing to God's infinite indulgence, unless indeed they persevere and die in a course of sin, and perhaps even then. There is no such place as hell, or at least punishment is not eternal. Predestination, election, grace, perseverance, faith, sanctity, unbelief, and reprobation are strange ideas, and, as they think, very false ones. This is the cast of opinion of men in general, in proportion as they exercise their minds on the subject of religion, and think for themselves; and if in any respect they depart from the easy, cheerful, and tranquil temper of mind which it expresses, it is when they are led to think of those [Catholics] who presume to take the contrary view, that is, who take the view set forth by Christ and His Apostles, . . . [and] who are the witnesses and preachers of those awful doctrines of grace, which condemn the world, and which the world cannot endure. . . .
>
> Its highest idea of man lies in the order of nature; its pattern man is the natural man; it thinks it wrong to be anything else than a natural man. It sees that nature has a number of tendencies, inclinations, and passions; and because these are natural, it thinks that each of them may be indulged for its own sake, so far as it does no harm to others, or to a person's bodily, mental, and temporal well-being. It considers that want of moderation, or excess, is the very definition of sin, if it goes so far as to recognize that word. It thinks that he is the perfect man who eats, and drinks, and sleeps, and walks, and diverts himself, and studies, and writes, and attends to religion, in moderation. The devotional feeling and the intellect, and the flesh, have each its claim upon us, and each must have play, if the Creator is to be duly honoured.

It would be unfair, I think, to point a finger at Kingsley and say, "Thou art the man." For did he not describe himself as "an old-fashioned High Churchman"? and pride himself on belonging to the Church of England *"as by law established"?* and quote the Prayer Book? and emphasize the value of the Creeds and the efficacy of the Sacraments? That is the man his curate, William Harrison, described—only to add, however, that "the two most distinctive features of his religious teaching were, I think, that the world is God's world, and not the Devil's, and that manliness is entirely compatible with godliness." Precisely. And those distinctive features, which symbolize everything we have been exploring, are not consonant with the Christianity of the Creeds. It is *not* unfair, therefore, to see in Newman's passage the real bearing of Kingsley's work; or, to put the same thing differently, the real drift of Liberal Protestantism. For however superior to this at its best and at its start, in men like Coleridge, Arnold, and Maurice, this is the end of the road. This is the child grown up, and now, in Kingsley, showing his true character, and about to break out of the orthodox home and go forth, in his own right, to spread the Gospel through the Protestant Churches. And how wonderfully Newman exposes his real nature, so that we see the disguised naturalism. One thinks of the dubious praise of Kingsley in the funeral sermon preached by A. P. Stanley: "He was we might almost say, a layman in the guise or disguise of a clergyman."

If we must choose between the great antagonists of 1864, can there be any question? A thousand times rather let us follow Newman, even to Rome, than accept this patched-up excuse for a genuine religion. And for the Victorians, as I pointed out earlier, that was the only choice because, when the Protestant revival of Wesley had been sapped by its pietistic and philanthropic strain, the only bulwark against Liberalism was Catholicism. But today, when the reaction against Liberalism, if not widespread, is at least emphatic among our leading theologians, we need not choose Newman in order to avoid Kingsley. For if Protestantism can return to its sixteenth-century heritage and build again on its theological foundations, we can achieve a firm and living Christianity which shall be neither liberal nor Roman.

# 3

# *Trollope, Bagehot, and the English Constitution*

———◆———

## Asa Briggs

*EDITORIAL NOTE. No collection of essays on the Victorian period would be adequate without a contribution from Asa Briggs, distinguished author of such works as* Victorian People *and* Victorian Cities. *The present selection attempts to define the special ethos of mid-Victorian England, a period which is marked off at one end by the opening of the Crystal Palace (May 1, 1851) and, at the other, by the "political engineering" of Gladstone's First Ministry (1868–74) which tidied up the situation left by the Second Reform Bill of 1867 and brought Great Britain into a recognizable "modern" political and administrative world.*

*The writers who most adequately convey the ethos of this period are, for Asa Briggs, Walter Bagehot (1826–1877) and Anthony Trollope (1815–1882). Trollope was, incredibly, the author of forty-seven novels, more than the combined output of Dickens, Thackeray, and George Eliot. Bagehot's collected works occupy many volumes and are now being reissued under the aegis of* The Economist, *the weekly which he edited and founded. He was a first-rate reporter and literary critic, an authority on the international money market* (New Lombard Street) *and the author of* The English Constitution *as well as* Physics and Politics: Thoughts on the Application of the Principles of Natural Selection and Inheritance to Political Society. *In politics, these middle years are frequently designated as "the Age of Palmerston" after the statesman who seemed to embody the character and outlook of the ascendent commercial and industrial middle classes. His program appeared unbeatable: conservatism in domestic affairs and jingoistic liberalism abroad. It proved impossible to make any substantial changes in the "constitution" or to extend the First Reform Bill until after Palmerston's death in 1865. With one five year gap he held the highest offices in the land from 1830 until 1865—Foreign Secretary (1830–1851); Home Secretary (1852–1855); Prime Minister (1855–1865). Asa Briggs offers a revealing portrait of the nineteenth century equivalent of "the Eisenhower years."*

# I

The middle years of Victorian England have been variously labelled. Two of the most frequent labels, which have been attached by tidy-minded historians, have been 'the age of Bagehot' and 'the age of Trollope.' The brilliant diagnosis of *The English Constitution* and the steady observation displayed in the forty-seven novels of Trollope seem to point to a common set of interpretations and conclusions. Both writers described the same superficially secure and comfortable England: for both of them Young England had passed into the world of dream and Chartism into the world of nightmare.[1] The fire of the 'forties had burnt out: if there was fear in society, it was not fear of the machine-breaker or the demagogue, but of the grocer and the merchant. As far as politics was concerned, 'a sense of satisfaction permeates the country because most of the country feels it has got the precise thing which suits it.'[2]

Neither Bagehot nor Trollope would have chosen the particular labels attached by their enthusiastic disciples. For both the central political figure of their times was Palmerston, and the age they were describing was 'the age of Palmerston.' Characteristically they

---

[1] See W. L. Burn, *The Age of Equipoise,* a paper read to the Anglo-American Historical Conference, July 1949.
[2] *The English Constitution* (1867), Ch. V.

did not pitch his claims too high. He was not considered a hero so much as a symbol. Bagehot found the secret of his success in the fact that though he was not a common man, a common man might have been cut out of him. 'He had in him all that a common man has and something more.'[3] Trollope, who wrote a little-known biography of Palmerston, said similarly that 'he was by no means a man of genius, [and was] possessed of not more than ordinary gifts of talent ... He was a man who from the first was determined to do the best with himself; and he did it with a healthy energy, never despairing, never expecting too much, never being in a hurry, but always ready to seize the good thing when it came.'[4] Palmerston was supreme precisely because he never expected too much. 'He was a statesman for the moment. Whatever was not wanted now, whatever was not practicable now, he drove quite out of his mind.'[5]

The normal politics which both Bagehot and Trollope described was the politics of the period of Palmerston's ascendancy. The stormy issues of the past were allowed to lapse: there was no undue interest in the future. Fortune favoured the politician who left too rapid improvement alone. It was not the business of politics to define political issues but to provide honest leadership and sound administration. In *The Prime Minister* the Duke of Omnium is disturbed when his restless leader of the House of Commons suggests that the government might be well advised to find a policy for the new session. It soon becomes clear, however, that Sir Orlando Drought has no policy to propound, save a mild increase in armaments, to which people would not bother to object. He himself indeed goes on to confirm that the main work of Parliament was to raise supplies. 'When that has been done with ease . . . Ministers are very glad to get rid of the Parliament . . . To get a session over and done with is an achievement and delight.' Bagehot presented the same picture. The legislative aspect of the work of Parliament came third in normal times, subordinate in importance to the executive management of the state and the political education pro-

---

[3] *Biographical Studies* (1881), p. 341.
[4] Lord Palmerston (1882), in the *English Political Leaders Series*, p. 9.
[5] *Biographical Studies* (1881), p. 342.

vided for the whole nation. If the governments were anxious to
avoid contentious legislation the members of the House of Commons
were loath to seek too frequent dissolutions. Elections were expen-
sive and too frequent contact with constituents was demoralizing.
And so the politically experienced Palmerston, who knew how to
lull rather than to arouse the minds of his followers, became the
dominating figure in the life of his age.

'Dear old Brock,' says one of Trollope's characters, 'he was the
very model of an English statesman. He loved his country dearly,
and wished her to be, as he believed her to be, first among nations.
But he had not belief in perpetuating her greatness by any grand
improvements. Let things take their way naturally—with a slight
direction hither or thither as things might require. That was his
method or ruling . . . He never broke his heart because he could not
carry this or that reform. What would have hurt him would have
been to be worsted in personal conflict. But he could always hold
his own, and he was always happy. Your man with a thin skin, a
vehement ambition, a scrupulous conscience, and a sanguine desire
for rapid improvement, is never a happy and seldom fortunate
politician.' [6]

Fortune is usually more fickle in its dealings with politicians than
Trollope suggested, but it was consistent enough in the middle
years of the century. Scrupulous consciences operated in private
rather than in public: they called upon the active service of the
voluntary body rather than the state. Sanguine desires for rapid
improvement were at best tinged with expediency. The great cry
of parliamentary reform, for instance, which had divided England
in the early nineteenth century was kept alive, as Bright once suggested, by its enemies as much as by its friends. Its survival as an
issue is best explained in terms of the delicately balanced political
situation within the House of Commons rather than in terms of
sustained pressure from outside or of the persistent attraction of a
fundamental theory. The reform bills of ministers were less triumphant vindications of principle than useful political manœuvres
which had the special advantage of being very unlikely ever to come

[6] *The Prime Minister* (1876), Ch. XI.

off. 'In politics at least the old antithesis of principle and expediency is absolutely forgotten,' wrote Sir Robert Cecil. 'Expediency is the only principle to which allegiance is paid.'[7] Even after the formation of Palmerston's ministry of 1859, which prepared the way for the emergence of the Liberal Party, politics remained in a state of truce, of arrested development. 'Never had the British mind shown itself so *decousu,* so unravelled, at sea, floundering in every sort of historical shipwreck,' wrote Henry Adams of the year 1863.[8] It was only after the passing of the Reform Bill in 1867, which could be regarded either as the crowning triumph of expediency or the belated victory of principle, that politics took a new turn.

# II

Both Bagehot and Trollope recognized that the peculiar characteristics of the English constitution in the middle years of the century depended upon a social as well as upon a political balance. The two main features of the social balance, as Bagehot stressed, were 'old deference' and the appeal of 'dignified parts' of the constitution, 'parts, that is, retained not for intrinsic use, but from their imaginative attraction upon an uncultured and rude population.'[9] Deference and dignity were safeguards of parliamentary government in a society in which 'primitive barbarism lay as a recognized basis to acquired civilization.' But they were more than safeguards: they were pre-conditions. 'A deferential community, even though its lowest classes are not intelligent, is far more suited to a cabinet government, than any other kind of democratic country, because it is more suited to political excellence. The highest classes can rule in it; and the highest classes must, as such, have more political ability than the lower classes . . . A country of respectful poor, though far less happy than where there are no poor to be

---

[7] Quoted W. L. Burn, loc. cit. Trollope suggested in a bitter aside in *The Three Clerks* (1858) that Peel had begun the dominion of expediency in 1846. Bagehot was wise enough to see, as Trollope came to see, that Peel's changes of opinions and policies were proofs of conscientiousness, not indications of a want of it. The two men agreed that the problems of the middle years of the century demanded a flexibility in the art of government which might easily taper off into expediency.

[8] *The Education of Henry Adams* (1918), Ch. XII.

[9] *The English Constitution,* Ch. VI.

respectful, is nevertheless far more fitted to the best government. You can use the best classes of the respectful country; you can only use the worst where every man thinks he is as good as every other.' [10] Happiness is considered neither as a pre-condition of nor as a prior objective of 'the best government.' The 'best government' is that based on discussion; it is most effectively managed by 'a select few,' men who have enjoyed 'a life of leisure, a long culture, a varied experience, an existence by which the judgment is incessantly exercised and by which it may be incessantly improved.'

The select few were the members of Parliament. Although some of them were 'the finest brute votes in Europe,' they were for the most part prepared to debate wisely and above all to choose responsible members of the cabinet. They were never eager 'to press the tenets of their party to impossible conclusions.' Together they made up 'a deliberate assembly of moderate and judicious men.' They chose rulers 'as we wish rulers to be chosen. If they did not, in a speaking and writing age, we should soon know.'

Trollope accepted the social pre-suppositions of Bagehot and explored them more fully in his novels. For him it was essential that the members of the select few should always be 'gentlemen.' He was very sensitive on this point and laboured it both in his novels and in his *Autobiography*. 'He would be defied to define the term ['gentleman']—and would fail should he attempt. But he would know what he meant, and so very probably would they who defied him.' [11] While Bagehot, the essayist, stressed the simple contrast between the many and the few, Trollope the novelist explored the gradations, the boundaries, and the no-man's lands which separated them. At one end of the scale were the 'coarse, dull, contracted multitude,' who only existed to serve and minister to the middle ranks of society and the upper classes. Trollope's poor have a language of their own, but little independent life: in so far as they have aspirations they make themselves ridiculous, as does Mr. Bunce in *Phineas Finn*. And the lower ranks of the middle classes are almost as ridiculous; in attempting to meddle with politics, they find them-

---

[10] *The English Constitution*, Ch. VIII.
[11] *An Autobiography* (1883), Ch. III.

selves, like Mr. Tappit, in *Rachel Ray*, getting into a series of scrapes and finally consoling themselves that political activity 'is just what gentlefolks is fit for when they're past their regular work.' It is only a few members of the middle classes who rise above the level of their station and mix freely with the squirearchy in a world of politics, which does not ask too many questions, provided that 'you are a gentleman.'

Although the world described by both Bagehot and Trollope seems surprisingly static, it contained within itself seeds of change, which compelled both writers to qualify their picture of a society divided into the many and the few. Changes in the distribution of wealth were more important than changes in politics in challenging the existing basis of the constitution. Bagehot defended the deference structure of English society because it saved the country from the rule of wealth, 'the religion of gold,' but he saw clearly that the kingdom of wealth was extending its boundaries with dangerous rapidity and challenging traditional social structure. 'Every day our companies, our railways, our debentures and our shares, tend more and more to multiply these *surroundings* of the aristocracy and in time they will hide it.' [12] Trollope went further along the path of criticism than the author of *Lombard Street*. For Trollope the world of wealth was associated not with the creation of valuable real capital but with senseless speculation, dangerous bubbles and 'the infamous trade of stock-jobbing.' In its intrusions into politics it destroyed old values without suggesting new ones. In all Trollope's novels the share-pusher is a conventional villain, leading the simple and the frail down the slippery slopes of temptation. The slopes are considered so slippery that Trollope often takes as his text, both in the *Autobiography* and in many of the novels, the phrase *facilis descensus averni*. Many man like Alaric Tudor in *The Three Clerks* could persuade themselves that they were rising in the world when all the time they were on the verge of destruction. 'What if a man be going down, down to Tophet, and yet think all the while he is scaling the walls of Heaven?'

This was indeed a very pertinent question in mid-Victorian Eng-

---

[12] *The English Constitution*, Ch. IV.

land. The social bases of the constitutional stability of the age of
Palmerston often appeared to be undermined by dangerous patches
of shifting sands. The expansion of the world of wealth was making
it difficult to distinguish between fortune hunting and real industry,
between social aspiration and legitimate self-help. All Trollope's
themes revolve around the ease of individual advancement in a
fluid society and the much greater ease of individual disaster.
Integrity appears as a rare gift rather than as a common denomina-
tor of action. *The Way We Live Now*, which is usually considered apart
from the rest of his novels, is an angry attack on the social shams of
his day. Society revolves around Melmotte, a financial magnate who
becomes a social potentate merely because he is rich and can make
others rich too. Trollope could never bring himself to appreciate
Bagehot's optimistic conclusion that the expansion of the world of
wealth was worth while, even though it let in 'a dirty crowd of little
men,' because it prevented England from becoming 'sleepy.' Unlike Bagehot he cared little for analogies between science and
politics and glib consolations that 'the rough and vulgar structure
of English commerce is the secret of its life; for it contains "the
propensity to variation," which, in the social as in the animal
kingdom, is the principle of progress.'[13] For Trollope it was the
impact of society and politics on personalities which was of fundamental importance, and not a general law of social progress.

    There was a second question which was as important as the first.
How could individual advancement in society be reconciled with the
maintenance of a necessary social balance between groups and
classes? Palmerston believed—and his belief was in line with the
orthodoxy of the age—that there was no great difficulty. 'We have
shown the example of a nation in which every class of society accepts
with cheerfulness that lot which Providence has assigned to it, while
at the same time each individual of each class is constantly trying to
raise himself in the social scale—not by injustice and wrong, not
by violence and illegality—but by persevering good conduct and
by the steady and energetic exertion of the moral and intellectual

[13] *Lombard Street* (1873), Introductory. Compare *Physics and Politics* (1872), Ch. VI.

faculties with which the Creator has endowed him.'[14] Smiles could have spoken no more persuasively. Trollope, although he showed the pitfalls and dilemmas which checked an automatically beneficent operation of individual exertion, accepted the general principle. So did Bagehot, very specifically, in his essay on Sterne and Thackeray, where he distinguished between social systems founded upon caste and those founded upon equality. The English system of 'removable inequalities, where many people are inferior to and worse off than others, but in which each may hope *in theory* to be on a level with the highest below the throne,' was superior to both. Indeed the English system allowed each individual 'reasonably and without sanguine impracticability' to gain one step in social elevation and to be at least on a level after a period of striving with those who had been originally slightly above him.[15]

Such appreciations of the peculiar excellencies of the English social system attempted to reconcile self-help and social order, but they were as effectively challenged and undermined by the passing of the second Reform Bill in 1867 as was the Palmerstonian constitution itself. Lowe was following Smiles,[16] Trollope and Bagehot when he pointed out that a large measure of parliamentary reform would be unnecessary if every working man £8 householder abstained from the consumption of twenty quarts of beer a year and acquired the suffrage by effective, but not excessive, self-help. Such an argument was swept away in a welter of political excitement which transformed the whole basis of the constitution. Not a brick of the Palmerston house was left standing. The change was 'a change not in one point but in a thousand points . . . a change not of particular details but of pervading spirit,'[17] and the danger of the future ap-

---

[14] Quoted W. L. Burn, loc. cit.

[15] *Literary Studies* (1879).

[16] *Duty*, written in 1880, long after the passing of the second Reform Bill, best expresses Smiles' point of view. 'Men cannot be raised in masses, as the mountains were in the early geological states of the world. They must be dealt with as units; for it is only by the elevation of individuals that the elevation of the masses can be effectively secured.' See my article in the *Cambridge Journal*, June 1949: *Samuel Smiles and the Gospel of Work*.

[17] *The English Constitution*, Preface to the second edition (1872).

peared to lie not only in constitutional upheaval but in the complete overthrow of the deference structure of society.

## III

Within the framework of the unreformed constitution there was one particular problem which Trollope explored more realistically and profoundly than did Bagehot—the problem of electioneering. Like Bagehot he was conscious of the honour of becoming a Member of Parliament, of belonging to the inner circle of the political élite, but he realized that elections were somewhat unsatisfactory means of getting into Parliament, because they were sordid and corrupt exercises in bribery and cajolery rather than rational verdicts of the local will. If society really was constituted as both he and Bagehot believed, the would-be Member of Parliament had to lower himself at election times in order to raise himself when the election was over. The way to the Palace of Westminster led through the pig-sty. From his own actual experiences as well as from his meditations on society Trollope acquired a lively and provocative picture of the place of elections in politics.

In his *Autobiography* he wrote that he had always thought that to sit in the British Parliament should be the highest object of ambition for every educated Englishman. 'I do not by this mean to suggest that every educated Englishman should set before himself a seat in Parliament as a probable or even a possible career; but that the man in Parliament has reached a higher position than the man out,—that to serve one's country without pay is the grandest work that a man can do,—that of all studies the study of politics is the one in which a man may make himself most useful to his fellow-creatures,—and that of all lives, public political life is capable of the greatest efforts.' [18] In his commentary on Trollope, Michael Sadleir refuses to take this remark seriously, and for no apparent reasons calls it 'a quaint declaration.' [19] In fact it was in keeping with the whole of Trollope's attitude to politics and society. He had never found in the public service of the Post Office that prestige

[18] *An Autobiography*, Ch. XVI.
[19] *Trollope, A Commentary* (1927).

which membership of the House of Commons gave. He realized, despite all his success as a public servant, that, in Bagehot's famous phrase, 'a clerk in the public service is "nobody;" and you could not make a common Englishman see why he should be anybody.'[20]

Seeking the social prestige and the political distinction of the House of Commons, Trollope decided in 1867 at the age of fifty-two to enter Parliament. 'I had an almost insane desire to sit there,' he wrote, and although he failed to secure nomination for a safe seat in Essex, he went to the very corrupt borough of Beverley in Yorkshire a year later to try out his fortune. He had no illusions about the dangers and difficulties of his enterprise; indeed his agent there began by telling him that not only would he not get elected, but that also he would lose a vast sum of money in the process of trying. 'You will spend £1000 and lose the election. Then you will petition, and spend another £1000. There will be a Commission and the borough will be disfranchised. For a beginner such as you are, that would be a great success.' Trollope did not flinch. 'In the teeth of this, from a man who knew all about it, I persisted in going to Beverley.'

Now Beverley was by no means unique among small English boroughs, where corrupt practices long survived the Reform Bill of 1832, but it had a long standing record of corruption which was made public for all to see after the famous 1868 election. There had been previous election petitions in 1837, 1857 and 1860. The petition presented after the 1868 election was examined by a High Court judge who found that 104 persons had been guilty of corrupt practices. The most influential manipulator of a highly corrupt electorate was a draper who acted as Conservative agent: his method was to buy votes not during parliamentary elections, as in days of more blatant corruption, but during town council elections, on the sensible supposition that convinced voters would remember their duty and their bribes. A Royal Commission which went on to examine the state of Beverley more thoroughly in the summer of 1869 not only uncovered corrupt practices during six preceding elections but brought to light a traditional structure of corruption. One witness

[20] *The English Constitution,* Ch. iv.

even produced an account book for the 1807 election which showed that of 1010 electors who voted for one of the candidates, only 78 received no money. These revelations led to the disfranchisement of the borough in 1870.[21]

Trollope described the fourteen days of his canvassing in Beverley as 'the most wretched fortnight of my manhood.' 'In the first place,' he declared, 'I was subject to a bitter tyranny from grinding vulgar tyrants. They were doing what they could, or said that they were doing so, to secure me a seat in Parliament, and I was to be in their hands at any rate for the period of my candidature . . . From morning to evening every day I was taken round the lanes and by-ways of that uninteresting town, canvassing every voter, exposed to the rain, up to my knees in slush, and utterly unable to assume that air of triumphant joy with which a jolly successful candidate should be invested . . . But perhaps my strongest sense of discomfort arose from the conviction that my political ideas were all leather and prunella to the men whose votes I was soliciting. They cared nothing for my doctrines, and could not even be made to understand that I should have any.' On the two issues concerning which his most radical supporters felt strongly—the ballot and the permissive drink Bill— Trollope disagreed violently with them. But it was not issues which decided the election, but bribes. 'It had come to pass that political cleanliness was odious to the citizens. There was something grand in the scorn with which a leading Liberal there turned up his nose at me when I told him that there should be no bribery, no treating, not even a pot of beer on our side! It was a matter of study to perceive how at Beverley politics were appreciated because they might subserve electoral purposes, and how little it was understood that electoral purposes, which are in themselves a nuisance, should be endured in order that they may subserve politics.' 'The use of the borough seems to be realized and approved in the borough in general. The inhabitants have taught themselves to think that it was for such purposes that boroughs were intended.'

---

[21] See *Copy of the Minutes of Evidence taken at the trial of the Beverley Election Petition (Parliamentary Papers,* 1868–9; *XV,* No. 90): *Election Expenses (Parliamentary Papers,* 1868–9, *XVII,* No. 424).

From Trollope's account it is clear that he shared, as a result of experience, Bagehot's reluctance to transfer political power from Parliament to the constituencies, from the men who knew to the men who did not know. He went further than Bagehot however in showing that constituents were not only potentially dangerous but also actively corrupt. Only the glory of the goal made the struggle worth while.

Even before he contested Beverley Trollope had described parliamentary elections in his novels. *Rachel Ray,* for instance, written in 1862, describes an election in the small borough of Baslehurst, where the expected costs of campaigning, petitioning, and scrutiny amount to over £6000. Voting behaviour depends upon custom and the supply of drinks and gifts rather than on political propaganda or persuasion. When the Conservative candidate is a little worried about his bad speaking, his agent tells him, 'It don't matter. It's only done for the show of the thing and to fill up the day. If Gladstone were here he wouldn't talk a vote out of them one way or the other, nor yet the devil himself.' The result appeared indeed to be a foregone conclusion before the poll. 'It was all known and thoroughly understood as though the matter was past a doubt.'

The description of the election in Baslehurst was merely a foretaste of what Trollope would do when he had added personal experience of an election to acute observation from outside. For in *Ralph the Heir,* written in 1870–71, Trollope took his revenge on Beverley. *Ralph the Heir* contains the best election episodes in English fiction and introduces us to one of the most sympathetic candidates who ever presented himself to a corrupt electorate—Sir Thomas Underwood.

Sir Thomas has been in Parliament before and has held minor office; he wishes to get back again, even though he knows the difficulties involved. 'I dare say I am a fool for my pains. It will cost me some money that I oughtn't to spend. If I get in, I don't know that I can do any good or that it can do me any good.' But he clings on despite illness, violence, and ultimate unseating by petition. As in Beverley the end of the story is the disfranchisement of the borough.

The account of the campaign is fascinating. Percycross had been fortunate to survive even the Reform Bill of 1832. It had in its Tory

agent, Trigger, a consummate political manipulator who dealt in
votes as easily as pioneers dealt in oil. Underwood came to loathe
Trigger but he had to depend upon him, particularly in keeping in
touch with the local network of business interests, represented by
the mustard-maker, the paper-maker, and two manufacturers of
boots. When Sir Thomas declared himself in favour of purity of
election one of his most influential supporters was shocked into
sickness. 'The idea of purity of election at Percycross made him feel
very sick. It was an idea which he hated with his whole heart. There
was to him something absolutely mean and ignoble in the idea of a
man coming forward to represent a borough in Parliament without paying the regular fees . . . It might be all very well in Manchester and such-like disagreeable places. But that candidates should
come down to Percycross and talk about purity there, was a thing
abominable to him.' Blessed with such supporters Sir Thomas began
to feel a strange but understandable sympathy for the raw and in-
genuous Radical candidate, Ontario Moggs, who disassociated
himself completely from his Whig colleague and stood for the advanced doctrines of Purity and the Rights of Labour. Moggs soon
realized too, however, that there were far too many men in Percycross 'who hate the very name of Purity and who know nothing of
the Rights of Labour.' [22]

*Ralph the Heir* recapitulated the gloomy experiences of Beverley,
and in a sense all Trollope's other political writings were substitutes
for political action, 'his compensation for disappointment.' [23] If he
could not air his political views in the House of Commons, he could
air them in his novels; but it was not the defeat at Beverley that
turned him to political writing so much as a growing interest in
politics which turned him to the election. What the defeat at Beverley did was to quicken his insight and to goad his pen. Just as the
election in *Ralph the Heir* is more vividly described and more corrupt
in its character than the election described in *Rachel Ray*, so *Phineas
Redux*, written in 1870, is more bitter in its tone than *Phineas Finn*
written in 1868.

[22] *Ralph the Heir* (1871), Chs. XX, XXI, XXVI.
[23] See Michael Roberts, *Trollope's Political Novels* in *Standpunte*, January 1950.

Trollope's political novels reflected his experiences, but they also reflected the constitutional theories of Bagehot. *The English Constitution* appeared just when Trollope's series of political novels was beginning. It was probably seen by Trollope at an early stage, for it first appeared as a series of articles in *The Fortnightly,* a review which Trollope had helped to launch in 1865.

Trollope's novels bring to life through illustrative examples Bagehot's notions of responsible power. They are concerned with the niceties of party and the perils of coalition, with the maintenance of majorities in a period when 'majorities were collected God knows how, voting God knows why,' and with the conventions of dissolution. But they are concerned too with problems which Trollope could explore more sensitively than Bagehot, problems of personality—the attempts of men like Phineas Finn, Monk and Palliser to keep their ethical standards from being dragged down to the level of those of purely professional politicians. The greatest tragedy of all to Trollope was that men should want to get seats in Parliament to protect their interests as directors of companies.[24] This was political prostitution of the worst sort and a sign that public life was not all that it ought to be, even after the business of fighting elections was over and done.

## IV

Both Trollope and Bagehot lived long enough to see the second Reform Bill of 1867 and the Ballot Act of 1872, but they did not live long enough to witness the cleaning up of the electoral system or the growth of powerful party organizations which re-designed political machinery and forced new issues into the open. Bagehot died in 1877 and Trollope in 1882: the sharp political cleavages and the re-definition of the content of politics still lay ahead. But both were sensitive to change, particularly to the slow but sure process of adaptation which passed for change in high-Victorian England.

---

[24] See *The Prime Minister,* Ch. II. Membership of the House of Commons 'assists a man in getting a seat as the director of certain Companies. People are still such asses that they trust a Board of Directors made up of Members of Parliament.'

Neither of them was a Tory, clinging to the traditions of the past. Trollope called himself an 'advanced Conservative-Liberal,' for both he and his generation liked political hyphens more than we profess to do today. Bagehot was Liberal enough to welcome the fundamental 'march of improvement' of the nineteenth century, but Conservative enough to believe that reform should produce greater stability and not an accelerating demand for further change. Neither in short was committed irrevocably to a party label. The political conditions of their day allowed them a position of intellectual detachment, which they would have found difficult to maintain even fifteen years later. As Palliser put it in *Phineas Redux:*

> When some small measure of reform has thoroughly commended itself to the country—so thoroughly that all men know that the country will have it—then the question arises whether its details shall be arranged by the political party which calls itself Liberal—or by that which is termed Conservative. The men are so near to each other in all their convictions and theories of life that nothing is left to them but personal competition for the doing of the thing that is to be done.

In their capacity to weigh arguments and in their balance of hopes and fears Bagehot and Trollope expressed more clearly than any other two writers the equipoise of mid-Victorian England, and although there were many problems which they both ignored, they saw quite clearly the central problems of the English constitution in a highly distinctive period of English social and political history.

# 4

## Tennyson's Ulysses: A Reconciliation of Opposites

### John Pettigrew

EDITORIAL NOTE: *Tennyson was born in 1809 and began publishing poetry at the age of eighteen; he continued to publish with undiminished energy until his death in 1892. It was an extraordinary career as well as a long one; he almost outlived the Age of Tennyson and became a legend in his own time. There has always been an argument about the way in which this great body of verse should be estimated. One group of readers respond to the esoteric and lyrical poems which treat of situations of psychological estrangement, withdrawal and despair—"The Lady of Shalott," "The Lotos-Eaters," "Tithonus," "Tears, Idle Tears" are representative examples. Another group of readers prefer poems which offer a more didactic and public statement of the poet's moral and social commitment to his society.* The Princess *and* Maud *and the "domestic idyls" address themselves more directly to subjects of contemporary interest. (One could argue that the last great public occasional poem in English is the "Ode on the Death of the Duke of Wellington.") It seems apparent, in any event, that Tennyson was strongly drawn towards two conflicting poetic roles—the artist as romantic recluse, withdrawn from vulgar concerns, and the artist as spokesman for his tribe, "Poet of the People." This*

*uncertainty about poetic ambitions he shared with other writers; it is expressed*
*time and again in his verse and contributes to the interest and drama of his*
*career. All these matters find expression in John Pettigrew's careful examina-*
*tion of the familiar "Ulysses," which appeared in 1842. The first half of his*
*essay is on the history of criticism of the poem; the last part presents Pettigrew's*
*version. Readers who are not concerned with previous readings may wish to*
*skip.*


"Tennyson," writes Professor Brooks, "was not always successful
in avoiding the ambiguous and the paradoxical; and indeed, in some
of his poems his failure to avoid them becomes a saving grace," into
which he "may be thought to have blundered" [1] (like the Light Bri-
gade?). While no one would argue that all of Tennyson's poems are
as susceptible of being turned into metaphysical poems and therefore
pronounced satisfactory as "Tears, idle tears," Brooks's implication
that Tennyson consistently and conscientiously avoided enriching
his poetic texture through irony is refuted by poem after poem in
which Tennyson's own fondness for the qualities which so much
modern criticism holds dear is clearly displayed: one has only to
think of the handling of comic irony in "Saint Simeon Stylites" or
"Locksley Hall," the paradoxical association of love and war (emphasized by the martial ballads sung by the heroine) as regenerative
forces in *Maud*, the inversion of the conventional values of the myth
in "The Holy Grail," the swift undercutting of the apparent theme
in the conclusion of "Vastness." But perhaps no Victorian poem
packs such an infinity of riches into a little room as "Ulysses"; what
I wish to do here is to develop and support a view of that poem which
seems to be emerging from some recent criticism, a view which sees
"Ulysses" as considerably more comprehensive and complex than
earlier comments had suggested. [2]

[1] Cleanth Brooks, *The Well Wrought Urn* (New York, 1947), p. 153. My paper is a revision
of one read at the 1961 meeting of the Association of Canadian University Teachers
of English. For much helpful criticism I wish to thank Professor F. E. L. Priestley.

[2] Much that is essential in my interpretation of "Ulysses" is suggested, directly and in-
directly, in Charles C. Walcutt, "Tennyson's *Ulysses*," *Explicator*, IV (1946), item 28;
E. D. H. Johnson, *The Alien Vision of Victorian Poetry* (Princeton, 1952), p. 41; W. B.
Stanford, *The Ulysses Theme* (Oxford, 1954), pp. 202–204; Robert Langbaum, *The*
*Poetry of Experience* (London, 1957), pp. 89–93; Jay L. Halio, " 'Prothalamion,'
'Ulysses,' and Intention in Poetry," *College English*, XXII (1961), 390–394.

"Ulysses" is one of the few Victorian poems to excite almost universal admiration; "a perfect poem" Mr. Eliot called it in his essay on Dante of 1929,[3] and from the moment of publication it has been highly praised. Carlyle, for instance, thought it the best poem in the 1842 volumes, and was persuaded that if only its author would give up poetry and get down to *Work* something might come of him.[4] The interpretation of "Ulysses" implicit in Carlyle's comments has been generally accepted, by all commentators for a hundred years after the poem's composition, and by most modern readers; for them the major key of the poem with its noble strength and vigorous resoluteness affords a striking contrast to the more characteristically Tennysonian minor key with its suggestions of indecisive weakness and lethargic melancholy. In "Ulysses," Tennyson's spokesman utters a clarion call to action and expresses a heroic aspiration "to strive, to seek, to find, and not to yield." In violent opposition to the conventional view, however, is E. J. Chiasson whose capacity for vilifying Ulysses is at least the equal of Thersites': "Ulysses" for him is "a dramatic portrayal of a type of human being who held a set of ideas which Tennyson regarded as destructive of the whole fabric of his society"; the speaker is "a hard, self-contained individual, contemptuous of his people, impervious to the softer affections, the sheer incarnation of 'Renaissance' *superbia.*" Tennyson works by indirection to embody his "conviction that religious faith is mandatory for the multitudinous needs of life."[5] Yet a third clearly distinguishable attitude towards the poem is presented by a small group of writers who react, like Chiasson, against the traditional view, but who direct their criticism not at the character but at the poem itself. Clearly the initiator of this attitude is—as so frequently when an individual talent modifies a tradition—Old Possum. For Mr. Eliot, "Ulysses" is "too *poetical*"; Tennyson "has to get his effect with a certain amount of *forcing.*"[6] Friedrich Brie, complaining that the style was too romantic for the subject, expanded on Mr. Eliot's suggestions, and in

---

[3] *Selected Essays,* 3rd ed. (London, 1951), p. 248.

[4] See Edward FitzGerald's comment, quoted in the notes to Tennyson, *Works,* ed. Hallam Tennyson (London, 1908), II, 337. Hereafter cited as Eversley Edition.

[5] "Tennyson's 'Ulysses'—A Re-Intrpretation," *UTQ,* XXIII (1954), 402–409. Quotation from pp. 402, 403, 405.

[6] *Selected Essays,* p. 248.

remarking that Tennyson seemed to have shifted absentmindedly from soliloquy to dramatic monologue, he suggested a further weakness in form.[7] Brie's criticism seems mild, however, when one turns to the violent onslaught on the poem made by Professor Paull F. Baum in *Tennyson Sixty Years After.*[8] Professor Baum, appalled at the general reader's respect for the poem, summons up all his resolute determination to dislike Tennyson and finds "Ulysses" but a "whited sepulchre," undermined by many inconsistencies. The fairness of outward view, "the triumph of rich color," is marred for him by "bad drawing," he is bothered by questions as to where Ulysses is and to whom he is speaking, by formal incongruities like those detected by Brie, and—one recalls the "dead men's bones" in the Biblical whited sepulchres—by unfortunate echoes of Milton's Satan and Byron's Childe Harold which clash hideously with Tennyson's attempt to present an altogether admirable character. We have, then, three sharply opposed conceptions of "Ulysses": to oversimplify slightly, most readers hear a trumpet-like voice declaiming something like *Rule, Britannia!*; Chiasson hears a Machiavellian villain; Baum comes close to hearing a wretched cacophony, with the conductor of the intended *Pomp and Circumstance* jarring the harmony by forgetting his audience, losing his place, rattling dead men's bones, and singing the odd sentimental strain.

A fourth conception of "Ulysses," one that steers between the seductively simple Scylla of most readers and the chaotic Charybdis of captious critics, it is the aim of this essay to develop. I suggest that the three opinions distinguished above, while unsatisfactory in themselves as final statements, reflect partial truths, and that, taken together—discordant and antithetical as they appear to be—they point to the larger synthesis, the reconciliation of opposites, effected within the poem itself. If, for instance, Chiasson's views are extreme, they are nevertheless a major contribution to fuller appreciation of the poem's riches: if he has tended to ignore any possibility of development in Tennyson's views by consistently tripping Ulysses up by reference to attitudes expressed in later poems, he has at least seen

---

[7] "Tennyson's *Ulysses*," *Anglia*, LIX (1935), 441–447.
[8] (Chapel Hill, 1948), pp. 92–95, and especially pp. 299–303.

"Ulysses" as part of the main stream of Tennyson's poetry and not as a kind of sport in complete contrast in its vigor to the more characteristically Tennysonian melancholy; if he is somewhat insensitive to the whole poem's texture and thus disagrees too violently with the general reader about theme, sentiment, and hero, he has also focused attention on aspects of Ulysses' character in particular which have too frequently been ignored; if he has exaggerated the poem's indirection, he has done it the justice of treating it as a dramatic poem; if his views are sharply opposed to Tennyson's own comments about the poem, he has not taken the conventional view of Tennyson's intention as an infallible guide to its understanding. The difficulty of responding freshly to the badly hackneyed poem is intensified with "Ulysses" by the dogmatic conviction—so strong and traditional as almost invariably to be accepted as axiomatic—that the poem presents a magnanimous hero "going forward, and braving the struggle of life," [9] and by the closely related conviction that Tennyson and Ulysses may be identified. Whether or not the conception of Tennyson's intention which lies behind these convictions is right or wrong, the convictions have certainly obscured the poem's intention, especially when associated with the natural and inevitable tendency of criticism to simplify the complex, to reduce several levels of meaning to one, to turn poetry into prose. And, while Chiasson's views clearly need modification, so too, in the light of the essential rightness of parts of Chiasson's attack on it, does the conception of the simply noble hero. Moreover, judgments asserting the poem's greatness have ignored the incongruities which depreciators of the poem have, so rightly, detected; and, on the other hand, the depreciators (also believing that Tennyson meant to portray a noble hero) have, I believe, drawn the wrong conclusions from the right evidence. For the inconsistencies which they see as indications of the *poem's* failings are rather indications of the *character's* failings. This is a dramatic poem. And only if the object is seen as it really is, do the apparently opposed views taken of "Ulysses" fit into place as indications of the poem's depth of characterization.

[9] Quoted by Hallam Tennyson, *Alfred Lord Tennyson: a Memoir* (London, 1897), I, 196 (hereafter cited as *Memoir*). See also Tennyson's own note in Eversley Edition, II, 339.

It is necessary to insist on the obvious fact that "Ulysses" is a dramatic poem because it has usually been treated as a lyric, a key with which Tennyson unlocked his heart; and while we no longer prove Tennyson mad by equating him with the speakers of "Locksley Hall" and *Maud*, the tendency (to which Tennyson strenuously objected) to confuse the poet with his characters is still rife, as comments on "Ulysses" in particular bear witness. Mr. W. W. Robson, for instance, complains that in it, "Tennyson, the responsible social being, the admirably serious and 'committed' individual, is uttering strenuous sentiments in the accent of Tennyson the most un-strenuous, lonely and poignant of poets," [10] without ever seeming to realize that the accent may tell us something of Ulysses' character; and Professor Georg Roppen, defending Ulysses' attitude towards Telemachus, remarks, "It would be strange indeed if Tennyson, whose besetting fear was of chaos and disorder, in this personal allegory should heap ridicule on 'the useful and the good,'" [11] a remark which assumes that the poem is a "personal allegory" in a rather narrow sense, that Ulysses is noble, that Ulysses is Tennyson, and that Tennyson is deficient in dramatic power. If, however, one can get rid of the beliefs that lead to the stock responses usually involved in reading "Ulysses" and simply read it as a dramatic poem, one comes to see its speaker as a highly complex individual, drawn with such superb poetic and dramatic skill that he partakes of the web of this life, good and ill together, a figure whose strengths and weaknesses are as finely fused as in Shakespeare's Henry V. Just as surely as obviously powerful feelings are objectified in J. Alfred Prufrock, and just as surely as the incongruities in Mr. Eliot's poem are not manifestations of the poem's weakness but dramatic devices revealing the divided personality of the speaker, so are they in "Ulysses." [12] In its

[10] "The Dilemma of Tennyson," in *Critical Essays on the Poetry of Tennyson*, ed. John Killham (London, 1960), p. 159. Robson echoes Brie's strictures.

[11] "'Ulysses' and Tennyson's Sea-quest," *English Studies*, XL (1959), 84. Roppen admirably analyzes Tennyson's handling of the quest as "good and necessary" or "futile" in what he calls the "Homo viator" poems. The ambiguity of the quest Roppen sees in this group of poems, but not in "Ulysses" itself.

[12] All the incongruities which Baum criticizes so heavily in "Ulysses" have their parallels in "Prufrock" and even the most cursory comparison of the critical treatments which each poem has received does well illustrate the perversity of so much "Ulysses" criti-

seventy lines, the poem comprehends much of the wealth of varied characteristics surrounding one of literature's most ubiquitous and ambivalent individuals; Tennyson's character is as many-sided as Homer's "man of many turns," as complex as Dante's mighty sinner. And everywhere the poem is loaded with ore from the tradition inherited and invoked by the poet.

As W. B. Stanford has stressed in his *Ulysses Theme,* authors dealing with Ulysses have varied widely in interpreting his character, but the better writers have naturally encouraged from their readers an extremely mixed response towards him—critics still argue furiously, for instance, about the relative proportions of heroic and satirical elements in Homer's Odysseus. Of more immediate relevance to Tennyson's poem, however, is Dante's Ulisse, who provides the main model for Tennyson's figure. Ulisse, it seems generally to be agreed, is one of the finest of Dante's creations, a complex figure who is very much the plain sailor in his use of matter-of-fact understatement, and at the same time the mighty sinner, his grandeur stemming from his superb determination and pride. He is led to his death by an insatiable thirst for knowledge, and Dante finds him in the ditch to which evil counsellors are assigned in the eighth circle of Hell, the circle reserved for those who have abused the gift of reason for evil purposes. The implications of Tennyson's choice of model are interesting (they have, I think, too frequently been ignored), for the general reference to the situation and character described in *Inferno,* xxvi, does raise the question as to whether Tennyson's Ulysses is to be seen in relation to Dante's Ulisse, one of the chief of sinners, a master of guile whose cunning and rhetorical skill have doomed so many others beside himself. Is Ulysses' address to his mariners to be seen in this context? Is Ulisse's dereliction of duty in undertaking his final voyage, emphasized heavily in his opening words, to affect one's

cism. While, for instance, the conception of "Ulysses" as autobiographical document has dominated critical treatment of it, no one (except when, like Mr. Graves in *The Crowning Privilege,* being deliberately naughty) would dream of treating "Prufrock" in the same way, despite the fact that in many respects (in archetypal quality, in time and milieu, in years) Tennyson's persona is more distant from his creator than Eliot's. Yet, so strong are the prejudices about Tennyson and "Ulysses," that even Mr. Eliot makes the error of identifying Tennyson and his persona in his brief remarks about "Ulysses."

reading of the character presented by Tennyson? While no final answer to such questions is possible, it is certainly clear that the reader who does recall Dante's Ulisse can hardly take a simple view of Tennyson's Ulysses as a noble hero. No one, of course, would suggest that a new handling of an archetypal figure need necessarily involve assimilating all that figure's characteristics, but if no poem has its complete meaning alone, if it is a part of all that it has met in the tradition, an affirmative answer to the questions raised above is at least possible. Moreover, to ignore Dante's treatment of Ulisse in reading Tennyson's poem is made extremely difficult by the poet's obvious awareness of it in writing the poem. On Tennyson's (and Hallam's) respect for, and familiarity with, Dante, there is no need to enlarge—Tennyson is quite clearly familiar with Cary's translation and may well have known Boyd's too;[13] and that Tennyson intended the reader to read his poem in the light of Dante's is suggested by his telling Frederick Locker-Lampson, who had spoken admiringly of "Ulysses," "Yes, there is an echo of Dante in it," by the specific parallels in the verses of the two poets,[14] and, most obviously, by Tennyson's own note in the Eversley Edition (ll. 338–339), calling one's attention to *Inferno*, xxvi, and quoting the first thirty lines of Ulisse's speech, lines which include his report of the oration by which he stirred up the mariners for their "witless flight." Whether or not, however, one admits that the Dantesque conception affects the reading, as it affected the writing, of "Ulysses," the tradition as a whole leaves no doubt, especially in view of the depth

---

[13] Sir Charles Tennyson, *Alfred Tennyson* (London, 1950), p. 32.

[14] *Memoir,* II, 70. The general situation of the old man embarking on a last voyage is similar, though Tennyson stresses, even more than Dante, the neglect of family duty and "return of love, / That should have crown'd Penelope with joy" (ll. 94–95), by having Ulysses embark from Ithaca instead of Circe's island, thus particularizing and making concrete a situation not tangibly presented in Dante. Both figures are conscious of "the short remaining watch, that yet / Our senses have to wake" (ll. 112–113); Tennyson's "untravell'd world" recalls Cary's "unpeopled world" (l. 114); both characters draw contrasts between a brutish life and an active, vigorous one (ll. 115–117); both claim to be pursuing knowledge (l. 117); Tennyson's "sinking star" would seem to derive from Ulisse's star "so low, that from the ocean floor / It rose not" (ll. 124–125). Ulisse's address is clearly a piece of rhetoric designed to incite his mariners to a "witless flight" (ll. 118–121). All references are to lines in Cary's translation of *Inferno*, xxvi.

of Tennyson's knowledge of it, that the character Tennyson inherited was such as to make probable a complex rather than a simple figure.

The weight of external evidence from Tennyson's own personality and situation, reflected in other poems written late in 1833, also supports a complex view of Ulysses, a fact which needs stressing since it is such biographical external evidence that almost invariably provides the starting-point, expressed or implied, for critical treatments of Ulysses which see him as a simple person. The strong conflicting tendencies (from which springs, as E. D. H. Johnson has emphasized, much of Tennyson's best poetry) to withdraw into self and to mix with action, tendencies which are at their strongest in Tennyson's formative years, were never so sharply opposed as they were at the time "Ulysses" was written. The poem was completed in virtually its present form within twenty days of Tennyson's receiving news of Hallam's death,[15] and that news intensifies the force of the conflicting impulses, with "The Two Voices," written within weeks of "Ulysses," providing the most obvious example of the intensification: the impulse to withdraw taking its ultimate form in the temptation to suicide, and the repudiation of that temptation coming in what is represented by the family on its way to church. "Ulysses" reconciles the two voices in one. Its speaker says with the still small voice:

> Why inch by inch to darkness crawl?
> There is one remedy for all, (ll. 200–201)

and:

---

[15] "Ulysses" is dated October 20, 1833, in J. M. Heath's commonplace book. Tennyson added three lines to the version of "Ulysses" transcribed by Heath, revised one other line in it, and made a few other extremely minor changes. What would appear to be the first draft of "Ulysses" is in the Harvard Library (MS Eng 952), notebook 16, a notebook which includes other poems which are dated by Heath in September and October, 1833. J. H. Buckley's references to the Harvard draft in his *Tennyson* (Cambridge, Mass., 1960), pp. 60–61, seem to me misleading. Buckley writes, for instance, that Ulysses "has nothing to say of Telemachus," but a version of the Telemachus passage, not very different from that in the published poem, is in the Harvard MS; and though it stands there as an afterthought, nothing suggests it is not an immediate afterthought.

> This is more vile . . .
> To breathe and loathe, to live and sigh,
> Than once from dread of pain to die. (ll. 103–105)

Ulysses, however, clearly speaks with the other voices as well. He wishes

> To search thro' all [he] felt or saw,
> The springs of life, the depths of awe,
> And reach the law within the law; (ll. 139–141)

he too can say:

> 'Tis life, whereof our nerves are scant,
> Oh life, not death, for which we pant;
> More life, and fuller, that I want. (ll. 397–399)

Further manifestations of the sharpening of the conflicting impulses as a result of Hallam's death are easy to discern. There is, for instance, on the one hand Tennyson's impulse to withdraw into the world of poetry, which can perform for him a cathartic function, "the sad mechanic exercise . . . numbing pain," and, on the other hand, the increased sense of social involvement which finds its expression in the political poems of the period—it is as if, deprived of Hallam's support, Tennyson finds an internal prop in these bad days in writing poetry, and an external prop in his sense of being at one with mankind. There is too the seemingly paradoxical fact that the grief-stricken period of eighteen months or so following Hallam's death is perhaps the most productive period in Tennyson's life—a fact that seems frequently to be neglected or forgotten.[16] That much of Ten-

---

[16] See Joyce Green, "Tennyson's Development During the 'Ten Years' Silence' (1832–1842)," *PMLA*, LXVI (1951), 672–674. The rather too reverent silence of the *Memoir* has led, I think, to too great an emphasis on Tennyson's prostration before the fact of Hallam's death. In an unfortunately unpublished Yale University dissertation (1946), "Tennyson: Studies in the Ten Years' Silence (1833–1842)," Miss Mary Joan Donahue makes a very convincing case for a Tennyson spurred into activity by Hallam's death, against the conventional view of a Tennyson collapsing into something resembling a jellyfish. In this connection see, for instance, a letter of November 1833, which—even if its jocularity is somewhat forced—is rather difficult to square with the conventional view, in Mary Joan [Donahue] Ellmann, "Tennyson: Unpublished Letters, 1833–1836," *MLN*, LXV (1950), 223–228.

nyson's poetry stems from the kind of divided sensibility suggested above is now a commonplace of criticism; at no time however is the division more extreme than at the time of the composition of "Ulysses," a poem which consequently reflects and incorporates the "romantic," withdrawing, passive Tennyson, and the "classical," outgoing, active Tennyson, and which thus, as Chiasson has suggested for different reasons, stands squarely in the main path of Tennyson's development.

Among passages from poems of the "Ulysses" period which reflect interestingly on the poem and on Tennyson's state of mind, are some stanzas from the political poem "Hail, Briton!" [17] The thirty-third stanza (later incorporated in *In Memoriam*, CXIV) gives us the knowledge that Ulysses claims to be following:

> Who loves not knowledge? Who shall rail
> Against her beauty? may she mix
> With men and prosper! who shall fix
> Her pillars? Let her work prevail.

What if, however, the pursuit of knowledge involves conflict with the values represented by Telemachus in "Ulysses"? Other stanzas of "Hail, Briton!" point to what Ulysses is repudiating in the quest after knowledge:

> Not he that breaks the dams, but he
> That thro' the channels of the state
> Convoys the people's wish, is great:
> His course is pure, his name is free.

> He cares, if ancient usage fade,
> To shape, to settle, to repair
> With seasonable changes fair
> And innovation grade by grade. (Stanzas 36–37)

A similar, though indirect, expression of these beliefs comes in another interesting gloss on "Ulysses" in "The Lotos-Eaters" (usually, I think incorrectly, regarded as thematically opposite to "Ulysses")

---

[17] First published by Miss Donahue in "Tennyson's *Hail, Briton!* and *Tithon* in the Heath Manuscript," *PMLA*, LXIV (1949), 385–416. Stanzas 36 and 37 quoted here also appear in "The Statesman," *Memoir*, I, 110–11.

in a section added to the 1832 version, probably in 1834, which
stresses the moral turpitude of the mariners. The mariners suggest,
attempting to excuse their selfish retreat from a world of responsible
action:

> surely now our household hearths are cold:
> Our sons inherit us: our looks are strange:
> And we should come like ghosts to trouble joy.
>
> • • • • •
>
> Is there confusion in the little isle?
> Let what is broken so remain.
> The Gods are hard to reconcile:
> 'Tis hard to settle order once again. (ll. 72–74, 79–82)

While Ulysses is unquestionably more heroic and more sympathetic
than the mariners, and while condemnation of his attitude is only
partial and is expressed even more indirectly than in the "Lotos-
Eaters," these lines do illuminate the opening sentence and the
Telemachus passage of "Ulysses," throwing into relief as they do
the element of selfishness in Ulysses' retreat from a world of responsible action. As a final example, there are the lines from "Tithonus,"
composed in its early form, "Tithon," probably within a year of
"Ulysses": [18]

> Why should a man desire in any way
> To vary from the kindly race of men,
> Or pass beyond the goal of ordinance
> Where all should pause, as is most meet for all? (ll. 28–31)

While Tithonus' attitude clearly contrasts with that of Ulysses, the
ambiguous value attaching to Ulysses' last voyage is pointed up by
these lines; and it is not without interest that Tennyson called
"Tithonus" "a pendent to the 'Ulysses,'" thus suggesting a relation
between the poems of affinity rather than contrast, a suggestion
which may be reinforced by Locker-Lampson's rather baffling remark that Tennyson "gave 'Tithonus' the same position as
'Ulysses.'" [19] Both Tennyson's comments would seem to support

[18] Dated 1833–34 by Donahue, "Tennyson's *Hail, Briton!* and *Tithon*," p. 400.
[19] *Memoir*, I, 459; II, 70.

Robert Langbaum's suggestion that the central emotional content of "Tithonus" and "Ulysses" is similar, the contrast between the poems lying in the fact that in the latter, "the emotion is couched in the contrasting language of adventure, giving an added complexity of meaning to the poem." [20]

In the context of Tennyson's remarks about the relation between "Ulysses" and "Tithonus," and of his unquestionably complex sensibility when he wrote them, the poet's direct comments on "Ulysses" take on fresh meaning. The poem, he wrote, "gives the feeling about the need of going forward and braving the struggle of life perhaps more simply than anything in *In Memoriam*";[21] he did not write that Ulysses is a hero going forward and braving the struggle of life, as the conventional interpretation of his statement would suggest. To feel the need of going forward is very different from actually doing so; Ulysses clearly feels the need, but whether he does go forward and brave the struggle is obviously another question—as with the "I" of "Locksley Hall" or "The Two Voices" or *In Memoriam,* the feeling may well be extremely complex and involve inseparable impulses to retreat. More revealing as a guide to the richness of "Ulysses" is Tennyson's comment to Sir James Knowles: "It *[In Memoriam]* is a very impersonal poem as well as personal. There is more about myself in 'Ulysses,' which was written under the sense of loss and that all had gone by, but that still life must be fought out to the end. It was more written with the feeling of his loss upon me than many poems in 'In Memoriam.'" [22] The stress here lies more on the feeling of loss than on that of fighting life out to the end, and the statement is extraordinarily difficult to reconcile with the usual conception of Ulysses as simply noble, vigorous, heroic. If "Ulysses" is as personal as Tennyson said it was (and there seems to be general agreement that it is an intensely subjective poem), if there is more of him in it than in *In Memoriam* (and no one has denied the capacity for despair in that poem), if the generally held conception

[20] *Poetry of Experience,* p. 90.
[21] Eversley Edition, II, 339; and, in almost identical form, *Memoir,* I, 196.
[22] "Aspects of Tennyson, II. A Personal Reminiscence," *Nineteenth Century,* XXXIII (1893), 182.

of Tennyson's personality is anything like true—then one is clearly justified in suggesting that "Ulysses," in itself and in its speaker, is more likely to embody a divided and complex character than a single-minded and simple one. I suggest, then, that biographical evidence supported by the tenor of other verse of the "Ulysses" period and by the implications of Tennyson's statements about the poem, is a much more reliable guide to the interpretation of "Ulysses" than the usual starting-point: a statement of the poet's intention based on selections from two brief comments.

Although Tennyson avails himself of his right to use the tradition for leverage and enrichment, and although biographical reference provides a helpful indication of the poem's complexity, the poem itself, without any reference to external evidence, insistently forces mixed responses to its speaker and to the values which he embodies. Ulysses complains of being unemployed but he hardly seems to be looking for work, for although he speaks grandly of work of noble note that may yet be done, we hear very little about it in the course of the poem, and instead we see that Ithaca obviously stands in urgent need of such work (we perhaps remember Tennyson's reiterated emphasis on the need of man's doing the duty that lies nearest him). Why is Ulysses idle? Why does he not do something about that savage race and its unequal laws, and attempt to make mild, useful and good his rugged people?—he might perhaps even make a beginning by lighting the fire in that still hearth. Ulysses claims that he is yearning to follow knowledge, but stress falls rather on the wish to escape his feeling of world-weariness in a constant accumulation of new experiences, and on a concern with intellectual oblivion in unceasing activity. Ulysses' motives for undertaking the voyage are further complicated by the contrast between his expressed desire for fuller and richer life, and the implicit extension of the urge to escape into an urge to die.[23] Again, is Ulysses simply following the gleam, or is he rather pursuing the grail?—and one notes that while the grail did exist and had value, the object of Ulysses' quest is left

---

[23] That Ulysses' motives for undertaking his last voyage are complex has frequently been suggested. See, for instance, Walter E. Houghton, *The Victorian Frame of Mind* (New Haven, 1957), pp. 295–297; and Langbaum, *Poetry of Experience,* pp. 89–92.

extremely vague, seems strangely unreal.[24] (I have always had a certain sympathy with the student who concluded a lengthy peroration on Ulysses' virtues with the sentence, "And so Ulysses resolves 'to strive, to seek, and not to find.'") In short, is Ulysses going forward, braving the struggle of life, being true to himself, embarking on a glorious search for knowledge? Or is he seeking extinction, courting death, being false to other men, and fleeing from duty? The mere paraphrasable content of what Ulysses says, especially when heard in its clearly defined situation, calls for such questions as these. And working beautifully to reinforce, to hammer home, the content's suggestion of rich complexity are the poem's structure, ambiguity in diction, syntax, and image, meaningful variations in the quality of the diction and the rhythm, and echoes of other works of literature.

"Ulysses" falls into four clearly defined parts, two of which present an essentially heroic Ulysses, two of which display less attractive characteristics. The first paragraph (ll. 1–5) suggests one extreme difference between Homer's Odysseus, always yearning for home, and Tennyson's Ulysses, who can't stand it. In presenting Ulysses' view of his present situation, he reveals anything but the noble Ulysses of popular imagination, for the bitterness is so intense as to make him odious rather than pathetic, and the expression of contempt for land, wife, and people is given real bite by the harsh grating monosyllables. The Biblical echo in "It little profits," while faint, is suggestive, and along with the sharp "mete and dole" brings to mind a self-centered petty tradesman. The undeniable snarl in "Match'd with an aged wife" is scarcely fair to poor old Penelope, whose own marital loyalty has been displayed during the years of Ulysses' absence by her weaving a magic web as steadily as the Lady of Shalott (with the additional hardship of having to take the work out every night). While the reference to the "still hearth" has a

---

[24] The contrast between Telemachus and Ulysses is rather like that between Arthur and the knights whose pursuit of the grail, even with those whose honor and motives are personally unexceptionable, is one of the most important causes of the destruction of Arthur's social order. The vagueness of the object of aspiration is an obvious frequent characteristic of Victorian literature, but while the vagueness weakens, say, "The Scholar-Gypsy," it has dramatic value here, just as it does in, for instance, *Middlemarch*, where the vagueness of Dorothea's aspiration is both a criticism of her milieu and the source of much gentle irony at her expense.

special poignancy for one who recalls that Homer's Odysseus repeatedly thinks of home in terms of the peaceful image of rising smoke, the phrase may well remind one of the lotos-eaters' excuses, and the paragraph as a whole makes relevant, indeed inevitable, the questions previously raised as to why Ulysses is idle when the legal system and the savage race are so obviously in need of reform. Moreover, the extremely heavy and regular iambic beat of the fifth line sharply stresses Ulysses' pride through his resentment that his people (imaged as animals) [25] no longer know him; the phrase "know not me" might be neutral, might even be spoken wistfully, were it not that the rigid movement of the line inevitably strongly emphasizes the "me" with which the paragraph ends (Sir Lewis Casson makes a valiant attempt, on the Caedmon recording, to read this line as if it were spoken by a magnificent old warrior; the attempt, the deed, and Tennyson's rhythm all confound him).

The second paragraph (ll. 6–32) sustains the note of pride struck at the end of the first; it explains Ulysses' disgust with his present situation and his hopes for the future in his Tennysonian passion of the past and regret for the days that are no more. Its primary relation to the first paragraph, however, is one of contrast, its main purpose in the poem as a whole being to establish the heroic aspects of Ulysses. While the diction is still largely monosyllabic, we have here the grand style rather than the savage bite of the opening paragraph; and, despite the romantic, un-Greek motif of the glorious quest, the Homeric tends to dominate the Dantesque, as the reader's imagination is released from the confines of Ithaca to the wide world of excitement and activity of classical epic, reflected in the echoes of Homer and Vergil and in the freer-flowing rhythms. The capacious grandeur of the speaker is primary and unmistakable—a line like "Far on the ringing plains of windy Troy" is in itself enough to give the lie to Chiasson's interpretation of Ulysses—but the grandeur (which is so obvious that I assume it in what follows) is nevertheless qualified, for the texture of the passage is complicated by the inter-

[25] The image and tone may well remind one of the soul's comments in "The Palace of Art," ll. 199–202: "I watch the darkening droves of swine / That range on yonder plain. / In filthy troughs they roll a prurient skin, / They graze and wallow, breed and sleep."

weaving of other threads which give additional depth to the characterization by insistently emphasizing the less praiseworthy aspects of Ulysses impressed in the opening movement, and by suggesting further characteristics. There is certainly intense pride. The concentrated use of appetitive terms ("drink / Life to the lees," "hungry hearth," "drunk delight of battle") may, as Roppen suggests,[26] stress Ulysses' capacity for enthusiasm, but it also reinforces the impression of a restless wanderer and strongly implies that the enthusiasm is rather for self-gratification than for pursuing knowledge. The Faustian element in Ulysses' quest has often been noted, and, in the light of Tennyson's work as a whole, one would feel surer of Ulysses' nobility if he were following "wisdom" rather than "knowledge." [27] The impression of resolute vigor is somewhat weakened by the slow movement of the lines comparing experience to an arch—as Matthew Arnold remarked in misquoting the lines horribly in "On Translating Homer," "these three lines by themselves take up nearly as much time as a whole book of the *Iliad*." The complexity of Ulysses' motives and character is further indicated near the end of the second paragraph in the phrase "like a sinking star." The star may well recall that of Dante's Ulisse, and the syntactical ambiguity of the phrase certainly complicates the apparent meaning. The phrase may modify "follow" and/or "knowledge." [28] If read as modifying "follow" it is an unhappy prognostic when the fate of Ulisse is recalled; if read as modifying "knowledge," the primary meaning of the image (one that takes us back to the fading margins,

---

26 " 'Ulysses' and Tennyson's Sea-quest," p. 81.

27 In the fullest treatment of "Ulysses" as personal allegory, Edgar Hill Duncan, "Tennyson: A Modern Appraisal," in *Tennessee Studies in Literature*, IV (Knoxville, 1959), 13–30, suggests (p. 30n.) that Tennyson first clearly distinguished "knowledge" and "wisdom" in "Locksley Hall," ll. 141, 143, and that in "Ulysses" "knowledge" has the kind of oracular connotation later involved in Tennyson's use of "wisdom." While the point is of more relevance to Tennyson's intention than to any reader's response, I would nevertheless agree with G. Robert Stange, "Tennyson's Garden of Art: A Study of *The Hesperides*," *PMLA*, LXVII (1952), 732–743, that the distinction is already implicit in some of the early poems. Stange's analysis of the symbolism in "The Hesperides" is illuminating for "Ulysses."

28 The ambiguity is discussed by Baum, *Tennyson*, p. 300, and by Halio, " 'Prothalamion,' 'Ulysses,' and Intention in Poetry," p. 393. A comma followed "knowledge" in the first edition, but Tennyson later omitted it.

and forward to "the baths / Of all the western stars") is qualified by
one's sense that the white star of truth seems to be in an unfortunate
place—the morning star to which Tennyson's sailor boy whistles,
or the rising stars which "lighten'd into view" in "The Voyage"
would certainly be more appropriate symbols for a pursuit of renewed life. The essentially noble voice of the second paragraph is,
then, counterpointed throughout by the still small voice; the passage
is an exciting example of the subtlety of Tennyson's dramatic
powers.

The third paragraph (ll. 33–43) has aroused much critical dis-
agreement. Most readers believe that Ulysses wisely leaves work for
which he is unsuited to a son whose merits he well recognizes, while
others stress Ulysses' dereliction of duty, and find contempt and
scorn in his attitude towards Telemachus. Both conceptions are
clearly possible, but the dominant tone, though considerably muted,
is rather like that of the first paragraph, to which we are taken back
by the reference to a present social context, and by a certain similarity in Ulysses' attitude towards Ithaca and its people. Whether or
not there is anything reprehensible in Ulysses' abdication—an
either/or response to the passage is, I think, undesirable—Ulysses'
indifference to the kind of work left to Telemachus and to the kind
of value represented by him is admirably stressed by the "un-
Tennysonian" extreme abstractness and poverty of the diction and
the flat, flabby rhythms, qualities emphasized by the richness and
surface vigor in the surrounding paragraphs. It is interesting that
while Ulysses attributes to Telemachus the quality of "slow pru-
dence" so prominent in the Homeric Odysseus, the negativeness and
adjectival drabness of "blameless" and "decent not to fail" scarcely
reflect much enthusiasm, the verb "subdue" is hardly tactful, the
dull prosiness of "the useful and the good" makes them sound almost
unpleasant, the adjective "common" applied to Telemachus' duties
has that telling ambiguity which is so fatal to any simple conception
of Ulysses' character, and Telemachus is even given the task of saying Ulysses' prayers for him. The unpleasant aspects of Ulysses'
character dominate in this paragraph.

The certain similarity in tone of the Telemachus paragraph to the opening sentence should not however obscure the difference in tone, for the opening's extreme bitterness and caustic contempt is certainly subdued here. The change in tone corresponds, I believe, to a change in form, occurring with the gesture implicit in "This is my son, mine own Telemachus," from interior to exterior monologue. Awareness of the Victorian genius and fondness for the dramatic monologue tends to make one forget how very tentatively Tennyson moved in its direction (witness "Oenone" and "The Lotos-Eaters"), and how very *new* "Ulysses" is in form. The reader of 1842 must have begun the poem by reading in terms of the familiar soliloquy and not of the relatively unfamiliar exterior monologue, especially since the presence of the mariners is not directly indicated until late in the poem. The first two paragraphs read like soliloquy, and evidence suggests they must be that. One would surely need to be excessively foolhardy and courageous to describe one's wife to her face as "aged"; and while Alexander Hamilton referred to his people as a great beast, he did not do so on a public platform, nor was he exactly an outstanding example of political tact—Ulysses speaks here of a "rugged people" and not of a "savage race." Most important of all, the master of rhetorical persuasion who speaks the poem's final paragraph would hardly convince an audience listening to the first two paragraphs of anything but his own bitterness, egocentricity, and restlessness, all qualities conspicuously absent from the final paragraph.[29]

The presence of soliloquy is suggested by Professor Baum, puzzled by Ulysses' location and audience: "It may be that the poem consists of three quite separate dramatic fragments, the first (ll. 1–32) a soliloquy *pure et simple,* the second (ll. 33–43) a farewell speech to his countrymen, and the third (ll. 44–70) a hortatory address to his

[29] The first critic to suggest the presence of soliloquy was Brie, who thought the shift to exterior monologue came with line 44. Walcutt, "Tennyson's Ulysses," thinks the poem improved if read as the reverie of a man *"dreaming* of a last adventure." He based his view on the melancholy of the poem, but ultimately rejected it because of the general Dante reference. My treatment of the third paragraph and the shift to exterior monologue is strongly indebted to Baum, *Tennyson,* pp. 299–300; I think, however, that he invents the difficulty of Ulysses' location.

fellow mariners. If this is so, we should expect some indication in
the text, or at least a plainer division in the printing, instead of consecutive paragraphs unspaced." [30] Sixty-four years before *Tennyson
Sixty Years After,* however, Tennyson blocked out the poem almost
as Professor Baum wishes he had: he divided it into four paragraphs
and left spaces between them. Editors always write that "Ulysses"
was unchanged after first publication and print the poem wrongly in
almost every modern edition; "Ulysses" appeared in its new format
in the New Collected Edition (London, 1884), and that format was
followed in every important subsequent edition in Tennyson's lifetime, and in the Eversley Edition.[31] The revision is admittedly slight,
but does help to support the suggestion of a shift from interior to exterior monologue; it throws greater weight on the first five lines by setting them off from the following passage; it heightens, by forcing the
reader's eye to pause between paragraphs, the kind of contrast between parts of the poem which I have been outlining above. To see
Ulysses as shifting from interior to exterior monologue also serves to
indicate that the Telemachus section is a revised version for public
consumption of the private opening movement, and the final paragraph a splendid piece of oratory which, keeping the mariners well
in mind, presents a nobler, less egocentric concept of the voyage than
Ulysses' private meditations in the second paragraph. One of the
great merits of "Ulysses" is certainly its perfectly controlled structure. The first private half of the poem is transposed into a new key in
the second, public half, the third and fourth paragraphs balancing
the first and second respectively. The Janus-like aspects of Ulysses
are further revealed through the contrast between the halves of the
poem, and between the predominantly ignoble Ulysses of the first
and third paragraphs, and the predominantly noble Ulysses of the
second and fourth.

[30] *Tennyson,* pp. 300–301.
[31] Until 1884, "Ulysses" was divided into three unspaced paragraphs at lines 33 and 44.
No change occurred in the one-volume *Works* (London, 1884), issued in January. The
change made in the New Collected Edition, issued later in 1884, is carried on in the
New Library Edition (London and New York, 1888) and in the Eversley Edition.
In these, there are four spaced paragraphs, beginning at lines 1, 6, 33, 44; only the
third and fourth are indented.

The final movement (ll. 44–70) is even more magnificent than the second, but again the splendor of Ulysses needs qualification. If the slow-moving verse gives Ulysses dignity and power, it also again somewhat undercuts the impression of hardy vigor:

> The lights begin to twinkle from the rocks:
> The long day wanes: the slow moon climbs: the deep
> Moans round with many voices.

These lines, and others of similar quality, have recently been frequently criticized as being too Tennysonian, too romantic, too poetical; the melancholy music is said to be inappropriate and martial music to be required: how *could* Tennyson, writes Mr. Robson, "have been content with the style of a minor poet." [32] The lassitude in these lines is, however, admirably dramatic in its capturing of the extent to which the motives for undertaking the voyage stem from world-weariness and the urge to escape, are negative rather than positive. If the movement of the verse evokes an elegiac mood, the complexity of the poem and its speaker is further underlined by other elements. "Men that strove with Gods" certainly works in two ways. Ulysses' setting out at night (so often attacked as being un-Greek!) may stress the romantic splendor or the classical foolhardiness of the voyage. Also functioning ambiguously are the symbols of the voyage, the Happy Isles, and the sea. The voyage may involve flight from duty or a search for it, a call to life or death or dreamful ease, a following of knowledge or a Byronic wallowing in experience. The Happy Isles, the dwelling of the virtuous after death, suggest a goal of renewed life in opposition to the gulfs; the context, on the other hand, hints that they may well be identified with Lotos-Land or with the "summer isles of Eden lying in dark-purple spheres of sea" to which the hero of "Locksley Hall" thinks of escaping, as well as with Avilion. The passage ultimately reflects Ulysses' fearlessness of death, his desire for renewed life, his wish for escape, his suicidal urge to pass to that "newer world" "beyond the sunset" of his life. The sea has many voices too—is it the south sea of escape or the Lincolnshire sea of life in "Locksley Hall"? Certainly here no "mighty wind arises,

---

[32] "The Dilemma of Tennyson," p. 159.

roaring seaward"; the landscape is still and hushed, the vessel only
puffs her sail, the seas gloom and are dark. In "Crossing the Bar"
the poet wishes that there be no moaning of the bar when he puts out
on a sea of death and of renewed life; in "Ulysses" "the deep moans
round" and its many voices speak perhaps more of death than of life.
In short, the final paragraph reveals a great deal more than a man
going forward and braving the struggle of life, for its atmosphere is
redolent of death, and death is associated now not with Ithaca, as
it was earlier in the poem, but with the world beyond it and with
the voyage.

A further factor enriching the texture of "Ulysses," which I have so
far only touched on, is the unusually insistent presence of echoes from
other works of literature. Besides the direct references to classical
epic, several echoes of Homer and Vergil summon up their worlds of
heroic action: "the rainy Hyades / Vext the dim sea," "delight of
battle," "windy Troy," "I am a part of all that I have met," "sitting
well in order smite / The sounding furrows," "the baths of all the
western stars." All these frequently noted echoes occur in the two
paragraphs which I have described above as presenting a predominantly heroic Ulysses; they are clearly deliberate; their function is
obvious; but another group of echoes is not as simple to deal with
because it raises the question as to when an echo becomes an allusion,
as to when the original context of a borrowing affects one's response
to the new context. Professor Baum, noting the presence of this group
of echoes, believes they mar the poem: "The Byronic was probably
not intended for our ears," he remarks, and, catching Ulysses in the
act of sounding like Milton's Satan, he writes, "We were not supposed to catch this echo, or even to recognize the Byronic over-
tones." [33] The display of optical and aural gymnastics involved in
this way of reading a poem seems to me rather strange. It is surely

[33] The number of things Professor Baum thinks one ought to notice but ignore is quite
remarkable. We find again that "we rarely observe the contradictions" between the
realistic on the one hand, and the romantic and picturesque on the other, in the final
paragraph. The contradictions "are in a sense irrelevant; it seems almost indecent
to take note of them. It is even bad taste to remark that neither Odysseus in Homeric
times nor Ulisse in mediaeval, would be likely to push off at nightfall" (p. 302). As I
have suggested, the contradictions and the time of departure should be noticed: they
tell us a great deal about Ulysses.

impossible for the modern reader, especially as reconditioned by
Mr. Eliot to recognize and appreciate an allusive technique, not to
treat clear echoes as allusions, and since "Ulysses" relies fairly exten-
sively on them, it may be that the poem has in some measure
changed its meaning, is perhaps a good example of the way in
which the old work can be modified by the new one. However this
may be, the fact is that if the poem's dimensions and Ulysses'
stature are enlarged by the classical echoes, the stature is reduced
by the pervasive general reference to Dante's Ulisse, and by more
particularized echoes.

"What shall it profit a man, if he shall gain the whole world, and
lose his own soul?"—considering what follows, the echo of Mark in
the opening line is immensely apposite. As Professor Douglas Bush
has noted,[34] the opening lines also recall the soliloquy beginning
"How all occasions do inform against me," in which Hamlet contrasts his own inactivity with Fortinbras' energy (IV, iv, 32ff), the
contrast partially comprehending Ulysses' divided personality, and
with its wealth of suggestion again making the echo meaningful. The
resemblance of image and feeling in "I will drink / Life to the lees"
to Macbeth's "The wine of life is drawn, and the mere lees / Is left
this vault to brag of " (II, iii, 91–92) is perhaps more tenuous, but if
the echo is admitted, the parallel and contrast with Macbeth's
statement gives added depth to Ulysses' words. The frequently noted
reminder of Shakespeare's Ulysses helps to reinforce the impression
of the languor of Tennyson's. Tennyson's hero remarks:

> How dull it is to pause, to make an end,
> To rust unburnish'd, not to shine in use!

The lines echo:

> Perseverance, dear my lord,
> Keeps honor bright; to have done, is to hang
> Quite out of fashion, like a rusty mail
> In monumental mockery. (*Troilus and Cressida,* III,
>                                                    iii, 150–153)

On the relation between these two passages, Mr. Stanford makes the

[34] "Tennyson's 'Ulysses' and *Hamlet,*" *MLR,* XXXVIII (1943), 38.

perfect comment: "The imagery is the same, but the context is significantly different. Shakespeare's Ulysses, an eminently extrovert figure, had addressed these words to Achilles in his sulky sloth. Now ... Tennyson's Ulysses has to address the exhortation to himself." [35] The same passage also recalls, as does the tenor of much of the second paragraph in particular, the restless self-centered Byronic wanderer of *Childe Harold:*

> Their breath is agitation, and their life
> A storm whereon they ride, to sink at last,
> And yet so nursed and bigoted to strife,
> That should their days, surviving perils past,
> Melt to calm twilight, they feel overcast
> With sorrow and supineness, and so die;
> Even as a flame unfed, which runs to waste
> With its own flickering, or a sword laid by,
> Which eats into itself, and rusts ingloriously.[36]

"He works his work, I mine" will for some readers recall Count Cenci's "He does His will, I mine!" (*The Cenci*, IV, i, 38) a remark made at God by Cenci as he curses his child Beatrice and gestures at heaven—the impression of Ulysses' scorn for Telemachus and of his rather slighting references to the Gods is certainly intensified if one admits the echo. And even the splendid resoluteness of the poem's final line is undercut with superb irony as, not for the first time, the shade of Milton's Satan is summoned by it: "And courage never to submit or yield" (*Paradise Lost*, I, 108).

How far Tennyson intended the echoes to have the effect they do on the modern reader is perhaps difficult to decide. Later in his life Tennyson was to call Churton Collins "a louse upon the locks of literature" [37] for so over-emphasizing his debts to previous writers that Tennyson felt he had been "most absurdly accused of palgiarizing." "People accused Virgil of plagiarizing," he remarked to Herbert Warren, "but if a man made it his own there was no harm in

---

[35] *The Ulysses Theme*, p. 203.
[36] *Childe Harold*, iii, stanza 44. Compare also *Childe Harold*, i, stanza 27; iii, stanzas 42–43; and "I live not in myself, but I become / Portion of that around me" (iii, stanza 72), with "I am a part of all that I have met."
[37] Charles Tennyson, *Alfred Tennyson*, p. 490.

that (look at the great poets, Shakespeare included)." [38] It would surely be strange if the poet who so loved two of the most allusive of English poets, Milton and Pope, was not well aware of the values of allusion; and, moreover, a number of notes in Tennyson's early volumes and in the Eversley Edition specifically draw attention to borrowings, and "Morte d'Arthur," written shortly after "Ulysses," is thickly sown with them. That Tennyson intended the classical echoes in "Ulysses" to be recognized is proved by his notes on the poem in the Eversley Edition, and the echoes of more modern poets are so pervasive as to suggest their being consciously intended. But whatever Tennyson's intention, the effect on the modern reader is clear enough.

And the same thing is true of the poem as a whole. We should no longer need warnings against the intentional fallacy; the question as to what extent Tennyson intended the complexity of utterance, feeling, and character that lies at the center of the greatness of "Ulysses" is inevitable because of its fascination, unanswerable because no artistic intention is ever fully to be comprehended, and ultimately unimportant because the poem speaks for itself. Even if one assumes, however, that Tennyson meant to find an objective correlative for braving the struggle of life, he chose as that correlative a figure who had in time played many parts, and embodied the traditional ambiguities surrounding Ulysses in his poem. He chose him at a time when his feelings about braving the struggle of life were far from simple, so that Ulysses became the correlative not for one simple feeling but for a complexity of feelings, a unified product of a divided sensibility, a fine example of Coleridge's "balance or reconciliation of opposite or discordant qualities." No single poem of Tennyson's reveals more of his poetic and dramatic powers; "Ulysses" marks his poetic coming of age as surely as "Chapman's Homer" marks Keats's, or the "Nativity Ode" Milton's.

---

[38] *Memoir*, II, 385.

# 5

## Two Styles in the Verse of Robert Browning

Robert O. Preyer

EDITORIAL NOTE. *Robert Browning was born in 1812, in a suburb of London. His education was haphazard, a matter of tutors, general reading in his father's extensive and curious library, and a few weeks at the new London University. Much of his life was passed abroad—in France, in Italy. (His son was to marry an American heiress and pass his days in one of the largest palaces on the Grand Canal.) Browning was an autodidact, an artist, and a cosmopolite, precisely the man one would expect to be celebrated in the second of Ezra Pound's* Cantos. *A great deal of ink has been spilled in efforts to comprehend Browning's "philosophy" and many essays devoted to his presumed ethical and religious teachings. Santayana, in a famous attack, has held him up as the poet of barbarism; others have attempted to place him firmly in a conventional Victorian setting. Robert Langbaum's* The Poetry of Experience *supplies a brilliant account of his development of the dramatic monologue which has become, in our time, virtually the sole mode of lyric poetry. The present study redirects attention to the language and resources of style, those aspects of his work which account for his puzzling reputation as*

*a genuine but flawed artificer of verse, perhaps the most original poetic voice
of the period.*

## I

We are faced at the start with a curious embarrassment. Browning's style, like his personality, is often depicted as either too simple or too complex.[1] The simplicity is somehow related to the Happy Warrior aspect of the verse; complexity appears when he adopts the role of Profound Metaphysician. These remarks are too general, as they stand, to be useful for the literary critic. They do suggest, however, the presence of two styles—"simple" and "difficult"—and imply that these styles are paired off with two sorts of subject matter. This paper will begin by inquiring whether we can in fact identify elements of two styles in Browning's poetry (later on I shall consider a middle stylistic term). Then it will proceed to examine the notion that each style consorts (happily or unhappily) with specific kinds of content.

Let us begin the discussion with a brief account of the elements that compose the "simple" style. I am thinking now of the fast-paced, pounding and jiggling *narrative* style of "Cavalier Tunes" (1842), "The Flight of the Duchess" (1845), *Christmas Eve and Easter Day* (1850), "Holy Cross Day," "The Heretic's Tragedy," "Transcendentalism" (all from the 1855 *Men and Women* volume), much of *Pacchiarotto* (1876) and of the volume published on the day of his death, *Asolando* (1889). A great many titles could be added; the list is given, in part, to suggest that this style remained with him throughout his literary career. (I exclude from consideration the plays and also the early continuous narrative confessions *Pauline*

---

[1] Browning's personality remains an enigma. Hardy's comment is well known: "How can smug Christian optimism worthy of a dissenting grocer find a place inside a man who was so vast a seer and feeler when on neutral ground?" G. K. Chesterton remarked in his little book on Browning (1903), "His work has the mystery which belongs to the complex; his life the much greater mystery that belongs to the simple. He was clever enough to understand his own poetry . . . but he was also entirely unconscious and impulsive, and he was never clever enough to understand his own character. . . . Robert Browning . . . combines the greatest brain with the most simple temperament known to our annals." (pp. 1, 3). Henry James' short story is built around this enigma.

(1833), *Paracelsus* (1835), and *Sordello* (1840). These works offer
special problems which have been dealt with elsewhere.[2]) If we
read through the remaining corpus of poems (well over two hundred
titles) certain obvious features emerge. There is, to begin with, a
playful insistence on the formation of curious linkages between
images rarely associated elsewhere in English literary tradition.
Between the tenor and vehicle of his comparisons there appears to
be little pre-existing congruence either of meaning or of connotation.
The imagery also exhibits a fascination with odd and monstrous
growths, with creatures and objects rarely named and described in
English verse after the time of Shakespeare:

> And pitch down his basket before us,
>   All trembling alive
> With pink and grey jellies, your sea-fruit;
>   You touch the strange lumps,
> And mouths gape there, eyes open, all manner
>   Of horns and humps,
> Which only the fisher looks grave at.
>
>                     *The Englishman in Italy* (1845)

The images are invariably precise no matter how unexpected
the simile or how surprising the juxtapositions (horns, humps, jellies,
sea-fruit). Colloquial phrases—as well as epithets—abound; and
the diction is rich in learned and artistic terms. Technical terms also:
every character has an occupation and a specialized vocabulary
which goes with it. (Browning includes as occupations equipped with
technical vocabularies loving, murdering, idling, riding, as well as
law, medicine, the priesthood, etc.) There is little point here in re-
capitulating in detail what is available elsewhere in many fine
studies of Browning's imagery, characterization and diction.[3] These
are some of the known constituents of Browning's art. What we
need to do now is consider in more detail how rhythm and syntax

---

[2] Robert Preyer, "Robert Browning: A Reading of the Early Narratives," *ELH* vol.
26, Dec. 1959.

[3] I have found the following works especially useful: E. D. H. Johnson, *The Alien Vision
of Victorian Poetry* (Princeton, 1952); Roma A. King, *The Bow and the Lyre* (Michigan,
1957); Park Honan, *Browning's Characters* (New Haven, 1961); Harlan H. Hatcher,
*The Versification of Robert Browning* (Columbus, 1928); Robert Langbaum, *The Poetry
of Experience* (New York, 1957).

bind together his words, phrasal units (important for Browning), and interjected expletives and noises into the sentences that constitute the basis for the "simple" or basic style. Here are a few texts to keep before us as we proceed:

> The wolf, fox, bear, and monkey,
> By piping advice in one key—
> That his pipe should play a prelude
> To something heaven-tinged not hell-hued,
> Something not harsh but docile,
> Man-liquid, not man-fossil . . .
>
> *Pacchiarotto (1876)*

> All's our own, to make the most of, Sweet—
> Sing and say for,
> Watch and pray for,
> Keep a secret or go boast of, Sweet!
>
> *A Pretty Woman* (1855)

> I tried chaff, found I famished on such fare,
> So made this mad rush at the mill-house door,
> Buried my head up to the ears in dew,
> Browsed on the best: for which you brain me Sirs!
>
> *Ring and the Book,* XI, 1482-5 (1869)

> For see, for see,
> The dark is rent, mine eye is free
> To pierce the crust of the outer wall,
> And I view inside, and all there, all,
> As the swarming hollow of a hive,
> The whole Basilica alive!
> Men in the chancel, body and nave,
> Men on the pillar's architrave,
> Men on the statues, men on the tombs
> With popes and kings in their prophyry wombs,
> All famishing with expectation
> Of the main-altar's consummation.
>
> *Christmas Eve and Easter Day,* X (1850)

> Higgledy, Piggledy, packed we lie,
> Rats in a hamper, swine in a stye,
> Wasps in a bottle, frogs in a sieve,
> Worms in a carcase, fleas in a sleeve.
> Hist! Square shoulders, settle your thumbs
> And buzz for the Bishop—here he comes.
>
> *Holy Cross Day* (1855)

These passages are representative of the "simple" style in that *they exhibit an overall rational consecution (the narrative line) while at the same time realize themselves localy in random, occasionally irrational flights of free association.* The *Pacchiarotto* passage appears to be a kind of joke, a self-conscious toying with bathos and grotesque images and rhymes. We have here a poor example of what Northrop Frye terms "intentional doggerel," a sort of verse which gives the effect of a continuous parody of normal poetry.[4] A quite different effect is gained in the passage from *A Pretty Woman*. Here Browning employs identical or nearly identical triple and double rhymes and a complex metrical and stanzaic pattern. The effect achieved is one of epigrammatic wit, there is nothing ludicrous, no effect of parody. It is the product of a master technician. The third selection is unrhymed and heavily alliterative. "In such a passage" wrote Bernard Groom, "alliteration seems to be struggling to become the master-principle of the meter as it was in our ancient poetry . . . one feels that the spirit and manner of a long-forgotten past have mysteriously revived in this mid-Victorian writer." [5] One also notices the low-life diction and the syntax of vulgar speech, proliferation of detail, and the speed of the rhythm. The effect is lively, nervous and muscular, colloquial and not literary. Yet in all these cases it is evident that we have to do with a superb craftsman, a master of literary devices and a deviser of ingenious rhetorical and rhythmical effects.

In the last two selections the element of play and spontaneity is very strong. Leeway is provided for verbal surprises which can occur when the meanings and connotations of words (called up in the first place by similarities of sound) begin to interact. Thus the first line of "The Holy Cross Day" selection tells us where we are in the narrative. The verbs set going a catalogue of amusing and preposterous analogies, and these in turn develop an independent momentum and threaten to run away with the narrative. An abrupt transition ends the sequence and, with the effect of

---

[4] Northrop, Frye, *The Well-Tempered Critic* (Bloomington, 1963), p. 69. "We call the result intentional doggerel, because, as in real doggerel, the effective rhythm is prose and the features of rhyme and meter become grotesque."

[5] Bernard Groom, "The Formation and Use of Compound Epithets in English Poetry from 1579," *SPE Tract* # xlix (1937), p. 133.

changing gears (the tempo shifting drastically but the heavy ac-
centual beat remaining) we move off to the next syntactically discriminated scene called for by the plot. Two contradictory principles
of organization seem to be at work simultaneously. There is to begin
with an external narrative frame which is made visible in the
straightforward sentence structure. These sentences firmly announce
subject, verb and predicate; so firmly that Browning has leeway to
toss in innumerable repetitions of every sort and can afford to cut
corners by leaving out articles, eliding verb forms, employing con-
tractions, etc. Logical and grammatical connections remain; but
enough school room grammar has been dumped to give an effect of
immediacy and colloquialism, something which imitates rather well
the repetitive and circling way in which our thoughts emerge and
appear, half-organized, in informal conversation or chatter. Browning is not here attempting—as experimental writers like Faulkner,
Beckett and Joyce sometimes do—to compose in a language which
bypasses or falls short of syntactically conventional and articulate
communication. Within his rational sentence frames there is, however, an area of freedom, of spontaneous creation, which is both
occasioned and limited (in large part) by the exigencies of sound
and duration. Words and phrases are found and fitted in because
they rhyme or balance a block of sounds or fill out a metric time
interval; they seem to have been suggested by simple association.
Rumbling polysyllables play off against rattling consonants—it is
a noisy poetry, very dissonant, where the soft play of Keatsian or
Tennysonian assonances is rarely found. Accents and rhymes go
off like firecrackers. All this surface buzz and clamor impedes, as
it were, the forward momentum supplied by the vector force of active
verbs seeking to bind without dalliance a subject to its lawful predicate.[6] An element of tension results which is unlike anything we find

---

[6] It was Browning's habit to write down on a slate a prose outline of his poetic argument: later on he began the process of verse composition. (The source for this is *The
Preraphaelite Brotherhood Journal,* Feb. 28, 1850). A more favored way of beginning
art works is to start with the random and proceed to introduce elements of order.
(Cf. Action Painting or for that matter Beardsley's technique of spilling ink on a
blank sheet and dawdling with it until something that interested him began to
emerge.)

in conversation or childish prattle. One notices also that the main-spring of rhythm is tightly coiled and in no danger of relaxing its tension, unwinding into something as easeful and attenuated as the rhythms (and waters they depict) in "The Lotos-Eaters." Browning's style shows no evidence that he ever sought a Tennysonian singleness and intensity of effect. He does not construct verse patterns out of materials in which there lurks a similarity of "feeling tone." He is not attempting, in the Tennysonian manner, to exclude matter which is irrelevant to the composition of a total image, single, sus-tained, harmonious in its parts and therefore giving an impression of "inevitable" rightness and completion. Tennyson's associations are *visual,* not musical: he wanted to compose and perfect an image. Browning had a very different plan in mind. His poetry is *musical,* he wants to heap up dissonances and resolve them. The charac-teristic method of the visual artist allows no confusing excitements of gesture, no disconcerting or unharmonious objects to interrupt the effortless glide and return of cadences. The rhymes function to with-draw the reader

> Below the thunders of the upper deep;
> Far far beneath in the abysmal sea,
>                                   "The Kraken"

—they are part of a technique of incantation, enforcing an hypnotic concentration on the images that pass before the reader's senses. Browning, on the other hand, might be described as aggressively musical. (The only field of learning in which he received the advan-tages of professional instruction was music.)[7] We may apply to his works the two criteria of value which Coleridge formulated for all works of art, namely that it is successful to the extent that it recon-ciles *many* and *significant* discords in human experience. We should expect therefore to find his better poems filled with a choking energy that spills over into word-play, abrupt shifts of tempo and attitude,

[7] Browning's music teacher was John Relfe, musician in ordinary to the King. Relfe in turn was a pupil of the Abbé Georg Joseph Vogler (1749–1814) and taught his musical method. "Abt Vogler" and "Master Hughes of Saxe-Gotha" give a good indication of Browning's musical competence. See W. C. DeVane, *The Shorter Poems of Robert Browning,* (New York, 1942), pp. 354, 369, and Chapter VII in *Browning's Parleyings* (New Haven, 1927).

darting points-of-view, and exaggerations and variations of every
sort. A landscape in his hands is apt to decompose into a series of
grotesque, discordant images taken from the human, animal, and
natural realms:

> I crossed a ridge of short sharp broken hills
> Like an old lion's cheek teeth. Out there came
> A moon made like a face with certain spots
> Multiform, manifold, and menacing:
> Then a wind rose behind me. So we met.
>
> "Karshish," ll. 291–295

The rhythms are complex, the sounds difficult to pronounce; there
is nothing "inevitable," in the total effect. The analogies are surprising and call attention to themselves. One cannot chant these lines.
It requires practise to render a good oral performance of Browning's
"unmusical" music.

Another aspect of the "simple" (or musical) style deserves attention. Lines and stanzas composed on these principles possess a
remarkable carrying capacity. Like Dickens, Browning commands
a diction that can name and describe an infinity of surfaces without
slowing down. The nouns and epithets do not impede the force
imparted by the verbs.[8] Notice, in the following passage, how
Browning manages to freight his lines with a clutter of ludicrously
unpoetic objects and epithets and yet keeps the rhythm resilient,
the pace as fast and direct as anything in *Don Juan* or *Martin
Chuzzlewit*:

> In came the flock: the fat weary woman,
> Panting and bewildered, down-clapping
>    Her umbrella with a mighty report,
> Grounded it by me, wry and flapping,

---

[8] The "simple" style resembles what we find in Byron and Dickens in other ways as
well. In many of their works a vein of parody and hilarity is constantly on the point
of breaking through; on the other hand, they are frequently as sentimental as Browning can be in, for example, "The Guardian Angel." In all three sensibility (for lack
of a better word) operates at an abnormal speed and intensity. I have not found a
way of formulating these similarities. One gets the *impression* that there is a literary
form or intention that they share.

> A wreck of whalebones; then, with a snort,
> Like a startled horse, at the interloper . . .
>
> *Christmas Eve and Easter Day*

Operating here is that "natural momentum in the syntax" Yeats admired in Byron and which, he said, makes it possible for a poem to carry "any amount of elaborate English." [9]

An illustration of Browning's use of syntax to shape stanzas into a total form will conclude this account of the elements (and the effects) of the "simple" style. The text is Part II of *James Lee's Wife* (1864):

## By The Fireside

### I

> Is all our fire of shipwreck wood,
> > Oak and pine?
> Oh, for the ills half-understood,
> > The dim dead woe
> > Long ago
> Befallen this bitter coast of France!
> Well, poor sailors took their chance;
> > I take mine.

### II

> A rudy shaft our fire must shoot
> > O'er the sea:
> Do sailors eye the casement—mute,
> > Drenched and stark,
> > From their bark—
> And envy, gnash their teeth for hate
> O' the warm safe house and happy freight
> > —Thee and me?

### III

> God help you, sailors, at your need!
> > Spare the curse!
> For some ships, safe in port indeed,
> > Rot and rust,
> > Run to dust,

---

[9] Quoted in Donald Davie, *Articulate Energy* (London, 1955), p. 95.

> All through worms i' the wood, which crept,
> Gnawed our hearts out while we slept:
>     That is worse.

## IV

> Who lived here before us two?
>     Old-world pairs.
> Did a woman ever—would I knew!—
>     Watch the man
>     With whom began
> Love's voyage full-sail,—(now, gnash your teeth!)
> When planks start, open hell beneath
>     Unawares?

The metrical and stanzaic pattern here is unusual. We may diagram it thus:

> a–4
> b–2
> a–4
> c–2
> c–2
> d–4
> d–4
> b–2

It functions well to catch the nuances of the speaker's voice and mental process as she is drawn inexorably to expand and extend the unexpected, almost inadvertent parallel between the plight of poor sailors and herself. It is a reverie—another and terrible "By the Fireside"—and we can expect therefore that it will partake of the quality of such dreamy states.[10] One of the uses of reverie for literary purposes is that it allows the mind to be surprised into making connections which the vigilant will would have suppressed. This poem portrays such a process of discovery taking place in the consciousness of the speaker. I want now to draw attention to the way in which syntax operates to create this effect. Consider first the

---

[10] Northrop Frye, *op. cit.*, p. 78. "It is a general principle of rhetoric that dream states are expressed by intensified sound-patterns, as in *Pearl* or *Kubla Khan* . . . repetitions of sound that would simply be blemishes in a less associative type of verse . . . are in order when we are close to reverie. . . ."

varying syntactical roles played by the last line of each stanza in
the sentences of which they are parts.

> Well, poor sailors took their chance;
> I take mine.

Here the subconscious preoccupation with her personal state
spills out, inadvertently, in an appended clause. (The sailors retreat
into the  past—her situation is rendered in the present tense.) The
second stanza consists of one rushing yet discontinuous rhetorical
question: the object of the sailor's envy ("Thee and me") being
held in suspense until the end. Two abrupt imperatives and a
tentative, run-on implied comparison constitute the third stanza
which ends emphatically (after a colon) "That is worse." And so
on. The punctuation is always different; the final phrase, consti-
tuting the final line of each stanza, is always surprising and forceful
because it serves a different grammatical function in each sentence
of which it is a part. Thus a powerful syntactical conception pre-
vents an elaborately "artificial" stanzaic pattern from becoming
tiresome or merely "clever."

If, as in the following passage, "the speed of the wheels" generates
a wild (yet witty) Dickensian humor,

> Then a tall yellow man, like a Penitent Thief,
> With his jaw bound up in a handkerchief,
> And eyelids screwed together tight,
> Let himself in by some inner light.
> *Christmas Eve and Easter Day*

—we can still notice how the fine excess in the diction and conception is held firmly within the confines of a metronomic beat and a
wiry, flexible syntax. Whether writing in long continuous forms—
blocks of blank verse or rhymed couplets for example—or whether
restricting himself to stanzaic units, the clear sense and firm rhythm
are accompanied by, if they do not generate, a particularized excitement of gesture, a remarkable surface buzz and hum of implication which plays against the continuous narrative momentum. And
that narrative momentum, of course, is the product of a syntax
which can command a fleet of powerful, active verbs to haul and
push about the many epithets, expostulations, imprecations, and

the like which clutter his verse. There is little assonance and less
metaphor in this "simple" style. But there is everywhere visible the
active on-going musical process of dissolving dissonances through
restatement and qualification of the theme.

## II

Let us turn now to a few examples of what might be termed the
"difficult" style in Browning. We can begin with the famous anapes-
tic pentameter lines of *Saul*. Here is stanza xiv:

And behold while I sang . . . but O Thou who didst grant me that
    day,
And before it not seldom hast granted thy help to essay,
Carry on and complete an adventure,—my shield and my sword
 In that act where my soul was thy servant, thy word was my
    word,—
Still be with me, who then at the summit of human endeavour
And scaling the highest, man's thought could, gazed hopeless as ever
On the new stretch of heaven above me—till, mighty to save,
Just one lift of thy hand cleared that distance—God's throne from
    man's grave!
Let me tell out my tale to its ending—my voice to my heart
Which can scarce dare believe in what marvels last night I took
    part,
As this morning I gather the fragments, alone with my sheep,
And still fear lest the terrible glory evanish like sleep!
For I wake in the grey dewy covert, while Hebron upheaves
The dawn struggling with night on his shoulder, and Kidron
    retrieves
Slow the damage of yesterday's sunshine.

Here, in one of the most extraordinary syntactical *tours de force*
in Victorian poetry, Browning conveys a breathless forward-rushing
movement to a climactic moment of supreme religious awareness—
even as he carries us back in time and then forward and around the
visionary moment he is driving hard to reach. "While I sang" is
placed in the recent past; the next clause opens a perspective back
into a series of more distant pasts. "Still be with me" returns us
from a contemplation of that telescoped past to the moment of
utterance. At this point a series of recessed, parenthetical clauses
are introduced which further complicate temporal location: we are

entangled in a complicated syntactical "still . . . then . . . till" construction which includes Hopkinsesque inversions ("And scaling the highest, man's thought could, gazed hopeless as ever.") We advance excitedly upon the proffered timeless event and it vanishes; at the end of the stanza we are apparently beyond it. ("This morning" brings us the realization that it transpired the preceding evening, though in some sense it is still present since David fears "lest the terrible glory evanish like sleep.") It is, obviously, a calculated effect, not obscurity: we are left with the "feel" of an experience which is, by definition, inscrutable, incommunicable.

The rest of the poem bears this out. Section xvi consists of one line, an admission that the limits of art have been reached:

Then the truth came upon me. No harp more—no song more! outbroke—

and the remainder of the poem is barefaced theology, culminating, as so many of Browning's religious poems do, with a strained prophecy of the Christ.[11] The versification is competent, the theme traditional and the poetic energies exhibited earlier find no place here. "Let me tell out my tale to its ending—my voice to my heart" David cries out. But that will come later, in the anticlimactic conventional rhetoric of the final two sections. Stanza xiv portrays a *first response* to a shattering experience. It is a "gathering of fragments" not a consecutive narrative.

Substance and body are given to narrative by the conventions that, first, events occur in a carefully discriminated time sequence and second, that they bear a causal relation to one another. Displacement of the time sense and interjected rather than serial arrangement of clauses, inversions of word order and similar syntactical derangements disrupt the linear narrative we have been following. Yet stanza xiv is not, for all this, "obscure" in the modern sense of containing private reference and symbol for which no key is available. It can be riddled out on a second reading and found to make perfectly adequate prose sense. The difference

[11] See for example "Cleon," "An Epistle Containing the Strange Medical Experience of Karshish the Arab Physician," "Imperate Agusto natus est" (from *Asolando*).

between the difficult style and the simple style can be stated this way. When the auditor (or reader) hears the verses and almost simultaneously comprehends their narrative meaning we have the simple style. When syntactical and temporal displacements slow down the process of comprehension and when the rhythmical pace does not slacken so that we are allowed time to get our bearings, we are experiencing the difficult style. It is not incomprehensibility that we face but rather a deliberately created discrepancy between the rate at which we hear the verse and take in its meaning. Possibly Swinburne had something like this in mind when he protested that in Browning's verse "the difficulty arises from a quality the reverse of that which produces obscurity properly so called." For he goes on to praise "his sureness and intensity of perception, his rapid resolution of aim," concluding "His is the track of an intelligence that moves with . . . incessant rapidity. . . ." [12] These impressionistic observations somehow ring true; they do justice to the oral experience of this verse.[13] Perhaps a few more examples of obviously "difficult" passages will clinch the point. Here are the opening stanzas of "Two in the Compagna":

I

I wonder do you feel to-day
    As I have felt since, hand in hand,
We sat down on the grass, to stray
    In spirit better through the land,
This morn of Rome and May?

---

[12] H. F. C. Grierson, *Swinburne,* London, 1953, p. 22.

[13] It is not likely that Browning fully grasped the difficulty that even simple displacements (ellipsis, synopsis, displacement of modifiers, omission of articles, etc.) occasioned Victorian readers. When Ruskin complained of his obscurity Browning suggested that he read too slowly to get the right effect: "You ought, I think, to keep pace with the thought tripping from ledge to ledge of my 'glaciers,' as you call them; not stand poking your alpenstock into the holes, and demonstrating that no fool could have stood there;—suppose he sprang over there?" In the same letter he added, significantly, "The whole is all but a simultaneous feeling with me"—which indicates rather well what his technical problem in writing must often have been. (You can "see" a picture—all of it—simultaneously. You cannot "see" a poem but must read its parts serially, in time.) Both the above quotations are taken from the distinguished anthology edited by Walter Houghton and Robert Stange, *Victorian Poetry and Poetics* (New York, 1959), p. 152.

## II

> For me, I touched a thought, I know,
>     Has tantalized me many times,
> (Like turns of thread the spiders throw
>     Mocking across our path) for rhymes
> To catch at and let go.

If we read this at the pace we usually employ for poems written in the "simple" style it comes out as a transcription of the colloquial chatter employed by a person who expects to be understood by his companion, no matter how disconnected his associations and fancies might be. The minute we reflect, however, the passage becomes opaque, a nightmare of incoherence. The rhythm, the ambiguous syntax (note in this connection the disruptive positioning of "since" in the second line) and the odd placement of phrases and modifiers do not define or shape a subject. It is very difficult to discover when things happen: the tense swings back and forth from present to imperfect. There are other ambiguities as well. Instead of straying "hand in hand" the couple sit down that way and stray "in spirit." In the line,

> For me, I touched a thought, I know,

the "I know" points in two directions, modifying either "the thought" or the effect of the thought. The reader is never told of the relationship between the two persons (married? old lovers? old friends? new lovers?). There is no "interaction" at all—this is a dramatic monologue, not a narrative. The emphasis is on the *significance* of what is said and not so much on the implied narrative which might be constructed out of the relationship so sketchily adumbrated. It is an important distinction.

In the "simple" style, it will be recalled, Browning held the narrative line firmly with his left hand and allowed his right hand, in a manner of speaking, to improvise, freely associate. A good bit of the improvisation resulted from his willingness to play with words which rose up into consciousness apparently because they rhymed or alliterated or simply were needed to fill out a rhythmical schema or a design in sound. When successful, this method of composition resulted in an excited or surprising set of associations, a redemption of the fatigued appearance of objects and situations by viewing them in novel and unexpected combinations. The effect, as in so much of Browning, is a delightful surprise: we respond to the sheer power of invention. But once the narrative frame is dismantled, as it is in all the dramatic monologues, to varying degrees, a discrepancy between the speed of the presentation and the time of comprehension sets in. The result directly mimes the disorder, incompleteness, and puzzlement that clings to human activity and which is everywhere apparent in the mental maunderings by which we seek to complete and comprehend actions. If a writer pushes this technique to extremes—as in stanza xiv of *Saul*—it can be made to render something other than the disorder and ambiguity of living experience. It can confront us with experiences that are logically unorderable, which are not so much ambiguous as incommunicable. Usually, however, the gap between hearing and comprehending what we hear is provided in order to convey an experience that is not *adequately* grasped by the protagonist. This familiar situation is what we find in the next four stanzas of "Two in the Compagna," stanzas iii through vi:

### III

Help me to hold it! First it left
    The yellowing fennel, run to seed
There, branching from the brickwork's cleft,
    Some old tomb's ruin: yonder weed
Took up the floating weft,

### IV

Where one small orange cup amassed
    Five beetles,—blind and green they grope
Among the honey-meal: and last,
    Everywhere on the grassy slope
I traced it. Hold it fast!

### V

The champaign with its endless fleece
    Of feathery grasses everywhere!

> Silence and passion, joy and peace,
>     An everlasting wash of air—
> Rome's ghost since her decease.

## VI

> Such life here, through such lengths of hours,
>     Such miracles performed in play,
> Such primal naked forms of flowers,
>     Such letting nature have her way
> While heaven looks from its towers!

These lines exhibit a continual, obsessive attention to irrelevant detail, a chain of free association in a mind that seems to have momentarily lost the power of holding fast to a consecutive chain of thought. The speaker is an appalled spectator at his own undoing: "Such letting nature have her way" he cries!

## XI

>     . . . Must I go
> Still like the thistle-ball, no bar,
>     Onward, whenever light winds blow,
> Fixed by no friendly star?

It should be clear that stanzas three through six supply the content out of which the theme emerges. They enact the central experience of the poem, helpless efforts to recapture redeeming moments of grace which lift us out of the insipid banality of normal consciousness. The effort is bound to fail—not only because they are sent to us by Grace and are beyond the control of Will (the theological explanation) but also because it is logically impossible to reconstruct or even recollect an experience which appears to be outside the categories of time and space. It is the inscrutable, the blankly puzzling that Browning wants us to confront in this poem and indeed in many of his great dramatic monologues and epistles.[14] We are brought up sharply against the limitations of our perceptive equipment.

---

[14] Notably "Cleon," "Christmas Eve and Easter Day," "Sludge," "Bishop Blougram's Apology," and "Karshish."

## XII

Just when I seemed about to learn!
　Where is the thread now? Off again!
The old trick! Only I discern—
　Infinite passion, and the pain
Of finite hearts that yearn.


We might add, parenthetically, that the famous "irony" in the epistle of Cleon exists because the writer refuses to admit that he is beyond his depth, face to face with mystery. (But the reader knows better.) Anyone acquainted with the works of Gibbon and Adams or who has read *Middlemarch* and *The Portrait of a Lady* knows that Rome and its environment baffles the intellect and obsesses the imagination. It offers to the Anglo-American vision one of the most powerful images of contemplation, a human counterpart to the traditional natural images of recurrence, the waves of the sea and the seasonal changes. Browning linked this image with the baffling rhythm of human feelings, the intermittencies of the heart, which are equally problematic, equally moving and perennial. He was frequently drawn to write on situations and scenes which do not declare their significance, do not tell a story, which simply are in themselves significant. It is in the confrontation of the problematic that the devices of the difficult style find their highest expressive potential. Neither drama nor narrative verse can lead us so directly into this area of awareness as the form of dramatic monologue. And the style of the dramatic monologue is precisely what we have been discussing under the rubric "difficult" style.


## III

Any technical means, once mastered, can be misapplied. Browning is an uneven writer, frequently trite and hostile to discursive reasoning, a man who on occasion refuses to use his mind rather than a fine poet who has pursued a subject to the limits of the intellect and *there* stumbled upon the unknown, the mysterious. His energy rarely fails but his intellect is occasionally in abeyance. The result, in writing, is a curious variant on the Horatian purple

passage. Sensations and perceptions are often rendered with vividness and clarity but there is no ordering purpose that links them
together leading to some overwhelming question or surprising sur-
mise.

In certain passages of *By the Fireside* critics have discovered no
dramatic occasion for the proliferating clauses and the random
specifications that constitute their context.

### XI

For the drop of the woodland fruit's begun,
These early November hours,

### XII

That crimson the creeper's leaf across
    Like a splash of blood, intense, abrupt,
O'er a shield else gold from rim to boss
    And lay it for show on the fairy-cupped
Elf-needled mat of moss,

### XIII

By the rose-flesh mushrooms, undivulged
    Last evening—nay, in to-day's first dew
Yon sudden coral nipple bulged
    Where a freaked fawn-coloured flaky crew
Of toadstools peep indulged.

Emotion is doubtless there in the depiction of these objects—but
it is not gotten out of them and made to accumulate and play over
the poem as a whole. Of this passage Donald Davie remarked that
it was not at all clear if the "syntactical pattern acts out a train of
feeling significant to the burden of the whole." [15] One feels that
a habit of language and expression has got out of control, that a
hypertrophy of style has set in. The passage has a sort of vitality—
but it is the vitality of a weed or a fungus, not precisely spurious, but
then not particularly useful either. Such surrenders to the principle
of vitality in all things suggest that the author has not been able to
avoid the dangers implicit in the distortion of rational statement.

Enough has been said, I trust, to indicate that the stylistic re-

---

[15] Donald Davie, *op. cit.*, p. 74.

sources of Browning remain pretty much the same whether we consider narratives or dramatic monologues. The "difficult" passages introduce elements of displacement, but in either mode the poems have the look of constantly being on the point of overleaping their formal structure. This is right, not only as a matter of rhetoric but right in terms of the life he celebrates. For Browning belongs with the dithyrambic or daemonic poets. His faults are those common to the *genus*—at times the life process he celebrates breaks away from his technical control or breaks through narrative probability; at other times he unabashedly celebrates his own adequacy as a celebrant ("Prospice" for example).

There are, of course, incidental passages in Browning which exhibit other levels or degrees of style and which do not appear to fit into the categories here employed:

> Beautiful Evelyn Hope is dead!
>   Sit and watch by her side an hour.
> That is her book-shelf, this her bed;
>   She plucked that piece of geranium-flower,
> Beginning to die too, in the glass;
>   Little has yet been changed, I think:
> The shutters are shut, no light may pass
>   Save two long rays thro' the hinge's chink.

That is the mean or natural style and it is rare in Browning.[16] "Evelyn Hope" does not continue throughout in this vein—already in "the hinge's chink" we feel the pressure building up—but it does not have the usual look of constantly being on the point of overleaping its formal structure. One reason for this seems to be that Browning is not holding here to a relentless regularity of measure. The movement is duple-triple (in each line there are two metrical norms, not simply variations on a single norm) and this allows the usual rhythm of prose phrases to enter the verse without strain and unnaturalness. (It is the measure of several successful poems—"Home Thoughts from Abroad," "My Star," "The Statue and the Bust," the "Epilogue" to *Pacchiarotto*, "Life in a Love," and sections one and five of "James Lee's Wife," among others.) His usual fault is exhibited in "One Word More," "La Saisaiz," and

16 Another example: "Memorablia."

"Clive" where the relentless imposition of the trochaic pattern becomes tiresome or in "Fifine at the Fair," which consists of 2,358 verses arranged in alexandrine couplets, a meter which had scarcely been attempted since Drayton's dismal *Polyolbion.* In "Love Among the Ruins" a fine conception is spoiled by a provoking meter that constantly calls attention to itself. Yet another reason "Evelyn Hope" seems different is because the elements of playful association and spontaneity are held in check. The imagery and diction of "Caliban" or "Fra Lippo Lippi" are not in place; nor are the rhetorical patterns and literary allusions of a "Cleon" or a "Rabbi ben Ezra." There are not many poems in this vein, however; Browning is not often the poet of simple things and quiet lives. The bulk of his poetic failures occur when he begins to lose his powers of invention and improvisation, when he can no longer bring animation and intensity to the curious settings and situations he normally employs. Such failures are organic and not really amenable to critical analysis.

## IV

If we glance back at the examples given of the "simple" style it will be seen that they embrace a host of subject matters, some of them complex and portentous *(Christmas Eve and Easter Day)* and others quite simple, on the order of

Bang-whang-whang goes the drum, tootle-te-tottle the fife;
No keeping one's haunches still: It's the greatest pleasure in life.

It can also achieve a special sort of pathos. In "Youth and Art" a meeting takes place after a long interval and two successful and wordly people look back wryly on their idealistic student years and the very different life which they might have shared. The interest depends on a carefully controlled tone, a half-joking, rueful irony appropriate on such occasions. Here are the concluding stanzas:

Each life unfulfilled, you see;
    It hangs still, patchy and scrappy;
We have not sighed deep, laughed free,
    Starved, feasted, despaired,—been happy.

> And nobody calls you a dunce,
> And people suppose me clever:
> This could but have happened once,
> And we missed it, lost it forever.

Perhaps this sample from a sixty-eight line narrative will suggest what can be done with double and internal rhymes, a powerful repetitive rhythm, strong accents and heavy punctuation—some of the more obvious features of the verse texture we have been calling the "simple" style. It would appear then that the "simple" style is not limited to the expression of any given sort of subject matter.

The case is somewhat different with the "difficult" style. It appears regularly in association with a particular subject-matter: the mind's confrontation with perceptions that resist rational analysis and shrewd common sense. Invariably such "good moments," as Browning called them, failed to declare their content or for that matter remain steadily enough in focus so that he could absorb their aura of significance. The "good moment" was just as impenetrable (and problematic) as the Italian landscape referred to in *By the Fireside*:

> The place is silent and aware;
> It has had its scenes, its joys and crimes,
> But that is its own affair.

This tough-mindedness is very appealing—and the "difficult" style enables the poet to render, with considerable psychological realism, the rich ambiguity of such moments, the sense of their significance, evanescence, and sometimes, absurdity.

As has been pointed out, these effects, in large measure, are brought about by a displacement of the syntactical bindings and of the time sense. What claim Browning has as a "mystic" rests upon passages where such tactics are employed. After all, the most available technique for breaking into the Beyond must involve the transcendence or erosion of the conventions which give body and substance to a narrative. The "difficult" style is there to convey the "feel" of experiences that baffle perception and remain portentous, tantalizing. "Saul," "Cleon" and "Karshish" are successful precisely in that they take place in an atmosphere pregnant with revela-

tion. *Christmas Eve and Easter Day* which attempts to disclose the
*content* of revelation (in the guise of traditional literary "visions"—
section VI is a fair example) is tiresome and unreal. After such false
displays Browning relapses helplessly into the ludicrous:

> I felt my brain
> Glutted with the glory, blazing
> Throughout its whole mass, over and under
> Until at length it burst asunder
> And out of it bodily there streamed,
> The too-much glory, as it seemed,
> Passing from out me to the ground,
> Then palely serpentining round
> Into the dark with mazy error.   (section vii)

So long as Browning did not falsify these valued confrontations he
wrote very well. As much as any Victorian author he was fascinated
by "threshold experiences," knew they occurred and sensed that
they had consequences. Even Sludge the charlatan is allowed to
make such an avowal:

> This trade of mine—I don't know, can't be sure
> But there was something in it, tricks and all!

It comes with even more conviction from such a source. But the
protagonists in his poems have little to say of the discursive content
of any knowledge acquired in moments of vision. That is left to the
system makers, men like Boehme and Yeats. Browning makes it
clear (notably in "Transcendentalism") that the poet's activity
should be compared to that of a magician "who made things
Boehme wrote thoughts about." It is what led up to and what followed the Eternal Moment that interested him—the way it affects
recognizable human beings.

But the difficult style does not exist solely to mediate this special
subject matter. Elements of this style, as we have pointed out, exist
in all the great dramatic monologues. There is, after all, much that
is tentative, problematic, and puzzling in human behaviour and
Browning does not often find it necessary to call in mysteries from
Beyond to liven things up. Perhaps the strangest—certainly the
least known—aspect of human behaviour has to do with the devious
processes by which individuals seek to justify their ways not so much

to God or fellow citizens as to themselves. The dramatic monologue
is a form which penetrates directly into the workings of this problematic process; it seems to catch men at those rare moments when,
for some reason, (not usually specified) they feel impelled to consider their responses and beliefs and justify an identity which is
made apparent to the *voyeur* reader though not necessarily to the
protagonist:

> Over his wine so smiled and talked his hour
> Sylvester Blougram, styled *in partibus*
> *Episcopus, nec non*—(the deuce knows what
> It's changed to by our novel hierarchy)
> With Gigadibs the literary man,
> Who played with spoons, explored his plate's design
> And ranged the olive-stones about its edge,
> While the great bishop rolled him out a mind
> Long crumpled, till creased consciousness lay smooth.
> ll. 971–79 "Bishop Blougram's Apology"

So much has been written on the dramatic monologue that I
will content myself with a final reflection. It is, that the stylistic
devices considered in this paper were there fused in such a way
that they reflect with great immediacy the movements of a mind
as it struggles to see itself for what it is and simultaneously draws
back from such revelations, seeking to protect, justify and even
conceal its being. Rousseau had provided the characteristic literary
form in which this modern search for authenticity displays itself.
In the *Confessions* he sought to strip away the contents of consciousness and penetrate to the true—because individually experienced—
grounds of being. In the words of Kant, "Rousseau was the first to
discover, beneath the varying forms human nature assumes, the
deeply concealed essence of man and the hidden laws in accordance
with which Providence is justified by his observations. . . ." [17] Other
forms seemed trivial in comparison and Rousseau was followed by
a host of self-confessed, self-incriminating egotists who justified
themselves by the one virtue of sincerity. The literary landscape was

[17] Quoted in Henri Peyre, *Literature and Sincerity* (New Haven, 1963), p. 109. The passage is taken from Kant's *Fragments* (8,630).

littered by revelations and Browning, to his later mortification, had contributed thousands of lines to similar projects *(Pauline, Paracelsus, Sordello)*. Seeking a way out he stumbled upon the dramatic monologue where we watch the process in fictional characters, not ourselves. We observe this compulsion to declare the self and see how it is checked by many and various defensive mechanisms. Uneasy feelings are assuaged by long bursts of defensive rationalization which, being recognized, are dismissed, and the process of unburdening moves off on another tack. Irrelevancies obtrude themselves, scraps of recollection or specious analogies crop up to impede the search. It is a continuing process—partly conscious, partly subconscious—that is being depicted, and Browning's artistic problem ultimately becomes that of shaping this flux into a unity, giving it a shape, without destroying the impression of spontaneity. This is a structural matter, however, and the concern in this paper has been largely with style. One may frequently have misgivings about the structure of Browning's works—especially so if the effect of finality, of an "inevitable conclusion," bulks large in one's aesthetic sense of moral perfection. Some poems seem to go on too long, others appear cryptic. But there can be no question of the value and usefulness, the eristic quality, of Browning's remarkable stylistic procedures. With them he opened up new ground for English poetry, demonstrating with finality that the novelist had not superseded the poet. As Wordsworth had done before him, he renewed the expressive potential of verse and proved once again that it is not only useful but necessary to have two modes of literary art available for the exploration of experience.

# 6

## Matthew Arnold

———◆———

### Kenneth Allott

EDITORIAL NOTE. *This fine dialogue was composed by Kenneth Allott as the introduction to a selection of Arnold poems published in Great Britain in 1954. In it a whole range of important questions are raised, discussed, and finally answered—always with wit, good humor, and critical penetration. The two parties to the dialogue are obviously educated, intelligent, and busy men. One of them is a scholar who happens to know a great deal about Arnold's verse; his acquaintance is familiar in a general way with Arnold's reputation as a social critic (based on his prose writings) but wonders if there is much point in spending time reading the verse. Who, he asks, are the artists and critics who have had something pertinent to say about Arnold's verse? What values and what inadequacies have they indicated? How would his friend place Arnold's poetry in relation to the poetry of Tennyson, Browning, Swinburne, Hopkins? Why did Arnold stop writing verse in mid-career? How well do his "classical" ideas about art stand up? What are the essential poems? What sorts of excellence should he expect in reading them? Isn't there supposed to be something wrong with the "style"? What exactly? And finally: what is the point in reading Arnold's verse in the middle of the twentieth century? Kenneth Allott is a critic and scholar of rare distinction*

*and style who has taken to heart the lesson contained in Arnold's* Culture
and Anarchy *and "The Function of Criticism at the Present Time."*

'The dialogue of the mind with itself . . .'
MATTHEW ARNOLD

A. We're going to talk about Arnold's poetry, and in some sort I'm
   to represent the ordinary reader and ask questions. I take it
   we don't have to go into biography?
B. I don't think we need. Everyone knows that Matthew Arnold
   was the son of Dr. Arnold of Rugby and earned his living as an
   Inspector of Schools, And I'm going to suppose that everyone
   also knows that he was the most valuable literary critic of his
   time, that he had something important to say on political and
   social questions, and that his religious writings were controversial and widely read. If anyone wants more details, he or
   she can be referred to the Chronological Table.
A. Good. But please, before we start, there are a couple of preliminary points.
B. I am at your service.
A. First, I have often wondered if it is fair to any poet to offer people
   merely a selection from his works.
B. I can't see much force in that. Different readers have different
   needs. Of course the serious student will want every word of an
   author: the general reader feels that life is short and that poets
   do not always write at their best. As for Arnold himself—
A. Yes, what would he have said?
B. Well, he published a selection from his own poems in the *Golden
   Treasury* series in 1878, and he followed it up with selections from
   Wordsworth and Byron intended to introduce those poets to a
   wider public. That should be some comfort to you.
A. Tell me—why don't you now reprint Arnold's selection of his
   own poems?
B. Because he left out too much and yet included some things we
   don't want—for example, a stodgy group of inferior 'late' son-
   nets. Then he put in a poor narrative like 'Saint Brandan' and
   forgot 'The Sick King in Bokhara,' which is much finer. He

reduced 'Empedocles on Etna,' one of the very few satisfying long poems by a Victorian, to a handful of fragments—

A. I see—you think you can choose better than Arnold.

B. Why not? Better than the Arnold of 1878.

A. I think that needs to be explained.

B. Arnold's *New Poems,* his last collection of verse, came out in 1867. He wrote very little verse afterwards and he had not written much in the previous ten years. Almost all his best work falls between 1845 and 1857.

A. Yes?

B. Don't you see what it implies? Arnold found it more difficult to write poems as he grew older, which is another way of saying that Arnold himself changed. There is sometimes a whole generation between the Arnold who wrote a particular poem and the Arnold who considered in 1878 whether it should be included in his volume of selections.

A. Surely a man may change and become a better judge of his own work? No, leave that alone now. Tell me instead why Arnold found it more difficult to write verse as he grew older.

B. You had two preliminary points—you haven't yet raised the second.

A. Are you avoiding my last question?

B. Not in the least. It's a question that was bound to come up sooner or later. But you mustn't expect a simple answer—or a complete one.

A. Go on.

B. So many things come together to account for Arnold's failure to keep up poetry. After all he is not the only poet limited to one period of creative power—Wordsworth is another example—and such a period often comes fairly early in life. Then there's the nature of the Victorian age with what Arnold called 'its true *blankness* and *barrenness,* and *unpoetrylessness*': if he felt his age to be inimical to poetry, then it was so for him. There's earning a living as a school-inspector and what that meant in lack of leisure—Arnold hadn't a private income like Browning, or like Tennyson a Civil List pension while he was still a comparatively young man. There's his intelligence—

A. Is intelligence a hindrance to a poet?

B. I'll quote to you Arnold's own words to Arthur Clough: 'I often think that even a slight gift of poetical expression which in a common person might have developed itself easily and naturally, is overlaid and crushed in a profound thinker so as to be of no use to him to express himself.' Then, again, there's Arnold's war on low spirits—much of his poetry came from the part of his nature that he was trying to overcome. There's his rather numbing and intimidating sense of the full seriousness of the poetic vocation—have a look at his *Letters*. Now I suggest you read 'The Progress of Poesy' and tell me your other preliminary question.

A. We seem to have moved away from it, but my second question follows from the first. If *you* may select from a poet's works, how much of them in my role of the man-in-the-street ought *I* to read?

B. As much as will give you fairly immediate pleasure. Obviously the fraction varies from poet to poet. More of Arnold than of Swinburne must be read.

A. Absolutely more, or do you mean a bigger fraction?

B. Both. Please notice that would not be true of Tennyson—speaking absolutely, more poems by him than by Arnold are still alive—and Browning's a doubtful case; but in terms of what fraction survives in relation to a total of poetic work, Arnold is the most successful of the Victorians.

A. You seem to agree with the common opinion that Tennyson, Browning, and Arnold are the most considerable Victorian poets.

B. I do. Provided that we look on Gerard Manley Hopkins as a special case. As his *Poems* were not published until 1918, he was not a Victorian poet to the Victorians.

A. And of the three poets just mentioned, who is the greatest? No, don't pull a long face. That's the kind of question the ordinary reader wants to ask.

B. My dear chap, don't bully me. I can't answer unanswerable questions—

A. Dr. Garrod doesn't seem scared of it. He says quite plainly: 'Arnold is the greatest Victorian poet.'

B. If you like, I'll tell you what Arnold said about this. He said:

It might be fairly urged that I have less poetical sentiment than Tennyson, and less intellectual vigour and abundance than Browning; yet, because I have perhaps more of a fusion of the two than either of them, and have more regularly applied that fusion to the main line of modern development, I am likely enough to have my turn, as they have had theirs.

A. Thank you, but what do you say?

B. I find Arnold the most congenial Victorian poet. He has obvious limitations—a narrow emotional range with a consequent tendency to monotony, a lack of animal high spirits and vitality that may explain a sensuous thinness in much of his poetry. Arnold says of Sainte-Beuve's verse—and Sainte-Beuve was the master in criticism with whom he seems to have identified himself most closely—that it revealed 'some want of flame, of breath, of pinion.' I would be willing to apply that to Arnold. Henry James—

A. If I may say so, you seem to be retiring behind a smoke-screen of great names.

B. Let me finish. Henry James speaks of Arnold's 'slight abuse of meagreness for distinction's sake'—a phrase of exact and delicate justice.

A. You would not describe Arnold as 'an educated versifier'? That is Dr. Edith Sitwell's opinion.

B. It is true that Arnold was educated.

A. I seem also to remember a remark by Mr. F. W. Bateson, a critic of whom I have heard you speak highly: 'I can find no trace in all his intelligent and readable verse of any specifically poetic originality. The sensibility reflected in it is not that of Arnold himself but of his age.

B. I think that is an eccentric judgement on the poet who wrote 'The Scholar-Gipsy' and the *coda* to 'Sohrab and Rustum.' I go back to James: 'his verse has a kind of minor magic and always goes to the point—the particular ache, or regret, or conjecture, to which poetry is supposed to address itself.'

A. You do realize that you have not yet given me your own opinion. Is Matthew Arnold the greatest Victorian poet?

B. Yes and no. Tell me, is Dickens a greater novelist than George Eliot? There is no novel by Dickens that is so satisfying or so finished a work of art as *Middlemarch.* Yet Dickens surely reveals in his shelf of splendid and indifferent books a more powerful creative talent than George Eliot's. Put Tennyson in the place of Dickens, put Arnold in the place of George Eliot, and you have the elements of a comparison. Not an altogether fanciful one, I suggest. George Eliot admired Arnold's poetry and it was natural for her to do so: both of them scored heavily over contemporary rivals in the quality of the intelligence they brought to bear on their work.

A. What is Arnold's *Middlemarch?*

B. You put me on the defensive, but together 'Thyrsis,' 'The Scholar-Gipsy,' and 'Empedocles on Etna' should prevent the scales coming down too heavily on the other side. It's odd, isn't it, that Clough should have mentioned this question of the comparative effect of Victorian poet and Victorian novelist in an early review of Arnold's poems?

A. Which way did he incline?

B. Oh, to the novelist's side—he felt the public preference and agreed with it; but then he was already half-committed after his verse novel, *The Bothie of Tober-na-Vuolich,* to the contemporary subject, which is the novelist's usual field, and you know how strongly Arnold kicked against that bit of Time-Spirit in his 1853 Preface (p. 251). I don't think he ever liked Clough's *Bothie* as much as he should have done—in spite of the agreeable things he said about it . . .

A. All my questions are still to ask.

B. I'm sorry. Bring me back to the point.

A. I want to hear something of what critics say of Arnold's verse today, and, more generally, I want to know what kind of attention is now paid to Victorian poetry. I have the impression that I am more likely to find intelligent critical writing about Marvell or Pope, for example, than about Tennyson, Arnold, or Rossetti. I suspect that Victorian poetry is neglected by the younger critics, though they may be quite interested in the Victorian novel.

B. Your impression is very near the truth. Victorian poetry is neglected by most of the intelligent younger critics, and, where an interest in it is still cultivated, the results are often unhappy. The most depressing articles in our critical journals are those devoted to Victorian poetry.

A. Why?

B. You won't expect me to go into detail, will you? Put it like this. The depressing articles are written by people who refuse to admit that a revolution in poetic taste has taken place in the last thirty years. The revolution, which has largely been occupied with the correction of Romantic and Victorian taste by an examination of its underlying poetic assumptions, has discovered the value of certain qualities which are rare in nineteenth-century poetry but usual enough in the poetry of earlier periods: for example, the seriousness of wit in some Metaphysical poetry, or the compressed neatness of statement and play of irony in some Augustan poets. I think we read these older poets more intelligently than our grandfathers and great-grandfathers, but there is some loss as well as gain.

A. You mean that the younger critics concentrate too exclusively on poetry in which these rediscovered qualities are present?

B. Perhaps. Certainly I mean that we are more sympathetic to the poetic assumptions of almost any other age than we are to those of the Romantics and Victorians. We are more prepared to become Elizabethans to read Spenser than we are to become Victorians to read Tennyson. Now I am quite sure that the pendulum of taste had to swing, but perhaps it has swung too far. We are quite exceptionally aware of what Victorian poetry cannot give us, and sometimes we are too easily satisfied that it has few valid elements of lasting appeal.

A. Would it summarize your position to say that if we were prepared to read Victorian poetry within the framework of Victorian poetic assumptions, as we are prepared to read Augustan poetry in its own framework, then we would not only enjoy it more, but we would be more likely to see what is permanent in it?

B. Yes.

A. Of course Arnold's case is peculiar. Tennyson and Browning were poets all the time, but Arnold was also an important writer of prose. Do you think his poetic reputation is overshadowed by his other reputations—as literary critic, as social critic, and so on?

B. It was overshadowed in his own day and it may still be so, but there's a further complication. We can't draw comparisons between a poetic Browning and a prose Browning, but we can and do think of two Arnolds: we are more aware of the limitations of Arnold's poetic personality because we can see from his prose-writings that one part of himself—his sociableness, humour and satirical bent—could not find expression in his verse.

A. Would you blame Victorian poetic assumptions for that?

B. Partly. I've been thinking of your remark about Arnold's different reputations—I suppose Lionel Trilling's book, *Matthew Arnold* (1939) shows what can happen to a poet's verse when it is overshadowed by his prose.

A. I was about to remind you that I wanted to hear about Arnold's modern critics.

B. Lionel Trilling is one of the best of them. He is an American with a positive intelligence and a breadth of literary and social interests that may easily remind you of Arnold himself. Not surprisingly Trilling's concern is with the strutcure of Arnold's ideas. He has therefore an excuse for examining the poetry as if it were prose, but of course such an examination does not begin to be literary criticism of the poetry: for his purposes a good poem is no more interesting than a bad one, and he could have reached the same conclusions from a translated text of the verse.

A. But there must be some books about Arnold as a poet . . .

B. There is a formidable one, *Matthew Arnold: Poète* (1947), by the French scholar, M. Louis Bonnerot. It is quite admirable in tracing the connexions between different poems, between the poems and the prose works, between the poems and the letters, but it is hard for real criticism to grow up between the footnotes and the cross-references. The author has read too much and forgotten too little, and his golden key to open all locks is psychological interpretation. It is the best book on Arnold's poetry, but on the whole it must be said that M. Bonnerot has forgotten Mallarmé's remark to Degas.

A. What was that?

B. 'Ce n'est point avec des idées, mon cher Degas, qu'on fait des vers. C'est avec des mots.'

A. I would like you to mention one book on Arnold's poetry that is primarily critical in intention.

B. There isn't one. I can think of useful remarks here and there by critics who have made no special study of Arnold, I can add the titles of a few essays that are mainly critical, but that's all. Perhaps I am simple-minded, but I am still amazed at the lengths to which some scholars will go to avoid literary judgements. Take as an example *The Poetry of Matthew Arnold: a commentary* (1940) by C. B. Tinker and H. F. Lowry. It is packed with information that is available nowhere else, it is an essential book for the student, but it shies away from all criticism except in absurd little asides 'Requiescat' is 'the most beautiful and popular' of Arnold's short lyrics. Let me quote to you from the preface:

> 'We have prefixed no introductory essay dealing with the development and cessation of Arnold as a poet because that is, in effect, the unifying subject of the book, however fragmentary and disunited it may at first appear. A reading of our remarks on 'Resignation,' 'Rugby Chapel,' and 'Obermann Once More,' for example, will give a person who has not time or inclination for the perusal of the entire volume an adequate notion of what we conceive to be the relation between Arnold's poetry and his philosophy of life, as well as of his inevitable transition from poetry to prose.'

A. Well?

B. Does that strike you even as a particularly honest way of throwing up the sponge? Observe what that quotation apologizes for. Not for a failure to criticize Arnold's poetry—that is never mentioned—but merely for evading what is already a too common *pis-aller*: the establishment in clear terms of a relationship between a poet's poetry and his philosophy of life. I repeat with Mallarmé: 'Poetry is written with words, not ideas.'

A. Isn't this a mistake that Arnold himself encourages when he says that the 'noble and powerful application of ideas to life is the most essential part of poetic greatness'?

B. He also says: 'The superior character of truth and seriousness, in the matter and substance of the best poetry, is inseparable from the superiority of diction and movement marking its style and manner.' But I'm not here to score a debating-point. I freely admit that Arnold's usual way of speaking seems to encourage the separation of style and content, and that he lays more emphasis on the latter. By content, of course, he means more than subject-matter: he also means how the subject-matter is to be disposed, the structure of the work. But with that reservation I will admit that often, and notably in the 1853 Preface, he does speak as if finding a subject and conceiving an outline for its treatment were the greater part of poetic creation.

A. We're agreed then. I repeat my point. Doesn't that to some extent justify the critics of Arnold's poetry who talk mainly of his ideas?

B. No. It's possible to see why Arnold fell into this way of thinking and writing. His critics haven't the same excuse.

A. You mean that Arnold's eye was on the poetry of his own day, that his insistence on the importance of subject and structure was to counter a contemporary emphasis on details of expression— words, phrases, images?

B. Exactly. You have to remember how much Victorian poetry stems from Keats—the weaker, luxuriant side of Keats. If you think of Wordsworth and Keats as dividing Victorian poetry between them, then Arnold gives his allegiance to Wordsworth. He prefers the penny-plain to the tuppence-coloured. He's not the complete Wordsworthian. On the poetic subject he's a neo-classic—

A. Surely some of Arnold's best poems were written under the influence of Keats—isn't that common knowledge?

B. Let me take that up later. For a moment think of the 1853 Preface. Arnold saw that 'Isabella' was a badly-told story. In his opinion the fact that it contained 'a greater number of happy expressions which one could quote than all the extant tragedies of Sophocles' in no way made up for its feebleness of conception and construction. Arnold objected to the Spasmodic poets of his own day, he objected to Tennyson's 'elaborateness' of thought and expression. He was quite prepared to track this elaborate expression back to Shakespeare and to object to it almost as strongly in him. Shakespeare's true greatness lay in 'discerning and firmly conceiving an excellent action.' Arnold was even prepared to turn prophet and argue that 'had Shakespeare and Milton lived in the atmosphere of modern feeling, had they had the multitude of new thoughts and feelings to deal with a modern has . . . the style of each of them would have been far less *curious* and exquisite. For in a *man* style is the saying in the best way *what you have to say*. The *what you have to say* depends on your age. In the seventeenth century it was *a smaller harvest than now*, and sooner to be reaped: and therefore to its reaper was left time to stow it more finely and curiously.' That's from an early letter to Clough, and in another letter a little later he puts his whole attitude very forcibly:

> But what perplexity Keats Tennyson et id genus omne must occasion to young writers . . . yes and those d—d Elizabethan poets generally. Those who cannot read G[ree]k sh[ou]ld read nothing but Milton and parts of Wordsworth: the state should see to it.

A. In effect Arnold is saying this: our civilization is complex, therefore our poetry must be simple and direct. It's almost a paradox. Didn't T. S. Eliot argue more naturally when he claimed that poetry must reflect the complexities of civilization by becoming 'more allusive, more indirect'?

B. I cannot myself see that the complexity of civilization has any automatic bearing on how poetry ought to be written.

A. I suspect Arnold knew that he was fighting a losing battle. He thought poetic expression in his own day ought to be more direct, he feared that it was becoming more elaborate. That threw him off balance. It made him distrust Keats and 'those d—d Elizabethan poets.' It led him to pooh-pooh expression and to magnify the importance for the poet of unity of conception and intellectual grasp of his material.

B. You're exaggerating. He blamed equally Clough's attempts 'to *solve* the Universe' and Tennyson's 'dawdling with its painted shell.' If you think Arnold unduly disparaged expression, let me remind you of what he wrote when Clough seemed in practice to disparage it:

> Many persons with far lower gifts than yours yet seem to find their natural mode of expression in poetry, and tho: the contents may not be very valuable they appeal with justice from the judgement of the mere thinker to the world's general appreciation of naturalness—i.e.—an absolute propriety—of form, as the sole *necessary* of Poetry as such: whereas the greatest wealth and depth of matter is merely a superfluity in the Poet *as such.*

A. I did not claim that Arnold was always consistent.

B. There's no inconsistency if you remember that every pronouncement has its own intention.

A. Even so, since in his view the typical error of his age was to single out happy phrases and images, Arnold's emphasis was more often on what was said than on ways of saying it.

B. There were so many occasions when he discussed appropriate form and the 'natural magic' of style that I don't like to leave the admission unqualified. However, I must not bore you with my scruples . . .

A. Good. That gives us enough common ground. Would it be right, then, to hint that Arnold's own poetic style is often faulty—faulty because he assumed that 'natural' expression would follow a good idea?

B. It's difficult to generalize. He had several poetic styles.

A. That reminds me—haven't some critics argued that it was precisely in those poems where he fell most strongly under Keat's influence—and, as a result, allowed himself some elaborateness of expression—that Arnold was most a poet?

B. True, but we must distinguish. Some of Arnold's best poems are influenced by Keats, other poems—still among the best—show hardly any influence or none at all. Again, to say that "X" is a good poem and that you can find Keats in it, is not necessarily to exhaust its merits. In 'Thyrsis' and 'The Scholar-Gipsy,' for example, where the stanza is a modification of one used by Keats in some of his Odes, there are clear verbal echoes, as well as places where the meaning is developed in a Keatsian manner. But you have hardly begun to account for the value of the two poems if you limit yourself to considering their Keatsian qualities— quickness to render sensation, richness of the local texture of the verse: you have still to observe how brilliantly the poems are conceived, plotted, and developed, and how remarkably both poetic argument and expression are sustained. It is not fatuous to notice the length of Arnold's poems when it is suggested that they owe everything to the Odes of Keats; and, since one or two critics have argued—unconvincingly, I think—that Arnold's stanza is invertebrate in comparison with Keats's, it is worth asserting that in these two elegiac pieces Arnold is a sounder craftsman than Keats in several of the Odes. To take a very small point. I do not think Arnold would ever have changed his rhyme-scheme twice in five stanzas, either without knowing it, or without caring about it, as Keats did in the 'Ode on a Grecian Urn.'

A. I won't cross-examine, because I think the argument is widening awkwardly.

B. Thank you for pulling me up. I am maintaining that Arnold's poems have several kinds of excellence, and that the particular excellence of the 'Keatsian' poems is a complicated affair— various elements, of which the influence of Keats is one, jointly produce it. I would like to go further into the matter, but there is no time. That is one kind of excellence. Then there are satisfying poems like 'Stanzas from the Grande Chartreuse,' 'Resignation,' 'Dover Beach,' and 'Stanzas in Memory of the Author of "Obermann,"' which are quite free from derivative Keatsian felicities; and there are a few pieces—'Growing Old' is a good example—of an extraordinary plainness. In them austerity of language is a poetic resource: it tallies with a state of mind of unusual emotional honesty.

A. Recently I came across an observation by the novelist Mr. Robert Liddell. He claims that 'significant meaning' in the novels of Thomas Hardy and George Eliot has sometimes 'to be apprehended through the ugly texture of the prose.' He instances a passage in *Far From the Madding Crowd* which critics have disagreed about—one critic seeing it as 'imaginative' and 'compelling,' another holding that it is very badly written. Mr. Liddell remarks that *both* critics are right. Would you allow that something similar might be said about meaning and verbal expression in Arnold's clumsier poems?

B. Meaning and verbal expression are so intimately associated in poetry that it is much more dangerous to apply Mr. Liddell's observation to poetry than to prose. I can go a few steps with you. It is easy to find blemishes in Arnold's poetic style—it has been done in our own time by T. S. Eliot and F. W. Bateson—but we must recognize that a poem may survive some verbal clumsiness, some looseness of expression. I would admit that the long philosophic outburst by Empedocles in Act I of 'Empedocles on Etna' creaks and lumbers like passages in Hardy's prose, but it is not a piece of writing to wish away. It has odd poetic compensations, and the two songs of Callicles which frame it are enhanced in value by their position. Dr. Leavis tells us that it is in the songs of Callicles that 'the sap suddenly flows,' which is true; but a final assessment of the poem must take into view more than the existence of the songs—it must see how they qualify underline and annotate what is said by Empedocles, how simultaneously they are a necessary relief from it and—

A. I am following you. You think 'Empedocles on Etna' is a single poetic structure, not a prosy argument with embedded lyrical nuggets.

B. That is so, and it makes me wary of censuring Arnold for his 'manner of evasion.' It's not often a simple 'Oh, for the Adriatic rather than the slums of Bethnal Green.' In 'The Scholar-Gipsy' and in the songs of Callicles, Arnold is near enough to the pastoral convention, which implies a criticism of the actual. I am not surprised that the author of these poems should also have written *Culture and Anarchy* and *Mixed Essays.*

A. You mentioned some criticisms of style by T. S. Eliot and F. W. Bateson . . .

B. Curiously, their criticisms are illustrated by the same poem— 'Memorial Verses.' Eliot quotes:

> But where will Europe's latter hour
> Again find Wordsworth's healing power?

> Others will teach us how to dare,
> And against fear our breast to steel;
> Others will strengthen us to bear—
> But who, ah! who, will make us feel?
> The cloud of mortal destiny,
> Others will front it fearlessly—
> But who, like him, will put it by?

and comments on the weak composition. He finds the fourth
line clumsy, the sixth line bathetic. He is worried by the outbreak
of dashes and by the expression 'to put by' used of a cloud.

A. Do you agree that the lines are faulty?
B. How can I avoid doing so? Eliot is right, so is Bateson, who takes
to pieces very thoroughly an earlier passage in the poem; but
Bateson goes on to say—and this is interesting—'read hurriedly
it is not unimpressive.'
A. Why does that interest you?
B. Because Arnold was against 'thinking aloud' in verse—he held
that a poem was something it needed skill to make, that a poem
was more like a horseshoe than a dream—and in 'Memorial
Verses' he does think aloud. He struggled against Victorian
conceptions of the poetical, but he was still influenced by them.
If the atmosphere of a poem seemed 'right' when it was read
'hurriedly' or 'dreamily,' then the ordinary Victorian reader
tended to believe that it was curmudgeonly to niggle about the
craftsmanship in the manner of Dr. Johnson.
A. Now you're confusing me. I thought you were accepting Eliot's
and Bateson's reprobation of certain details, but arguing that a
poem could survive such fault-finding.
B. That is still my position. I think 'Memorial Verses' survives by a
rather narrow margin. I also think that there are better poems,
which nobody would want to condemn, with a good deal of
roughness in their grain.
A. So Arnold's stylistic successes are triumphs of tone and temper
rather than models of good composition?
B. Yes. I agree that Arnold's triumphs are of tone and temper. He
is not rich in imagery, he is not a poet whom one frequents for
the dazzling epithet or for artful marriages of sound and sense.

Too often his diction is a mongrel affair. I think his diction troubles me more than anything else.

A. Why?

B. Well, I don't care for nouns like 'teen' or 'marge,' or verbs like 'benumb' or 'upclose'; and I can hardly stomach 'erst' for 'formerly,' 'elf' for 'man' and 'deem' for 'think.' Scott and Keats use 'elf' in the same way and Milton is fond of 'erst'—it would seem that Arnold thought any word was good enough for use if you could find it in a good poet.

A. It's one theory of poetic diction.

B. It was not conscious enough to become a theory. Unconsciously he must have argued that poetry could use unusual words if they were not too unusual. He drew the line at 'eld' and 'liefly' in Francis Newman's translations of Homer.

A. Clough is just as misguided in his shorter poems as Arnold.

B. Certainly. He never had the courage of his colloquialisms except when he was writing hexameters.

A. Do you imply that Arnold should have written more colloquially?

B. No. He was not dealing with the appearances of contemporary life even when he was dealing with contemporary ideas. On the one hand his diction needed to be kept clear of colloquialisms, but on the other it would have been an advantage if he could have swept out of it all the words that no longer belonged to educated Victorian speech and so had become 'poetical.'

A. I think we've talked enough about this. What I want now is a good reason for reading Arnold's poetry. There are so many poets. Why should I read *him*?

B. Because in an essential respect his sensibility is modern. No, don't protest. I know 'modern sensibility' can mean almost anything, but I suppose myself to be using the phrase in an acceptable way. With me the stress is on feelings held in common, not on a common mode of expressing feelings. Obviously we have different conventions from the Victorians about that. They seem to have thought that the most effective method of expressing a complicated state of feeling was to edit it, to tidy it up for presentation by emphasizing the dominant element or elements in it, and suppressing or playing down fringe-elements which might weaken and confuse the effect of what was judged to be of primary importance. Now a favoured contemporary view is just the opposite of all this: namely, to give the complicated state of feeling in all its untidy, unedited immediacy, in the persuasion that it is worth risking some confusion to convince the reader that you are aware of complexity and a truthful reporter.

A. But you don't think one method is intrinsically superior to the other?

B. I happen to prefer the contemporary view, but that may mean only that people do get tired of one style of window-dressing and are pleased by a change.

A. Let me borrow your metaphor. You admit that Arnold has a Victorian style of window-dressing, but you insist that his stock— of feelings, kishes, anxieties and so on— is quite up-to-date. That is what you mean by describing his sensibility as modern.

B. Exactly so. If a poet can ever teach us to understand what we feel, and how to live with our feelings, then Arnold is a contemporary. To my way of thinking he expresses better than any other Victorian poet, and better than most poets, what it feels like to live in a world that has not been arranged to please its inhabitants. I do not want to be misunderstood. Please notice that I do not think that any questions of religious belief or disbelief are here involved. I am speaking of a mode of sensibility that may underlie in different people quite opposed views.

A. I am trying to understand you.

B. And I am trying to be plain. Consider the doubleness of our feelings. There is one set of facts that may be represented by the feeling-statement, 'The world is a pleasant place.' You will find this easily enough in the Arnold who talks of 'youth, and bloom, and this delightful world.' But the word 'bloom' is a symptom of something else: it tells of what is quickly rubbed off, of what is evanescent, and of course it is one of Arnold's favourite words. There is a second set of facts that may be represented by another feeling-statement: 'The world *appears* to be a pleasant place.' Here you may think of Arnold's 'something that infects the world' and also of our common notions of disappointment and frustration. Normally one would suppose a time-lag between the experience of such different feelings, and ideally perhaps one might hope to reach old age without being punished by a sense of the darker implications of the second statement. The simultaneous experience of the feelings associated with both sets of facts seems to me a fairly modern phenomenon. In Shakespeare's day young men talked bawdy like Mercutio and old men were grave and pompous like Polonius. You had the feelings appropriate to your age-group. But, as Blake says, 'When Nations grow old . . . all are born poor, aged sixty-three'. Didn't Shelley think that he had lived longer than his grandfather? Now this time-ridden sensibility and the disenchantment that it produces, our own disenchantment, Arnold was peculiarly gifted to express.

A. Aren't you forgetting something? Didn't Arnold in his own life make war on low spirits?

B. He did, but that is to speak of the level at which the will operates. The will has very little to do with poetry, and Arnold's poetic vocation was to express disenchantment—when he fully realized that, he chose silence.

A. Then perhaps that is the most important reason for his ceasing to write verse.

B. Yes—he 'thrust his gift in prison till it died,' as Auden says. He had no wish to go on reflecting doubleness and melancholy. He tried once in his poetry—at the end of 'Obermann Once More'—to go beyond his intuitions and be positive and joyful: I think we detect the ring of false metal at once in that part of the poem. But Arnold need not have felt so uneasy about the earlier and typical expressions of his sensibility. Mr. Eliot says that he had no real serenity, only an impeccable demeanour. It is quite true, but an impeccable demeanour is something: it is what Arnold has to teach us about living with feelings that we have no reason to enjoy. I do not think that we have any right to require serenity of our poets, but we can ask them to be truthful.

# 7. A Dickens Landscape

## C. B. Cox

◆

# 8. The Hero's Guilt:
# The Case of *Great Expectations*

## Julian Moynahan

◆

# 9. Dickens and His Readers

## Gabriel Pearson

EDITORIAL NOTE. *In* Victorian Fiction: A Guide to Research *(edited by Lionel Stevenson and sponsored by the Victorian Literature Group of the Modern Language Association of America, 1964) 109 pages are needed for the bibliographical essay on Dickens. The essays on other Victorian novelists run to between twenty and thirty pages. There are already in existence collections of essays on his works—notably two volumes edited by George Ford,* Dickens and His Readers: Aspects of Novel-Criticism since 1836 *(1955) and* The Dickens Critics *(1961; co-editor, Lauriat Lane, Jr.). * Dickens and The Twentieth Century *(edited by John Gross and Gabriel Pearson, 1962) and several student casebooks are also available.*

*The three selections from this vast literature will indicate, perhaps, some of the directions this interest has taken. C. B. Cox provides a close reading of a single passage from* Bleak House—*and makes one aware of an extraordinary poetic technique working in the novels. Julian Moynahan concerns himself with the feelings of guilt in Pip, the narrator of* Great Expectations. *His essay expands into a provocative and arresting account of Dickens' procedure as an artist. The third selection, "Dickens and His Readers," follows in the path of Edmund Wilson's remarkable essay "Dickens: The Two Scrooges" (in* The Wound and the Bow, *1941). This work, with its blend of psychological and social criticism, stands at the watershed between a new view of Dickens as a great, tormented creative artist much like Dostoevski, and the earlier conception of the "inimitable Boz," author of* Pickwick Papers *and entertainer-general to the world.*

121

# 7

## A Dickens Landscape

━━━◄●►━━━

### C. B. Cox

M<small>Y</small> Lady Dedlock has been down at what she calls, in familiar conversation, her "place" in Lincolnshire. The waters are out in Lincolnshire. An arch of the bridge in the park has been sapped and sopped away. The adjacent low-lying ground, for half a mile in breadth, is a stagnant river, with melancholy trees for islands in it, and a surface punctured all over, all day long, with falling rain. My Lady Dedlock's "place" has been extremely dreary. The weather, for many a day and night, has been so wet that the trees seem wet through, and the soft loppings and prunings of the woodman's axe can make no crash or crackle as they fall. The deer, looking soaked, leave quagmires, where they pass. The shot of a rifle loses its sharpness in the moist air, and its smoke moves in a tardy little cloud towards the green rise, coppice-topped, that makes a background for the falling rain. The view from my Lady Dedlock's own windows is alternately a lead-coloured view, and a view in Indian ink. The vases on the stone terrace in the foreground catch the rain all day; and the heavy drops fall, drip, drip, drip, upon the broad flagged pavement, called, from old time, the Ghost's Walk, all night. On Sundays, the little church in the park is mouldy; the oaken pulpit breaks out into a cold sweat; and there is a general smell and taste as of the ancient Dedlocks in their graves. My Lady Dedlock (who

122

is childless), looking out in the early twilight from her boudoir at a keeper's lodge, and seeing the light of a fire upon the latticed panes, and smoke rising from the chimney, and a child, chased by a woman, running out into the rain to meet the shining figure of a wrapped-up man coming through the gate, has been put quite out of temper. My Lady Dedlock says she has been "bored to death."

(Dickens, *Bleak House*, ch. 2.)

The conventional view of Dickens has often been of a man who could not resist facts, whose curiosity concerning the odd and the eccentric poured itself abundantly into his novels. In the last decades, the work of Edmund Wilson in particular has shown that Dickens never merely listed interesting facts. His great descriptions of places and people attain their peculiar hold upon our minds because every detail fits into an imaginative pattern. Much attention has been given to Dicken's psychological problems, and the ways these affect his selection of material; but there are many other sources for his striking originality.

In spite of the thousands of text-books written by psychologists, consciousness is still a mystery, and its nature is often best expressed in imaginative symbols, rather than by analytical description. Dickens knew that the state of an individual mind depends upon a quality of movement, quick or slow in apprehension; precision, clarifying its awareness or leaving all issues blurred; will-power, forcing an action onwards or shifting according to every wind of opinion; focus, relating events to particular needs or prevailing ideas. He recognised that when a character looks outwards, these factors and many others determine what he sees. Landscapes in his novels thus become projections of the mind, expressing by their tones and qualities the whole personality of one of his characters. The details of skies, fields and woods cannot describe a character going through a process of thought, or reacting in time to experience, but they can reveal profoundly a total response to life, the general attitude which defines a person whatever he may do. In Dickens's novels, adults do not often develop radically once they have settled down into some routine. His characters are defined by their surroundings, every detail of town or countryside representing some aspect of consciousness.

The extract we have printed here from *Bleak House* describes Lady Dedlock's view of her 'place' in Lincolnshire. Her marriage into the Dedlock family has broken her down, until for her all experiences have lost their significance. She has retained no sense of purpose, nothing firm and definite which can give meaning to her life. As in her mind, so in the Lincolnshire scene everything has lost precision and sharpness. The trees are wet through; they make no crash or crackle as they fall. Even a rifle shot has lost its sharpness. An arch of the bridge has been sapped and sopped away. Every image describes a breakdown of creative effort; there is no hardness, firmness, energy or order, for everything in Nature is being softened by the rain.

Men have a fundamental psychological need to deal with objects which are firm and precise; this provides one reason why extroverts in particular enjoy making things with wood, or giving a hard blow with a hammer. The hardness of exterior objects, against which we struggle, gives proof of a firmness in ourselves. Nothing for Lady Dedlock has such definiteness; the view from her windows is alternately a lead-coloured view, and a view in Indian ink. She is moving away from life, with its colour and vitality and purposes, towards the dulling of the faculties which precedes death; so the passage moves towards the church of the Dedlocks, whose odours seem to be rising from the grave to engulf Lady Dedlock, and to drag her down with the family ancestors.

The passage thus begins with a series of impressions of stagnation and frustration. The 'melancholy' trees recall the past beauty and uprightness of summer, now undermined by the water. The unending drip, drop of the rain forces Lady Dedlock to remain indoors, trapped in a sophisticated boredom which has lost all real contact with life. Only at the end does her gaze focus on a precise scene. Suddenly there is movement, as the child, chased by the woman, runs out into the rain; there is warmth, with the light of the fire; and the man returning home after his work is not frustrated by the rain. Another view of the landscape is offered, that of the countryman whose life has the purpose and order of Nature itself.

Lady Dedlock has placed herself outside this world; she has reached a condition of mind when all activity seems pointless, when

the hills and valleys of her life have flattened out into meaningless-
ness. This description is one of the best examples of Dickens's poetic
technique, his use of images of fog, rivers, cities or Nature to define
the complex factors which make up a particular consciousness. In
one sentence he can convey a frightening picture of Lady Dedlock's
total apathy and depression:

> The adjacent low-lying ground, for half a mile in breadth, is a
> stagnant river, with melancholy trees for islands in it, and a
> surface punctured all over, all day long, with falling rain.

# 8

## *The Hero's Guilt:*
## *The Case of Great Expectations*

---◄◆►---

### Julian Moynahan

Two recent essays on *Great Expectations* have stressed guilt as the dominant theme. They are Dorothy Van Ghent's 'On Great Expectations' (*The English Novel: Form and Function,* New York, 1953) and G. R. Stange's 'Dickens's Fable for his Time' (*College English,* XVI, October 1954). Mr. Stange remarks *inter alia* that 'profound and suggestive as is Dickens's treatment of guilt and expiation in this novel, to trace its remoter implications is to find something excessive and idiosyncratic;' and he has concluded that 'compared to most of the writers of his time the Dickens of the later novels seems to be obsessed with guilt.' He does not develop this criticism, if it is a criticism, but one might guess he is disturbed by a certain discrepancy appearing in the narrative between the hero's sense of guilt and the actual amount of wrong-doing for which he may be said to be responsible. Pip has certainly one of the guiltiest

126

consciences in literature. He not only suffers *agenbite of inwit* for his sin of snobbish ingratitude toward Joe and Biddy, but also suffers through much of the novel from what can only be called a conviction of criminal guilt. Whereas he expiates his sins of snobbery and ingratitude by ultimately accepting the convict Magwitch's unspoken claim for his protection and help, by willingly renouncing his great expectations, and by returning in a chastened mood to Joe and Biddy, he cannot expiate—or exorcise—his conviction of criminality, because it does not seem to correspond with any real criminal acts or intentions.

Snobbery is not a crime. Why should Pip feel like a criminal? Perhaps the novel is saying that snobbery of the sort practiced by Pip in the second stage of his career is not very different from certain types of criminal behaviour. For instance, a severe moralist might point out that snobbery and murder are alike in that they are both offenses against persons rather than property, and both involve the culpable wish to repudiate or deny the existence of other human beings. On this view, Pip reaches the height of moral insight at the start of the trip down the river, when he looks at Magwitch and sees in him only 'a much better man than I had been to Joe.' By changing places with the convict here, he apparently defines his neglectful behaviour toward Joe as criminal. Does this moment of vision objectify Pip's sense of criminality and prepare the way for expiation? Perhaps, but if so, then Pip's pharisaic rewording of the publican's speech, which occurs a few pages later while he is describing Magwitch's death in the prison, must somehow be explained away:

> Mindful, then, of what we had read together, I thought of the two men who went up into the Temple to pray, and I thought I knew there were no better words that I could say beside his bed, than 'O Lord, be merciful to him, a sinner!'

Even Homer nods, and Dickens is not, morally speaking, at his keenest in deathbed scenes, where his love of the swelling organ tone is apt to make him forget where he is going. Still, we ought not to explain anything away before the entire problem of Pip's guilt has been explored at further length.

Others answers to the question I have raised are possible. Consider the following passage, wherein Pip most fully expresses his

sense of a criminal 'taint.' He has just strolled through Newgate
prison with Wemmick and is waiting near a London coach office
for the arrival of Estella from Miss Havisham's:

> I consumed the whole time in thinking how strange it was that
> I should be encompassed by all this taint of prison and crime;
> that, in my childhood out on our lonely marshes on a winter
> evening I should have first encountered it; that, it should have
> reappeared on two accasions, starting out like a stain that was
> faded but not gone; that, it should in this new way pervade my
> fortune and advancement. While my mind was thus engaged, I
> thought of the beautiful young Estella, proud and refined, com-
> ing toward me, and I thought with absolute abhorrence of the
> contrast between the jail and her. I wished that Wemmick had
> not met me, or that I had not yielded to him and gone with him,
> so that, of all days in the year, on this day I might not have had
> Newgate in my breath and on my clothes. I beat the prison
> dust off my clothes as I sauntered to and fro, and I shook it out
> of my dress, and I exhaled its air from my lungs. So contaminated
> did I feel, remembering who was coming, that the coach came
> quickly after all, and I was not yet free from the soiling conscious-
> ness of Mr. Wemmick's conservatory, when I saw her face at the
> coach window and her hand waving at me.

Without question, Pip here interprets the frequent manifestations
in his experience of criminal elements—the runaway prisoner on
the marshes, the man with the two pound notes, the reappearance
of the same man in chains on the coach going down into the marsh
country, the reappearance of Magwitch's leg iron as the weapon
which fells Mrs. Joe, the accident making the criminal lawyer
Jaggers, whose office is beside Newgate prison, the financial agent
of his unknown patron—as signs that indicate some deep affinity
between him and a world of criminal violence. But a question that
the reader must face here and elsewhere in the novel is whether to
accept Pip's interpretation. If we conclude that Pip is in fact tainted
with criminality, we must rest our conclusion on a kind of symbolic
reading of the coincidences of the plot. Through these coincidences
and recurrences, which violate all ordinary notions of probability,
Dickens, so this argument must go, weaves together a net in whose
meshes his hero is entrapped. Regardless of the fact that Pip's
association with crimes and criminals is purely adventitious and

that he evidently bears no responsibility for any act or intention of criminal violence, he must be condemned on the principle of guilt by association.

Nevertheless, if the reader is himself not to appear a bit of a pharisee, he must be able to show good reason for accepting the principle of guilt by association in settling the question of the hero's criminality. Both Mr. Stange and Miss Van Ghent present readings of the guilt theme which are an attempt to validate this principle. Mr. Stange decides that 'the last stage of Pip's progression is reached when he learns to love the criminal and to accept his own implication in the common guilt.' He believes that one of Dickens's major points is that 'criminality is the condtion of life.' Pip, therefore, feels criminal guilt because he is criminal as we are all criminal. Along similar lines, Miss Van Ghent remarks, 'Pip . . . carries the convict inside him, as the negative potential of his "great expectations"— Magwitch is the concretion of his potential guilt.' The appearance of Magwitch at Pip's apartment in the Temple is 'from a metaphysical point of view . . . that of Pip's own unwrought deeds.' Finally, she maintains that Pip bows down before Magwitch, who has been guilty towards him, instead of bowing down before Joe, toward whom Pip has been guilty. In so doing Pip reveals by a symbolic act that he takes the guilt of the world on his shoulders— rather in the style of Father Zossima in *The Brothers Karamazov*. This is shown particularly by the fact that Pip assumes culpability in a relationship where he is, in fact, the innocent party.

Objections to these metaphysical readings can be raised. If criminality is the condtion of life, and if guilt is universal in the world of the novel, what world may Joe Gargery, Biddy, and Herbert Pocket be said to inhabit? Miss Van Ghent's theory of Pip's guilt as the negative potential of his great expectations is more promising, because it seems to exempt humble people from the guilt attaching itself to a society of wealth and power which thrives on the expropriation of the fruits of labour of its weaker members. But in her description of Pip's redemptory act, Miss Van Ghent insists upon the pervasiveness of guilt throughout the Dickens world. Less disturbing than this contradiction but still questionable is her assumption that Magwitch has been guilty of great wrong-doing towards Pip.

Metaphysics aside, how badly has he treated Pip? Does his wrong-doing stand comparison with the vicious practices of an Orlick or even a Miss Havisham? Who, in the light of the virtues of faithfulness and love, virtues which the novel surely holds up for admiration, is the better, Magwitch or his daughter Estella?

My final objection to these interpretations is Pip's language at Magwitch's deathbed. Pip, after all, tells his own story. Evidence that he has attained an unflawed moral grasp of experience in which the distinction between criminal and noncriminal forms of evil is transcended through the confession *mea culpa* must come, at least partly, from Pip himself. On the strength—on the weakness rather—of his biblical flight, this reader is not convinced that the evidence is clear.

Miss Van Ghent's and Mr. Stange's efforts to demonstrate Pip's metaphysical involvement in the criminal milieu of *Great Expectations* are dictated, rightly enough, by their concern for the unifying and inclusive significance of the guilt theme. Their readings provide a means of bridging the gulf between Pip's social sins and the more drastic phenomena of criminality presented in the novel—attempts to moralise the melodrama, as it were, attempts to make the complete narrative presentation revolve around the crucial question of Pip's moral nature. Sensitive readers of the novel will sympathise with this effort, but I do not believe they will agree that the gulf *is* bridged by making criminal guilt a universal condition and by insisting that this is what Pip comes to understand by the time his story is told.

## II

In my opinion, Pip's relation to the criminal milieu of *Great Expectations* is not that of an Everyman to a universal condition. It is rather a more concrete and particularised relation than the metaphysical approach would indicate, although the novel defines that relation obliquely and associatively, not through discursive analysis. Miss Van Ghent has suggested a metaphoric connection between Magwitch and Pip. Her proposal of such implicit relations between character and character, even though they do not become rationalised anywhere, is an illuminating insight into the artistic method of the mature Dickens. But her principle can be applied differently and yield rather different results.

I would suggest that Orlick rather than Magwitch is the figure from the criminal milieu of the novel whose relations to him come to define Pip's implicit participation in the acts of violence with which the novel abounds. Considered by himself, Orlick is a figure of melodrama. He is unmotivated, his origins are shrouded in mystery, his violence is unqualified by regret. In this last respect he is the exact opposite of Pip, who is, of course, filled with regret whenever he remembers how he has neglected his old friends at the forge.

On the other hand, if we consider Orlick in his connections with Pip, some rather different observations can be made. In the first place, there is a peculiar parallel between the careers of the two characters. We first encounter Orlick as he works side by side with Pip at the forge. Circumstances also cause them to be associated in the assault on Mrs. Joe. Orlick strikes the blow, but Pip feels, with some justification, that he supplied the assault weapon. Pip begins to develop his sense of alienation from the village after he has been employed by Miss Havisham to entertain her in her house. But Orlick too turns up later on working for Miss Havisham as gate-keeper. Finally, after Pip has become a partisan of the convict, it turns out that Orlick also has become a partisan of an ex-convict, Compeyson, who is Magwitch's bitter enemy.

Up to a point, Orlick seems not only to dog Pip's footsteps, but also to present a parody of Pip's upward progress through the novel, as though he were in competitive pursuit of some obscene great expectations of his own. Just as Pip centres his hopes successively on the forge, Satis House, and London, so Orlick moves his base of operations successively from the forge, to Satis House, and to London. From Pip's point of view, Orlick has no right to interest himself in any of the people with whom Pip has developed close ties. For instance, he is appalled when he discovers that his tender feeling for Biddy is given a distorted echo by Orlick's obviously lecherous interest in the same girl. And when he discovers that Orlick has the right of entry into Satis House he warns Jaggers to advise Miss

Havisham to get rid of him. But somehow he cannot keep Orlick out of his affairs. When Magwitch appears at Pip's London lodging half-way through the novel, Orlick is crouching in darkness on the landing below Pip's apartment. And when Pip is about to launch the escape attempt down the Thames, his plans are frustrated by the trick which brings him down to the marshes to face Orlick in the hut by the limekiln. Its lurid melodrama and the awkwardness of its integration with the surrounding narrative has made many readers dismiss this scene as a piece of popular writing aimed at the less intelligent members of Dickens's audience. But the confrontation of Orlick and Pip on the marshes is crucial for an understanding of the problem I am discussing, because it is the scene in which Dickens comes closest to making explicit the analogy between the hero and the novel's principal villain and criminal.

Orlick inveigles Pip to the limepit not only to kill him but to overwhelm him with accusations. Addressing Pip over and over again as 'Wolf,' an epithet he might more readily apply to himself, he complains that Pip has cost him his place, come between him and a young woman in whom he was interested, tried to drive him out of the country, and been a perpetual obstacle in the path of his own uncouth ambitions. But the charge he makes with the greatest force and conviction is that Pip bears the final responsibility for the assault on Mrs. Joe:

> 'I tell you it was your doing—I tell you it was done through you,' he retorted, catching up the gun and making a blow with the stock at the vacant air between us. 'I come upon her from behind, as I come upon you to-night. I giv' it to her! I left her for dead, and if there had been a limekiln as nigh her as there is now nigh you, she shouldn't have come to life again. But it warn't old Orlick as did it; it was you. You was favoured, and he was bullied and beat. Old Orlick bullied and beat, eh? Now you pays for it. You done it; now you pays for it.'

The entire scene has a nightmare quality. This is at least partly due to the weird reversal of rôles, by which the innocent figure is made the accused and the guilty one the accuser. As in a dream the situation is absurd, yet like a dream it may contain hidden truth. On the one hand Orlick, in interpreting Pip's character, seems

only to succed in describing himself—ambitious, treacherous, murderous, and without compunction. On the other hand, several of
Orlick's charges are justified, and it is only in the assumption that
Pip's motives are as black as his own that he goes wrong. We know,
after all, that Pip is ambitious, and that he has repudiated his early
associates as obstacles to the fulfilment of his genteel aspirations.
Another interesting observation can be made about Orlick's charge
that 'it was you as did for your shrew sister.' Here Orlick presents
Pip as the responsible agent, himself merely as the weapon. But
this is an exact reversal of Pip's former assumptions about the affair.
All in all, Orlick confronts the hero in this scene, not merely as
would-be murderer, but also as a distorted and darkened mirror-
image. In fact, he presents himself as a monstrous caricature of the
tender-minded hero, insisting that they are two of a kind with the
same ends, pursued through similarly predatory and criminal
means. This is what his wild accusations come down to.

# III

Is Orlick mistaken in representing himself in this scene as a
sort of double, *alter ego,* or shadow of Pip? Is he merely projecting
his own qualities upon him, or do Orlick's accusations, in any sense,
constitute a partially or wholly valid comment on Pip's actions? In
order to answer these questions we shall have to begin by analysing
the fantasy of great expectations which gives the book so much of
its universal appeal. This fantasy, so the psychologists tell us, is a
well-nigh universal imaginative flight of childhood. By creating for
himself a fiction wherein the world is made to conform to his desire
and will, the child succeeds in compensating himself for the fact that
his real position is without power and that the quantity of love and
nurture to which he believes himself entitled is greatly in excess
of the amount he actually receives. Out of this unbalance between
an unbounded demand and a limited supply of love and power
proceed the fairy godmothers as well as the vicious step-parents
and bad giants in which world legend abounds. The fantasy element *Great Expectations* shares with such stories as *Cinderella* and
*Jack and the Beanstalk* contains, then, two implicit motives: the

drive for power and the drive for more mother-love. However, of
the two, the power motive, since it involves the aggressive wish to
push beyond the authoritarian figures who hold the child powerless,
is apt to be more productive of guilt and, consequently, is likely to
be expressed with a certain amount of concealment. Thus, Jack in
the folk tale conquers authority in the fictional guise of killing the
wicked giant. But there is no attempt to disguise the fact that he
steals from the giant in order to live in affluence with his widowed
mother, enjoying her undivided love and admiration. We might
add that the type of love sought in this fantasy is a childish version
of mature love. It is largely passive. It is associated with a superabundance of the good things of life, often with the enjoyment of
great wealth.

In *Great Expectations,* the second motive is clearly represented
in the early stages of Pip's career. His early experiences follow the
fairy-tale pattern. Circumstances magically conspire to rescue him
from the spartan rigours of Mrs. Joe. In taking him up, Miss Havisham plays the rôle of fairy godmother, and later permits him to
continue in his belief that she is also the sponsor of his luxury in
London—until he is brought up short by the rough figure of Magwitch. Until the real world breaks in on him, Pip allows himself to
be pushed along, never challenging the requirement that he must
not look to closely into the sources of his good fortune. Likewise,
he is passive in his longing for Estella, who, in her metaphoric
associations with precious jewels and lofty stars, comes to symbolise
to him the final goal of his dreams of love, luxury, and high position.
Instead of trying to capture her through an aggressive courtship
he simply pines, assuming on very little evidence that one day she
will be bestowed upon him by Miss Havisham as everything else
has been.

Upon the return of Magwitch, Pip is forced to wake up and
recognise that life is not, after all, a fairy tale. He learns that his
own wealth comes from a criminal, that even the magical figures
of Satis House, Miss Havisham and Estella have criminal connections, and, as we have seen, that his callous treatment of Joe Gargery
was essentially criminal. This linking up of the criminal milieu and
the milieu of wealth and high position is a way of drawing the

strongest possible contrast between Pip's regressive fantasy-world, where wealth and good luck have seemed unremitting and uncompromised, and a real world where the dominant moral colouring is at best a dirty grey.

In terms of what we have called the love-motive, then, Dickens has shown fantasy in collision with reality. Pip learns that the world is not a vast mammary gland from which he can draw rich nourishment with moral impunity. He finds that he must hunger and struggle like all the rest. Furthermore, he must accept the unhappy fact that his participation in the old dream of great expectations has hurt real people. With his awakening to reality he develops a capacity for active, self-bestowing love. But the mature toughminded perspective from which the hero's development is viewed does not permit him to move on into happiness and fulfillment. In the final chapters of *Great Expectations* Pip wants to give himself, but there is no longer anyone in a position to accept his gift. Magwitch's fate is upon him; the circumstance of marriage has carried both Biddy and Estella beyond his reach. In bestowing himself upon the family of Herbert Pocket, Pip comes to rest in a kind of limbo. The book seems to imply that Pip is doomed to a lifetime of vicarious experience, because he lingered too long in his condition of alienation from the real.

This is not a complete account of Dickens's critique of the great expectations fantasy, that dream of huge and easy success which has always haunted the imagination of children and also haunted the imaginations of adults in the increasingly commercial and industrial society of nineteenth-century England. In *Great Expectations,* as in its legendary prototypes, the theme of ambition is treated under the two aspects of desire and will, the search for a superabundance of love and the drive for power. And it is in his presentation of the theme in the latter aspect that Dickens makes the more profound analysis of the immoral and criminal elements in his hero's (and the century's) favourite dream.

But Pip's ambition is passive. He only becomes active and aggressive after he has ceased to be ambitious. How then does *Great Expectations* treat the theme of ambition in terms that are relevant to the total action of which Pip is the centre? I have already begun to suggest an answer to the question. Ambition as the instinct of aggression, as the pitiless drive for power directed against what we have called authority-figures is both coalesced and disguised in the figure of Orlick. And Orlick is bound to the hero by ties of analogy as double, *alter ego* and dark mirror-image. We are dealing here with an art which simultaneously disguises and reveals its deepest implications of meaning, with a method which apparently dissociates its thematic materials and its subject matter into moral fable-*cum*-melodramatic accompaniment, yet simultaneously presents through patterns of analogy a dramatic perspective in which the apparent opposites are unified. In *Great Expectations* criminality is displaced from the hero on to a melodramatic villain. But on closer inspection that villain becomes part of a complex unity— we might call it Pip-Orlick—in which all aspects of the problem of guilt become interpenetrant and co-operative. The only clue to this unity which is given at the surface level of the narrative is Pip's obsession of criminal guilt. Pip tells us over and over again that he feels contaminated by crime. But we do not find the objective correlative of that conviction until we recognise in the insensate and compunctionless Orlick a shadow image of the tender-minded and yet monstrously ambitious young hero.

What is the rationale of this elusive method? In my opinion it enabled Dickens to project a radical moral insight which anticipated the more sophisticated probings of novelists like Dostoievsky and Gide without abandoning the old-fashioned traditions of melodrama and characterisation in which he had worked for more than a quarter of a century before *Great Expectations* was published. Pip, by comparison with Raskolnikov, is a simple young man. But through the analogy Pip-Orlick, *Great Expectations* makes the same point about ambition as *Crime and Punishment,* and it is a very penetrating point indeed. In the *Brothers Karamazov* Ivan comes to recognise during the course of three tense interviews with his half-brother, Smerdyakov, how he shares with that brother a criminal responsibility for the murder of their father, although Smerdyakov alone wielded the weapon. The comparable scene in *Great Expectations* is the limekiln scene. Orlick even adopts the tone of a jealous sibling during the interview, as in the remark, 'You was favoured, and he was bullied and beat.' But Dickens is not a Dostoievsky. Pip does not recognise Orlick as a blood-relation, so to speak. The meaning remains submerged and is communicated to the reader through other channels than the agonised confession of a first-person narrator. Indeed, the profoundest irony of the novel is not reached until the reader realises he must see Pip in a much harsher moral perspective than Pip ever saw himself.

## IV

Recognition that Pip's ambition is definable under the aspect of aggression as well as in terms of the regressive desire for passive enjoyment of life's bounty depends upon the reader's willingness to work his way into the narrative from a different angle than the narrator's. The evidence for the hero's power-drive against the authority-figures, the evidence of his 'viciousness' if you will, is embodied in the story in a number of ways, but a clear pattern of meaning only emerges after the reader has correlated materials which are dispersed and nominally unrelated in the story *as told*. Orlick, thus far, has been the figure whose implicit relations to the hero have constituted the chief clue to the darker meaning of Pip's career. He continues to be important in any attempt to set forth the complete case, but there are also some significant correlations to be made in which he does not figure. This is fortunate, if only to forestall the objection that the whole case depends upon an imputed resemblance between two characters whom generations of devoted readers have not, after all, found very much alike. Let us, then, present the rest of the evidence, and see whether Pip, in any sense, stands self-indicted as well as indicted for the bad company he occasionally—and most reluctantly—keeps.

We might begin with the apparently cynical remark that Pip, judged on the basis of what happens to many of the characters closely associated with him, is a very dangerous young man. He is not accident-prone, but a great number of people who move into his orbit decidedly are. Mrs. Joe is bludgeoned, Miss Havisham goes up in flames, Estella is exposed through her rash marriage to vaguely specified tortures at the hands of her brutal husband,

Drummle. Pumblechook has his house looted and his mouth stuffed
with flowering annuals by a gang of thieves led by Orlick. All of
these characters, with the exception of Estella, stand at one time or
another in the relation of patron, patroness, or authority-figure to
Pip the boy or Pip the man. (Pumblechook is, of course, a parody
patron, and his comic chastisement is one of the most satisfying
things in the book.) Furthermore, all of these characters, including
Estella, have hurt, humiliated, or thwarted Pip in some important
way. All in some way have stood between him and the attainment
of the full measure of his desires. All are punished.

Let us group these individual instances. Mrs. Joe, the cruel foster-
mother, and Pumblechook, her approving and hypocritical relation
by marriage, receive their punishment from the hands of Orlick.
Mrs. Joe hurts Pip and is hurt in turn by Orlick. Pip has the motive
of revenge—a lifetime of brutal beatings and scrubbings inflicted by
his sister—but Orlick, a journeyman who does not even lodge with
the Gargerys, bludgeons Mrs. Joe after she has provoked a quarrel
between him and his master. If we put together his relative lack
of motive with his previously quoted remarks at the limekiln and
add to these Pip's report of his own extraordinary reaction upon
first hearing of the attack—

> With my head full of George Barnwell, I was at first disposed to
> believe that *I* must have had some hand in the attack upon my
> sister, or at all events that as her near relation, popularly known
> to be under obligations to her, I was a more legitimate object of
> suspicion than anyone else—

we arrive at an anomalous situation which can best be resolved
on the assumption that Orlick acts merely as Pip's punitive instru-
ment or weapon.

With regard to Pumblechook's chastisement, the most striking
feature is not that Orlick should break into a house, but that he
should break into Pumblechook's house. Why not Trabb's? One
answer might be that Trabb has never stood in Pip's light. Pumblechook's punishment is nicely proportioned to his nuisance value for
Pip. Since he has never succeeded in doing him any great harm with
his petty slanders, he escapes with a relatively light wound. Al-

though we are told near the end of the novel that Orlick was caught and jailed after the burglary, we are never told that Pip reported Orlick's murderous assault on him or his confessions of his assault on Mrs. Joe to the police. Despite the fact that there is enough accumulated evidence to hang him, Orlick's end is missing from the book. Actually, it seems that Orlick simply evaporates into thin air after his punitive rôle has been performed. His case needs no final disposition because he has only existed, essentially, as an aspect of the hero's own far more problematic case.

Estella receives her chastisement at the hands of Bentley Drummle. How does this fit into the pattern we have been exploring? In the first place, it can be shown that Drummle stands in precisely the same analogical relationship to Pip as Orlick does. Drummle is a reduplication of Orlick at a point higher on the social-economic scale up which Pip moves with such rapidity through the first three-quarters of the novel. Drummle, like Orlick, is a criminal psychopath. At Jaggers's diner party the host, a connoisseur of criminal types, treats Drummle as 'one of the true sort,' and Drummle demonstrates how deserving he is of this distinction when he tries to brain the harmless Startop with a heavy tumbler.

But the most impressive evidence that Orlick and Drummle are functional equivalents is supplied by the concrete particulars of their description. To an extraordinary degree, these two physically powerful, inarticulate, and dark-complexioned villains are presented to the reader in terms more often identical than similar. Orlick, again and again, is one who lurks and lounges, Drummle is one who lolls and lurks. When Pip, Startop, and Drummle go out rowing, the last 'would always creep in-shore like some uncomfortable amphibious creature, even when the tide would have sent him fast on his way; and I always think of him as coming after us in the dark or by the back-water, when our own two boats were breaking the sunset or the moonlight in mid-stream.' When Startop walks home after Jaggers's party, he is followed by Drummle but on the opposite side of the street, 'in the shadow of the houses, much as he was wont to follow in his boat.' The other creeper, follower and amphibian of *Great Expectations* is Orlick, whose natural habitat is the salt marsh, who creeps his way to the dark landing below

Pip's apartment to witness the return of Magwitch from abroad, who creeps behind Biddy and Pip as they walk conversing on the marshes and overhears Pip say he will do anything to drive Orlick from the neighbourhood, who appears out of the darkness near the turnpike house on the night Pip returns from Pumblechook's to discover that his sister has been assaulted, and who, finally, creeps his way so far into Pip's private business that he ends by acting as agent for Compeyson, Magwitch's—and Pip's—shadowy antagonist.

Like Orlick, Drummle is removed from the action suddenly; Pip is given no opportunity to settle old and bitter scores with him. In the last chapter we hear that he is dead 'from an accident consequent on ill-treating a horse.' This is the appropriate end for a sadist whose crimes obviously included wife-beating. But more important to the present argument is our recognition that Drummle has been employed to break a woman who had, in the trite phrase, broken Pip's heart. Once he has performed his function as Pip's vengeful surrogate he can be assigned to the fate he so richly deserves.

Mrs. Joe beats and scrubs Pip until she is struck down by heavy blows on the head and spine. Pumblechook speaks his lies about him until his mouth is stuffed with flowers. Estella treats his affections with cold contempt until her icy pride is broken by a brutal husband. In this series Orlick and Drummle behave far more like instruments of vengeance than like three-dimensional characters with understandable grudges of their own. In terms of my complete argument, they enact an agressive potential that the novel defines, through patterns of analogy and linked resemblances, as belonging in the end to Pip and to his unconscionably ambitious hopes.

When Miss Havisham bursts into flames, there is no Orlick or Drummle in the vicinity to be accused of having set a match to her. In the long series of violence which runs through *Great Expectations* from the beginning to end, this is one climax of violence that can be construed as nothing more than accidental. And yet it is an accident which Pip, on two accasions, has foreseen. Before Miss Havisham burns under the eye of the horror-struck hero, she has already come to a violent end twice in his hallucinated fantasies—in Pip's visionary experiences in the abandoned brewery, where he sees Miss Havisham hanging by the neck from a beam. He has this vision once as a child, on the occasion of his first visit to Satis House, and once as an adult, on the occasion on his last visit, just a few minutes before Miss Havisham's accident occurs. What are we to make, if anything, of these peculiar hallucinatory presentiments and of the coincidence by which they come true?

The child first sees his patroness hanging from a beam after his first hour of service with her. At this point the novel dwells at length on his keen awareness that he has been cruelly treated, generalises on the extreme sensitiveness of children to injustice, and describes how Pip in utter frustration vents his injured feelings by kicking a wall and twisting his own hair. In these passages it seems to me that the reader is being prepared to interpret Pip's immediately ensuing hallucination as the child's further attempt to discharge his anger and grief against his adult tormenter. In fantasy Pip punishes a woman whom in fact he cannot disturb in any way, and, by hanging her, attempts to destroy the threat to his peace and security which she represents. This interpretation excludes the possibility of a supernatural element in the experience; the novel provides abundant evidence that the imagination of a child operating under a great stress of emotion is possessed of a hallucinatory power. When Pip carries stolen provisions to Magwitch on the marshes, his guilt-ridden imagination effects a transformation of the countryside through which he passes, until even gates, dykes, banks, cattle and a signpost seem to him to be pursuing him and crying out his guilt. Pip's hallucination, then, is an imaginative fantasy which both projects and disguises the boy's desire to punish his employer and to destroy her baleful power over him.

Pip experiences no recurrence of the hallucination during the long years of an association with Miss Havisham based on his mistaken assumption that she is the sole author of his good fortunes. The fantasy returns only after his eyes have been opened to the fact that nothing has come to him from Miss Havisham except unhappiness. On that last visit to Satis House he learns definitely of Estella's marriage. With this information the last link between him and his former employer snaps. The false fairy godmother kneels to

ask forgiveness for her crimes against him, and the duped hero
offers forgiveness sincerely, if sadly. Nevertheless, as Pip strolls
through the ruins of the estate he is not able to refrain from brooding over Miss Havisham's 'profound unfitness for this earth,' and
when he walks into the chilly, twilit brewery building he is not able
to prevent the return of the old hallucination of Miss Havisham
hanging from the beam. We are told that this was owing to the
revival of a childish association. But surely the episode represents
more than a curious psychological detail. It is profoundly right that
the fantasy should return at a time when he can see in complete
clarity and detail how his connection with Miss Havisham has
hurt him. It is profoundly right that he should forgive the false
patroness and yet not forgive her, behave generously toward her
and yet feel deeply that she has no right to live, treat her with some
degree of melancholy affection, yet hate her also in the depths of his
being.

We need not deny Dickens the insight necessary to the imagining
of so ambivalent a response in the hero of his great novel. And we
should not commit the anachronism of demanding that this response
be defined in the novel analytically and self-consciously—that the
hero should tell us, 'I forgave Miss Havisham as fully as I could, but
continued to think how well it would have been for me if she had
never set foot on this earth.' Pip's ambivalence is embodied dramatically. It must be known not as it is talked about, but as enacted.
A man forgives a woman, then hallucinates her death by hanging.
A man watches a woman burst into flames, then leaps bravely to
her rescue, but in the course of describing this rescue is forced to
remark, 'We were on the ground struggling like desperate enemies.'

How do these hallucinations, the second followed immediately
by Miss Havisham's fatal accident, add to the burden of the hero's
guilt? The answer is obvious. Because Pip's destructive fantasy
comes true in reality, he experiences the equivalent of a murderer's
guilt. As though he had the evil eye, or as though there were more
than a psychological truth in the old cliché, 'if looks could kill,'
Pip moves from the brewery, where he has seen Miss Havisham
hanging, to the door of her room, where he gives her one long, last
look—until she is consumed by fire. But here the psychological

truth suffices to establish imaginative proof that Pip can no more escape untainted from his relationship to the former patroness than he can escape untainted from any of his relationships to characters who have held and used the power to destroy or hamper his ambitious struggles, In all these relationships the hero becomes implicated in violence. With Estella, Pumblechook, and Mrs. Joe, the aggressive drive is enacted by surrogates linked to the hero himself by ties of analogy. With Miss Havisham the surrogate is missing. Miss Havisham falls victim to the purely accidental. But the 'impurity' of Pip's motivation, as it is revealed through the device of the recurrent hallucination, suggests an analogy between that part of Pip which wants Miss Havisham at least punished, at most removed from this earth for which she is so profoundly unfit, and the destroying fire itself.

## V

In this essay I have argued that Dickens's novel defines its hero's dream of great expectations and the consequences stemming from indulgence in that dream under the two aspects of desire and will, of regressive longing for an excess of love and of violent aggressiveness. In the unfolding of the action these two dramas are not presented separately. Instead they are combined into Dickens's most complex representation of character in action. Pip is Dickens's most complicated hero, demonstrating at once the traits of criminal and gull, of victimiser and victim. He is victimised by his dream and the dream itself, by virtue of its profoundly anti-social and unethical nature, forces him into relation with a world in which other human beings fall victim to his drive for power. He is, in short, a hero sinned against and sinning: sinned against because in the first place the dream was thrust upon the helpless child by powerful and corrupt figures from the adult world; a sinner because in accepting for himself a goal in life based upon unbridled individualism and indifference to others he takes up a career which *Great Expectations* repeatedly, through a variety of artistic means, portrays as essentially criminal.

After Magwitch's death, Pip falls a prey to brain fever. During his weeks of delirium it seems to me that his hallucinations articulate the division in his character between helpless passivity and demonic aggressiveness. Pip tells us he dreamed

> that I was a brick in the house wall, and yet entreating to be released from the giddy place where the builders had set me; that I was a steel beam of a vast engine clashing and whirling over a great gulf, yet that I implored in my own person to have the engine stopped, and my part in it hammered off.

It is tempting to read these images as dream logic. The hero-victim cries for release from his unsought position of height and power, but cannot help himself from functioning as a moving part of a monstrous apparatus which seems to sustain itself from a plunge into the abyss only through the continuous expenditure of destructive force. In the narrative's full context this vast engine can be taken to represent at one and the same time the demonic side of the hero's career and a society that maintains its power intact by the continuous destruction of the hopes and lives of its weaker members. In the latter connection we can think of Magwitch's account of his childhood and youth, and of the judge who passed a death sentence on thirty-two men and women, while the sun struck in through the courtroom windows making a 'broad shaft of light between the two-and-thirty and the judge, linking them both together.' But to think of the engine as a symbol of society is still to think of Pip. For Pip's career enacts his society's condition of being—its guilt, its sinfulness, and in the end, its helplessness to cleanse itself of a taint 'of prison and crime.'

When Pip wakes up from his delirium he finds himself a child again, safe in the arms of the angelic Joe Gargery. But the guilt of great expectations remains inexpiable, and the cruelly beautiful original ending of the novel remains the only possible 'true' ending. Estella and Pip face each other across the insurmountable barrier of lost innocence. The novel dramatises the loss of innocence, and does not glibly present the hope of a redemptory second birth for either its guilty hero or the guilty society which shaped him. I have already said that Pip's fantasy of superabundant love brings him at last to a point of alienation from the real world. And similarly

Pip's fantasy of power brings him finally to a point where with-drawal is the only positive moral response left to him.

The brick is taken down from its giddy place, a part of the engine is hammered off. Pip cannot redeem his world. In no con-ceivable sense a leader, he can only lead himself into a sort of exile from his society's power centres. Living abroad as the partner of a small, unambitious firm, he is to devote his remaining life to doing the least possible harm to the smallest number of people, so earning a visitor's privileges in the lost paradise where Biddy and Joe, the genuine innocents of the novel, flourish in thoughtless content.

# 9

## *Dickens and His Readers*

——◄◆►——

### Gabriel Pearson

Dickens the man, remains after a half-century of biography and much literary, social and psychological criticism, a baffling figure, as complex, dynamic and tragic as the age in which he lived. We think of his dominating the early Victorian period, not so much as a combatant in its ideological warfare but as a sort of folk hero, an embodiment of the resources and frustrations of a nation. It is almost a shock to realize that he died at the age of fifty-eight in 1870, so clearly do we envisage him as venerated and adored, so almost patriarchal in the modes of feeling he fathered, yet another of the tribe of long-lived Victorian sages. As a Victorian he died in what for most would have been prime middle-age; but he died a prematurely old man who, it could without fantasy be argued, committed what was virtually suicide. He had lived at just the pace of his society, and it had worn and worried him to death.

Dickens's life was not peripheral to his artistic career but one with it. In a complex variety of ways he managed, in his actual career, to embody nearly all the typical experiences of his age, and this

146

despite the fact that he was personally very neurotic with a private case-history of mental trauma. Yet somehow he was able to make his private conflicts and compulsions public, to integrate them with a wide social vision and to stir the imaginative depths of a vast national audience. What will be demonstrated here is the way in which his personality, his audience, and the popular forms he used combined into a typicality, a generality of appeal, which has never since, significantly, been equalled.

Pickwick is the starting point of the great career. His is the figure most immediately evoked by the adjective Dickensian. Much of *The Pickwick Papers* is set, as we remember, in Rochester and Rochester was the scene of Dickens's early childhood. It is a very significant part of his childhood, of his life indeed, for it became the symbol, not only of pre-industrial England, but of Dickens's own innocence before the fall, the trauma of the little drudge in the Blacking Factory, the son of a bankrupt father sheltering from a world of creditors in the Marshalsea debtor's prison, of "the child of singular abilities, quick, eager, delicate and soon hurt, bodily or mentally" who was always haunted by "the sense . . . of being utterly neglected and hopeless"[1] in the crowded desert of industrial London. No wonder then that the happy and carefree childhood of Rochester became in memory idealized as the age of good fellowship, good living, altogether of the good life. And the teens of the century, though indeed they have their black side, could be seen, at least in rural Kent, as the fast vanishing remnant of a more genial and spacious age. Dickens, as a writer, returned several times to Rochester, once as the tormented figure of litle Nell seeking a sanctuary in which to die, once as the Uncommercial Traveller (a title fascinating to ponder) but finally and momentously in his last work, the only half-completed *Edwin Drood*. It was a very different Rochester to which the exhausted novelist limped home, indeed it was no longer home. Cloisterham, its fictional pseudonym, in 1870 is a muffled and sinister ruin, where the relics of proud decay sway through miasma of the opium-dream suffered by the divided soul of an artist in the strange disguise of a cathedral organist. The

[1] Forster, Life of Charles Dickens, Chap. 2.

Orient, the victim of the new form of capitalist exploitation, has come to roost in the ideal world of childhood, there to poison and subvert its host.

What happened to the fictional Rochester, what happened through his suffering the sea-change of that symbol is, in general, what happened to England. As we have suggested, the childhood world is not without its foundation in historical reality. The change over from stage-coach to railway is not what we call the Industrial Revolution itself, but it must have been a palpable and all evident mainfestation of it. Likewise, the growth of cities, with the accompanying horror of tenement and disease, must have been in the earlier years of the century a very visible confirmation that England was passing through the throes of its transformation from an agricultural into a ruthlessly expanding industrial nation. This transformation Dickens, as we have seen, experienced through the subjective agony of thwarted childhood. He also experienced it, as one might say, professionally. It is indicative of the typicality of Dickens's career that in his earlier years, he was of that then most modern of occupations, a successful and very high-powered journalist. This, in the grand style, even when he had achieved established fame as the best-selling novelist of his day he continued to be. During the last twenty years of his life he half-owned and edited two weeklies, *Household Words* and *All The Year Round*. In his early years as reporter for the *Mirror of Parliament* and the *Morning Chronicle,* he was whirled from the Commons to the hustings, travelled all over England in search of sensational copy, was renowned for the devices he invented for pushing through news ahead of rivals and has a good claim as the originator of the "scoop." His career as a journalist had two important issues. It sent him out, actively as a young man and through widespread contacts as the controller and dominator of his own magazine later, into the arena of social transformation. It also gave him a miraculously sensitive finger to the national pulse. He developed preternatural sensitivity as to what constitutes a public, its demands and the extent to which its demands could be formed and its tastes governed. Dickens is the last great writer who was, in the fullest sense, a public figure. In his visits to America, he went as a sort of unofficial ambassador. He moved in the principal literary circles of his time. He knew most of the leading intellectuals, was made much of by the great and revered by the working-class. All this, of course tells us much of the quality of his sheer success. But there is another significance: his position, almost outside the class structure of his time yet living all its complex gradations, was experience. It is a tribute to his greatness as an artist that so much of what would have been for a lesser man the mere reward of preeminence, found its way back into the world of the novelist.

There was another aspect of his typicality which can only briefly be touched on. In his personal life he was in turn a typically Victorian husband and father begetting a host of children and later a rebel against sexual convention, separating from his wife and (the evidence is almost conclusive) taking as his mistress a young actress, Ellen Ternan.[2]

Through this world of experience he was then transformed into something like the representative of an epoch. But the most typical part of his life was his childhood. He remained true always to that shift from the world of innocence to that of experience. And it was the unity between his life and his art than enabled him to become the embodiment of the case-history of a nation in the throes of social revolution.

We have been arguing that on many levels Dickens embodied the life of his times. Yet in a very obvious way he was not typical, in that he did not participate to any outstanding degree in the intellectual life of the century. When we think of the sages, Arnold, Carlyle, Ruskin, they seem to us typical precisely because of the sturdy consistence of their diversity; it is the quality of their participation rather than its content that marks them. This is true of

---

[2] In the reputed confession made to Canon Benham many years after Dickens's death, Ellen Ternan declared that "she loathed the very thought of this intimacy." If these are in fact her words, they throw a curious light, on Dickens himself of course, but also on the whole sexual ethos of Victorian England. One may hazard that the mere fact that the relationship was necessarily illicit is a partial explanation of what was evidently a genuine personal failure. George Eliot of course may be cited as evidence of what sort of relationship could be achieved. But she was not, I think, typical in the way Dickens was; nor submitted to the kind of scrutiny a public idol would inevitably incur. The failure must also be related to Dickens' own psychological development of which there is ample illustration.

the pure creative talents also. George Eliot exists not only in relation to *Middlemarch* but to "topics" as well; to Puritanism and German Idealism, to Lewes and Spencer. It would be possible to summarise the "thought" of minds even as obviously unintellectual as Tennyson's and Browning's; or of Trollope and Thackeray, for that matter. Even a popular novelist like Bulwer Lytton was an intellectual in a way Dickens never was.

It would be possible to extract almost any number of opinions from Dickens's works. He could be characterized as an unconscious socialist, a radical individualist, a Carlylian authoritarian, and almost anything else under the sun, all with the immediate legitimacy that quotation affords. He was, at once, all of these and none. In trying to establish his "position" it is as well to assert what he wasn't.

In general, his imagination was caught only at the point where ideas impinge on the lives of ordinary people. Hence he was consistently concerned with popular science as the policy of his two weeklies, entirely in his own hands, proves. But he did not live the conflicts of ideology with anything like enough involvement to suffer the agonies of that typically Victorian malady, "Doubt." He was not, as Tennsyon was, terrorized by "the twin terrible Muses, Astronomy and Geology," nor does he seem to have had much time for the religious controversies of the period. Although it was *the* topic of one of the most sensitive periods of his career, the 'Thirties, he evinced no interest in the Oxford Movement. He disapproved of Anglicanism as being a buttress of the class system, of Catholicism which stood for the dogma and superstition which he loathed, and of Nonconformism in particular, which had so oppressive and thwarting an effect on the individual; he explored this effect in great detail in a novel, *Little Dorrit,* in a short story, *George Silverman's Explanation,* and satirized nonconformist preaching many times in his fiction.

His social attitudes are very complex indeed. He hated the state apparatus, and particularly Parliament ("the national cinderheap") yet was convinced that the State should intervene to control the rapacity of landlord and capitalist and to raise the standards of the working-class. At the same time he attacked the ideology of radicalism, Malthusianism and Utilitarianism, particularly in *Hard Times,* with a fervour that owes much to Carlyle. With Carlyle, a certain modified conservatism caused him to take the wrong side in the case of Governor Eyre; and yet he had no time for the divine dictator hero; on the contrary, he declared in 1869: "My faith in the people governing is, on the whole, infinitesimal; my faith in the people governed is illimitable." This is a long way from Carlyle's contempt for the people; likewise, it is not a socialist opinion. It could best be described, bearing in mind the period, as lower-middle-class common sense. Lower-middle-class is of course, if we have to make the assignment, Dickens's class position. But as is very frequently the case such a position goes with a distinct Anarchism. Of course, a careful division must be made between the kind of opinions that went with the public persona of the novelist, whose financial success, popularity and philanthropic activities combined into a general respectability (though never conformity), and the attitudes formulated in artistic terms which increasingly become more and more anarchistic as the novelist's social vision deepened. This Anarchism has, in certain aspects, much in common with that traditionally English working-class scepticism displayed towards institutions and the men that "work" them. In other ways, it was the product of a fundamental isolation, the lonely and irrational cry of a bruised and uncomprehending childhood. Basically, on the psychological as on the social level, it was the expression of a disappointed and ineffective idealism, which persisted through all the activity of an often startlingly successful mission to improve the lot of the common man. This Anarchism must have been a potent contribution to his popularity. It enabled him to reach the levels of revolt that were unformulated and hidden in the minds of a working-class not always very politically conscious. It explains further why he so disastrously misunderstood political activity such as Trade Unionism. His portrait of industrial conflict in *Hard Times* is narrow and unconvincing. It is significant that in this novel his working-class hero, Stephen Blackpool, is, for personal reasons, outlawed both from his own work-mates and the Capitalists. The only comment he can find to contain his situation is: "See how we die and no need, one way and another—in a muddle—every day!" This is almost the despairing cry of the ideological agnostic of all ages.

Another aspect of Dickens's anarchism accounts for his love-hate relationship to the idea of revolution. This had the obvious superficial attraction that sheer contemporaneity must bestow: the fear of revolution was an ever-present possibility throughout the larger part of the period of his most abundant activity. Of course, the same type of fascinated horror is to be found in Carlyle; the success of both *The French Revolution* and *A Tale of Two Cities* has the same source so far as the general imaginative context is concerned. With Dickens however, there was a further psychological incentive: the symbolic relationship between the actual, latent explosiveness of capitalist society and the destruction of the prison (the archetype here is the storming of the Bastille, which, as Lyonel Trilling has pointed out in his essay on *Little Dorrit,* is a dominant Nineteenth Century symbol for the liberating power of revolution); and the prison was quite precisely the Marshalsea, the debtor's jail where Dickens's father was imprisoned. In *A Tale of Two Cities* the theme of incarceration, of release, of the dead brought back to life permeates the fabric of the novel; there is, if one may use the term, a psychological objectivity in the exploration of this theme which survives the falsities of sentiment and the subjective haziness of characterization which is now an impediment to evaluation. Popular violence constantly dovetails with the theme of release. The mob has, so the conscious Dickens who has to get his ending "right" feels, in the end to be thwarted and repulsed; order has to be restored; and "order" is the complacencies of the individual existence. The novelists *social* participation is destructive. The high point in the description of the rising of the Paris mob is undoubtedly the storming of the Bastille itself. This, it could be argued, is historically *the* moment of exaltation any way. But in the much earlier *Barnaby Rudge* (1841), set in the Gordon Riots, there is the same fascination with mob violence, and again the high point is the burning down of the jail. The subjective symbol of the Marshalsea Prison (his childhood experience of it was unquestionably searing, relating as it does to the particular parental betrayal he believed himself to have suffered) thus had a real existence in the imagination of his audience; and his private anarchism relates closely to the latent though unspecified movements of revolt in his time.

In the preceding pages we have tried to define some of the qualities that in Dickens, the man and artist, tended to make for typicality. Equally important to this consideration are the literary forms that were available to him, their relationship to audience and the particular effect that they had on the workings of his creative imagination. The novel, when Dickens opened his career with the *Sketches* and *Pickwick*, was hardly a respectable form. Scott, it is true, had lent it his authority—at first, it is worth noting, anonymously. But it was a popular form. This was because part-publication (novels were generally published in twelve monthly parts before they achieved three-volume status) created an audience that feasted on the stimulus of suspense, that demanded excitement, entertainment and thrills. A popular form demands a popular (in all senses of the word) author, and this Dickens superlatively was. He was not, it is fair to say, at least not in the most superficial sense, a revolutionary in the matter of form. The genus he generally found ready-made; what he did was to breathe into the old body his at once personal and typical spirit. Most of the types of novel were ready to hand. Thus Pickwick is essentially a fusion of the rambling and disconnectedly episodic eighteenth century picaresque novel and a popular form of the time, the sporting sketches, whose most famous example is Surtee's *Jorrocks Jaunts and Jollities;* the complex, gothic novel often combined with a socially contemporaneous theme, unified through an altogether melodramatic plot, was a feature of the work of such "popular" novelists as Ainsworth and Bulwer Lytton. Examples of this kind could be multiplied. The point is that Dickens used his popular forms with such success because he believed in them, in his audience and, it should be added, because they could bring in big money. His treatment of his audience through the popular form always, even to the end, had something of the grand manner of the impresario. He depended on the support of a mass-audience to keep him really in business at all, yet he was always one step ahead; often it was a false step and he had to retrace and retract only to spring a new imaginative vision from the vantage-point of an apparent concession. The nature of part-publication called for a relationship between artist and public of an arduous sensitivity. Dickens could always feel just how his new line was "going down" by that crudest of barometers, sales! There were, of course, reviews which, though Dickens pretended never to read any, did have some influence on him; but to nothing like the extent they would have today. There was the advice of friends, but this was generally taken when it seemed to Dickens to represent a prevision of a public demand.[3] Of course, after the mid-fifties, Dickens's fame was so established (at least, he had never again to fear the type of failure, with its accompanying anxieties and its threat to his personal position that Martin Chuzzlewit evoked) that he had no need to angle for support when in fact he received worship. Nevertheless, the habits of the great popular novelist remained; his feel for an audience, lively, responsive and fascinated was a stimulus essential to the creative method. It is significant that his last, unfinished novel, *Edwin Drood,* was designed to be a detective thriller of the kind which a much younger novelist, Wilkie Collins, had made popular. Even at the end, he could not submit to the status of a revered anachronism.

The fact that Dickens's novels were published in installments had of course very distinct effects. Since it was being written and sold before it was finished, it demanded haste, a monthly crisis, and no pause for rewriting or manipulations towards an over-all pattern. This does much to account for the loose structure, diffuseness and often inadequately tided-up plot of what we think of as the typically Dickensian novel. It meant, also on the debit side, that before he had really established his impregnable position as the leading novelist of his day, and when the sales-barometer showed signs of sinking, Dickens was particularly drawn to non-literary devices designed to bolster demand. Thus, in *Martin Chuzzlewit,* when sales began to

[3] There are two good examples of this: (1) Jeffrey, venerable critic of the *Edinburgh Review,* along with the bulk of readers, was passionately euthusiastic about Little Nell in *The Old Curiosity Shop;* he did not like Martin Chuzzlewit; nor did the bulk of readers. His advice played a considerable part in causing Dickens to put another child's death in his next novel: the death of Little Paul in *Dombey and Son.* (2) Bulwer Lytton did not think the original "disillusioned" ending of *Great Expectations* would go down. Dickens agreed with him and substituted the more sentimental ending.

drop, he inserted the grand American excursion, reasoning that the recent notoriety of his *American Notes* would make an irresistible appeal. (In fact, the public refused to take the bait, and by so doing shewed excellent taste.) On the credit side, however, the monthly publications did have this extraordinary result; that by the extremely close touch they maintained (not only through the sales statistics, but through correspondence and more intangible forms of response as well) novelist and audience in a sense created the work together; instead of the artist merely offering the finished articles, he entered into the community of his readers and created for them and, to an extent, through them. The audience was the whole of early Victorian England. Dickens was read with equal avidity by intellectuals (though here, from the first, there were dissenters) and by working people. This was the period before the Education Acts and a public captured by mass-circulation journalism. Many of Dickens's audience were illiterate, but accessible through readers' clubs, where one member, literate, read to the rest. Dickens was also family reading, and on the whole he was careful to keep his tone approved and moral; he minded his d–mns and G–ds! It was through his preternaturally close contact with a mass audience, that Dickens was able, in the first half of his artistic career, to achieve what no other writer has succeeded since in approaching: he created genuine folk-figures, Pickwick, Fagin, Scrooge, Quily, which not only bear the clear stamp of their popular origin but have found their way back into a current mythology where they are still renewed through our modern mass-media, the film and the radio.

By 1850, this era of the creation of folk heros was over for Dickens. The reasons for this change are of course very complex, but they certainly have something to do with an increasing and irremediable urbanization with its accompanying loss of traditions, an increasing self-consciousness on the part of the novelist's public, and, most certainly, the development of Dickens himself towards a highly conscious artist of the modern type; though whether cause and effect can be separated is doubtful. This change is shewn very clearly in the fate of the Christmas stories. *A Christmas Carol,* for all its crudities and sentimentalities, possesses obviously, as its present seasonal popularity testifies, to an insistent degree, an archetypal popular appeal. Cashing in on their popularity, Dickens went on producing Christmas stories throughout his career. They continued to sell prodigiously; but they must strike us now as decidedly mechanical and mass-produced. They degenerated, almost admittedly, into pot-boilers; though they always retained the function of shewing which pot was being boiled. Dickens tried hard, in his last novels, to return to the type of folk-humour that early endeared him. After 1850, however, Fagin, Sairey Gamp, Sam Weller, all the typically "Dickensian" characters, somehow evaded his art; such late attempts as Silas Wegg, in *Our Mutual Friend* and the Wopsall-playing-Hamlet scene in *Great Expectations* are not really successful. Dickens was by then on to deeper and gloomier things.

Dickens's audience wanted, rather in the modern film-sense, "drama," and this the novelist provided in a very complex way. The more or less strict contemporaneousness of a Dickens novel does not provide the social content of the novels, rather, the symbolic structure that gives a specific significance to a general pattern of social vision. Thus, the "theme" of *Bleak House* is concerned with the evil effects of the venerable and decaying Court of Chancery (so *Oliver Twist* attacks the Poor Law; *Nicholas Nickelby* attacks Yorkshire schools; *Little Dorrit* satirizes the bureaucratic incompetence of the Crimean War through the Circumlocution office; and *Our Mutual Friend* uses as one of its symbols the actual dust-heaps that were sold at great profit in the London of the sixties)—and it could be said that that novel is concerned with remedying an obvious public scandal. Such particular attack was Dickens's dramatic fodder; in the earlier part of his career the novelist lived through a certain notoriety; and even when established his tendency to attack another soft section of the Establishment made him disliked in many official and conservative quarters. This actvity has, obviously, a good deal in common with the capacity for scoop journalism discussed above. It was another of the ways through which he held and fascinated his audience and by means of which he was able to compete with the contemporary sex-fiction (for it existed: cf. Ford, *Dickens and his Readers*) of this time. But most important it was a way of integrating his personal vision with an ever-present individual social reality. The Court of Chancery was a crying scandal whose anti-social practice Dickens sharply focused; what is typical of Dickens, however, is that he uses a decaying sector of society that is under attack as, in turn, a symbol for the whole of society. Around a central symbol or overt pre-occupation Dickens weaves a complex tapestry of unsuspected and unlikely relationships; extraordinary coincidences with an obscure connection, and a plot which manages to show that the aristocracy has an ultimate connection with the outcast and disowned (Lady Dedlock and Jo, the crossing-sweeper in Bleak House); that in the end all are reducible to the same social terms; Dickens manages in fine to image a society organic beyond all its rigidities and apparent stratifications.

Melodrama was the medium in which Dickens could come to terms with his audience through the contemporary theatre, as was farce and Shakespearian tragedy. It is no accidental part of his success that the novelist was constantly absorbed in some aspect of the theatre. Undoubtedly he learned, not in a very conscious manner it is true, much from Shakespeare, with whom Dickens had this in common: that he was professionally committed to literature at the most obvious level, that he held something for all in an heterogenous audience, and that he worked towards large symbolic structures, that could be "taken" as specific and mythical simultaneously. Thus, the boast that Dickens is a second Shakespeare is not just a wild hyperbole of evaluation; it is a quite exact parallel, descriptive rather than adulatory. Ben Jonson was his real love however; Jonson's grasp of the caricature of the humourous declares itself omnipresently in the pre-1850 Dickens. The novelist himself acted Ben Jonson, and composed, directed and acted farces (and romantic comedy) of his own composition and of questionable merit. He was in fact fascinated by the theatre, the feel of a live audience, the arranged unreality in which illusion is created and lived, through grease-paint and foot-light. This throws much light on the personality of the novelist who in "real" life was irritable, rather ruthless, domineering and gloomy. Given any sort of an audience however he breathed and expanded in a radiance of mimicry, high spirits and almost hysterical hilarity. It serves also to explain why, when he was secure (at least, outwardly; for he never lost the deep compulsion with its roots in his childhood trauma which drove him to bolster himself more and more with a drive towards money-making) financially and socially, and hence had lost something of his old sensitive intimacy with his readers, he was driven so naturally to the device of public readings. Through these he was enabled, during the last years of his life when composition had become agonizingly arduous, to achieve once again, in a new form, the exhilerating sense of the artist's power to control an audience, with the additional advantage of being able to see with his own eyes the physical effect. His readings were nearly all from the earlier novels and the Christmas stories—a striking example of their folk appeal. (He read to audiences that ranged from the mechanics of Manchester to the leaders of fashionable society). Not the readings themselves, but the fascination Dickens found in them lends them the effect of a last, portentously fascinating disease. We have on record Dickens's pulse-rate, and it soared alarmingly whenever he read. With his audience he acted out the hidden conflicts and compulsions of the age. The murder of Nancy in *Oliver Twist* became a favourite piece, and Dickens noted, with morbid satisfaction, the number of women who fainted during performances. He was forbidden to give any more performances by his doctors but he pressed on with a kind of intense frenzy. When he did heed the warnings it was too late, the damage was done, and he died exhausted and paralysed. In a sense his audience, or rather his lover's passion for it, destroyed him; but not before his artist's passion had, beneath the guise of the performer, moulded it and recreated it, and, in the process, the imaginative landscape of nineteenth century England.

# 10

# Thackeray's Narrative Technique

John A. Lester, Jr.

EDITORIAL NOTE. *Until recently Victorian scholars bothered very little about the state of the texts they studied. This meant, in Thackeray's case, that* The Letters and Private Papers *were not suitably collected until 1945-6 and that the two volume biography,* Thackeray: The Uses of Adversity *and* Thackeray: The Age of Wisdom, *did not appear until 1955 and 1958 respectively. The author of all these works was Gordon Ray, the American scholar. An annotated* Vanity Fair *based on collation of the manuscripts and the various printed editions made its appearance in 1963, the work of Geoffrey and Kathleen Tillotson. There had been, of course, a large body of criticism but much of it was tentative, specialized, or crotchety. A number of influential contemporary critics tended to dismiss Thackeray as an unsatisfactory novelist with an undeserved reputation—among them Dorothy Van Ghent, F. R. Leavis, and Arnold Kettle. Those who defended Thackeray (Geoffrey Tillot-son's* Thackeray the Novelist *is a good instance) did not seem to meet head on the objections raised against him. Thackeray remains, as a consequence, the most problematic of all the Victorian writers.*

*In the following essay John Lester attempts to remedy this situation. Lester offers a systematic survey of the narrative technique used in Thackeray's fiction and, in addition, explains why these techniques were employed, what ends they serve. He faces up to a major difficulty by offering some justifications for Thackeray's habit of breaking up an exciting passage of narration by intruding a talkative, and not especially intelligent, omniscient narrator. It is an important essay with implications for the study of Victorian fiction generally as well as for the novels of this author.*

## I

To one who would explore the range and variety of fictional technique, the Victorian novel presents an infinite resource. It shows us novelists in the exciting awareness of a new literary genre shaping under their hands,[1] aware of a vast new audience to whom they could appeal. They write often uninhibited by conscious theories of technique; they write with gusto and with what Edith Wharton once called the true mark of vocation in any art—abundance.[2]

Yet the exploration of the techniques of Victorian fiction has scarcely begun. Percy Lubbock, in *The Craft of Fiction* (1921), applied the single criterion of point of view to Victorian novelists (among others)— and found them wanting. E. M. Forster (*Aspects of the Novel,* 1927) and Lord David Cecil (*Early Victorian Novelists,* 1934) have advanced on a somewhat broader front, exploring aspects of characterization and plot, and the "range" of the major nineteenth-century novelists. What has hardly been attempted in any detail is a close and analytical study of the fictional techniques developed by individual authors. Fred W. Boege has considered Dickens' awareness of the advantages of a fixed point of view in fiction,[3] and has found Dickens far more aware of the effectiveness of that device than had been supposed. Several studies have been made of the influence of serialization and monthly-parts publication on Victorian fiction,[4] modes of publishing which frequently did force

---

[1] See Lionel Stevenson, "The Second Birth of the English Novel," *UTQ,* xiv (July 1945), 366–374.

[2] *The Writing of Fiction* (New York, 1925), p. 77.

[3] "Point of View in Dickens," *PMLA,* lxv (March 1950), 90–105.

[4] See, for Dickens, Gerald G. Grubb, "Dickens' Pattern of Weekly Serialization," *ELH,* ix (June 1942), 141–156; John Butt, "The Composition of *David Copperfield,*" *Dickensian,* xlvi (1950), 90–94, 128–135, 176–180; xlvii (1950–51), 33–38; for Meredith, Royal A. Gettmann, "Serialization and *Evan Harrington,*" *PMLA,* lxiv (Dec. 1949), 963–975; for Reade, Royal A. Gettmann, "The Serialization of Reade's 'A Good Fight,'" *NCF,* vi (June 1951), 21–32; for Hardy, Mary Ellen Chase, *Thomas Hardy from Serial to Novel* (Minneapolis, 1927).

the novelist to consider closely the effect of different technical methods. But there is a host of similar critical studies which might profitably be made. They offer a way of access not only to the creative genius of the Victorian novelists, but also to a fresh and expanding view of the craft of fiction.

The present article is based on a systematic survey of the narrative techniques used in Thackeray's fiction.[5] Special attention has been paid to two factors: (1) Thackeray's handling of chronological sequence in the story, and (2) his variations in method between telling the story personally, in his own words, and presenting it dramatically in scenes. These features lie close to the heart of Thackeray's distinctive narrative method and at the same time yield objective data which make possible a more accurate description of that method than has been possible before. Frequently they reveal Thackeray's conscious attempt to meet specific critical problems; more often they point to hitherto hidden traits of his temperament as an artist.

# II

Students of Thackeray have long observed in his novels a singular attitude toward time. He looks with an Olympian view on his characters and events, and sees the course of his story laid out as it were in panorama before him. Over this panorama he can look before and after, moving backwards and forwards freely in time, selecting detailed scenes here or there as he chooses. Percy Lubbock has remarked that time in the Thackeray novel "is not movement, it is tranquillity—time that stands still, as we say, only deepening as the years go."[6]

Using this freedom of motion, Thackeray characteristically doubles backwards and forwards in the course of telling his story. The redoublings are there in his first substantial work of fiction (*Catherine*, 1839–40), and they remain a major narrative device in his final

[5] Such a study has not previously been made of Thackeray's fiction as a whole. Two valuable detailed analyses have been made of *Vanity Fair:* Ludwig Baucke, *Die Erzählkunst in Thackerays "Vanity Fair"* (Hamburg, 1932), and Edwin Walter, *Entstehungsgeschichte von W. M. Thackerays "Vanity Fair"* (Berlin, 1908).

[6] Percy Lubbock, *The Craft of Fiction* (New York, 1945), pp. 108–109. Cf. Edwin Muir, *The Structure of the Novel* (London, 1946), p. 68.

and incomplete novel, *Denis Duval* (1864). The redoublings are most numerous in *The Virginians* (1857–59), which has 18 major redoublings (involving the major part of a chapter or more) and 46 minor ones. Lest we regard this as evidence of Thackeray's discursiveness in his later work, the novel second in number of redoublings in the narrative is *Vanity Fair* (1847–48), with 16 major and 44 minor redoublings.[7]

These characteristic redoublings may be ascribed in part to a natural bent, the Thackerayan "roundabout manner." In his non-fictional prose he often proceeds in the same back-and-forth fashion, not only in the *Roundabout Papers* but in *English Humourists* and *The Four Georges* as well.[8] The great majority of the redoublings in his fiction, however, stem from a deeper cause than this, and reveal Thackeray's subtle motives as a craftsman. A survey of the whole range of his reversals in chronology suggests two main types of motivation which may lie behind them. The first includes those redoublings which Thackeray employs in order to solve specific technical problems in telling his story; the second includes motives of thought and temperament of which one suspects Thackeray himself was not always fully aware.

## A. Motives of Technique

(1) Many of Thackeray's redoublings result from his instinct to plunge "into the midst of things." A dramatic scene, drawn from the

---

[7] The totals for the other important novels are: *Barry Lyndon* (1844), no major and 16 minor; *Pendennis* (1848–50), 13 major and 34 minor; *Henry Esmond* (1852), 2 major and 9 minor; *The Newcomes* (1853–55), 11 major and 38 minor; *Philip* (1861–62), 2 major and 47 minor. It goes without saying that in the course of these free redoublings Thackeray often falls into chronological discrepancies. W. A. Hirst to the contrary ("The Chronology in Thackeray's Novels," *Cornhill Mag.*, LXVII N. S., 553–563), there are clear errors in chronology in all Thackeray's major novels, with the exception of the fragment *Denis Duval*. Hirst himself provides more specific evidence against his thesis of "exquisite chronological accuracy" than he does for it.

[8] Examples of apparently random redoubling appear in *The Virginians,* Ch. xcii, pp. 792–793; *Philip,* Ch. xxi, p. 349; *Denis Duval,* Ch. v, pp. 503–505; and indeed in all Thackeray's fiction. (Page references throughout this article refer to the Biographical Edition of *The Works of William Makepeace Thackeray,* ed. Anne Ritchie, 13 vols., New York, 1903.)

full course of the action, brings the reader at once into the story. It stakes a strong claim on his interest. But at the same time it raises questions: who are these characters? what are their motives? The plunge in medias res brings as its inevitable consequence the doubling back, the recapitulation of what has gone before.[9]

The best illustrations of Thackeray's use of this device are found in the opening chapters of his novels. All of his major novels, with the exception of the first (*Barry Lyndon*, 1844), open with a "discriminated occasion," a scene dramatically portrayed,[10] and in each case the scene is followed by what George Saintsbury has called an "explanation-retrospect," [11] a doubling back to give the necessary background. The opening scenes of these novels—Becky Sharp flinging the dictionary from the coach, Colonel Newcome's visit to the Cave of Harmony, Major Pendennis at his club—are among the memorable triumphs of Thackeray's art. In the face of his many disavowals of the conventional tricks of novel-spinning,[12] one must recognize that he has thoroughly mastered the device of starting his novel in the midst of things, and of doubling back to gather up the background explanations later.[13]

The device is not confined to the opening of his novels, however. Thackeray carries it with him throughout the telling of his stories, as a means of keeping the narrative alive. Very rarely is the reader allowed to feel completely abreast of the story; nearly always as one theme is advanced, others are perceptibly left behind, to be caught

---

[9] The most specific recognition I have found of this technical problem by a Victorian novelist is Anthony Trollope's, in the opening paragraph of *Is He Popenjoy?* (1878).

[10] *The Virginians* varies slightly from the pattern in that two chapters are employed in the intial scene instead of one. Thackeray first used this method of commencing a story in *The Bedford-Row Conspiracy* (1840). Significantly, neither the opening scene nor the consequent redoubling is present in the French source for this story, Charles de Bernard's *Le pied d'argile*.

[11] *A Consideration of Thackeray* (London, 1936), p. 180. J. Y. T. Greig (*Thackeray: A Reconsideration*, New York, 1950, p. 112) fails to recognize the technical necessity of this device.

[12] Notably in "On a Peal of Bells," in *Roundabout Papers*. See also his letter to Mrs. Baxter, 10–23 April 1858, in Gordon N. Ray, ed. *The Letters and Private Papers of William Makepeace Thackeray* (Cambridge, Mass., 1946), IV, 80.

[13] Dickens also realized the importance of winning the reader's interest with the opening of the novel: "If you do not fix the people in the beginning, it is almost impossible to fix them afterwards" (*Nonesuch Letters*, III, 187).

up and advanced in their turn later on. Midway, for example, in his
account of Lady Jane Sheepshanks' visit to Miss Crawley, Thackeray writes, "In the autumn evenings (when Rebecca was flaunting
in Paris, the gayest among the gay conquerors there, and our
Amelia, our dear wounded Amelia, ah! where was she?) Lady Jane
would be sitting in Miss Crawley's drawing-room . . ." [14] Thus in
brief parenthesis we are reminded of two other themes still to be
brought up to date and are forewarned that soon the story must
redouble twice to account for them. [15] Continually, as he proceeds,
Thackeray stores up events and developments to be related later.
In Chapter xliii of *Vanity Fair* Dobbin asks for leave to return to
England; in Chapter lvii, after thirteen chapters concerned with
Becky and Amelia, we double back to find that he easily got his
leave and has in fact returned. Chapter lix of *Pendennis* is followed
by a chapter doubling back to give "Explanations"; Chapter lxii is
followed by Chapter lxiii, appropriately titled, "Which Accounts
Perhaps for Chapter LXII." About one-fifth of the redoublings in
Thackeray's novels can be accounted for by this device of advanc-
ing the story into the midst of new and partially unexplained circumstances, then turning back to provide the explanations by
following up other themes of the narrative. [16]

(2) One cannot long examine the chronological pattern of Thackeray's novels without becoming aware of a second technical problem
which confronted him—the necessity of adapting his narrative for
publication in instalments or separate parts. *Henry Esmond* was the
only novel of Thackeray's to make its first appearance in book form,
and it is significant that *Esmond* exhibits fewer chronological redoublings than any of the others. [17] The rest of Thackeray's major works

[14] *Vanity Fair*, Ch. xxxiv, p. 324.
[15] It does so in Chs. xxxiv (pp. 334-336) and xxxv (pp. 336–346).
[16] Occasionally Thackeray makes deliberate acknowledgment of this device. See *Pendennis*, Ch. vii, p. 72; *Virginians*, Ch. lxx, p. 596; *Denis Duval*, Ch. i, p. 448. To a degree,
some such redoubling is inevitable in narrative which aims to portray complex social
history. "Narrative," as Carlyle observed, "is *linear*, Action *is solid*" ("On History," in
*Critical and Miscellaneous Essays*, London, 1869, II, 351). The distinguishing traits of
Thackeray's method are the complexity of the social fabric he portrays (see pp. 397–
398) and his readiness to give prominence to many different strands of it.
[17] See n. 7, above.

of fiction all first reached the public in a series of single, usually monthly, instalments. There can be no doubt that this method of publication directly influenced the form and narrative technique of his fiction. From the time of his first extensive narrative published in instalments (*Catherine*, 1839–40), Thackeray was aware that his story had to be shaped accordingly.[18]

Very frequently Thackeray's method is to end an instalment or part with a sudden new turn of plot. It may be a leap forward to a scene well in the future,[19] requiring in the next instalment an explanation-retrospect of the sort we have considered. It may be simply a dramatic episode, whether it be the sudden re-appearance of George Warrington or the news of George Osborne on the field of Waterloo, "lying on his face, dead, with a bullet through his heart." [20] The essence is that the number end on a note of suspense, a promise of events to be explained and characters' reactions to be studied.[21]

Having devised a technique for planning the single serial part, however, Thackeray was by no means consistent in using it. It may be true, as Erwin Walter says, that much of the desultory progress of Thackeray's narrative may be attributed to the vogue of publication in parts. It may be true that the unity of *Henry Esmond*, on which virtually all critics agree,[22] is the result of its having been planned and written as a single book rather than in many parts. But such statements are true only in the most general sense, and insofar as they apply to Thackeray's notoriously dilatory habits of work. One finds on examination that in *Pendennis*, for example, out of 23 parts

[18] The influence of parts-publication on Thackeray's work as a whole has not previously been considered. Erwin Walter (see n. 5) on p. 133 touches briefly on the problem as it relates to *Vanity Fair*.

[19] See examples at the conclusions of No. xvi (Ch. lvi) of *Vanity Fair*, and No. xi (Ch. xxxv) of *Newcomes*.

[20] The conclusions of *Virginians*, No. xii (Ch. xlviii), and *Vanity Fair*, No. ix (Ch. xxxii), respectively.

[21] The same principle was recognized by Dickens (Butt, "The Composition of *David Copperfield*," *Dickensian*, xlvi [Spring 1950], 92), Meredith (Gettmann, "Serialization and *Evan Harrington*," *PMLA*, lxiv, 973), and Reade (Gettmann, "The Serialization of Reade's 'A Good Fight,'" *NCF*, vi, 28).

[22] See, e.g., John W. Dodds, *Thackeray: A Critical Portrait* (New York, 1941), p. 164.

only 4[23] show clear marks of having been planned as units. In the rest of the novels the number of parts which are patently constructed as separate units is much higher: 4 out of 11 parts in *Barry Lyndon,* 10 out of 19 in *Vanity Fair,* 6 out of 23 in *The Newcomers,* 9 out of 24 of *The Virginians,* and 10 out of 20 in *Philip.* There seems to be no regular pattern to Thackeray's technical procedure in this respect. Many numbers are planned as special units in the progress of the narrative; the substantial majority are not.

The bearing of the serial parts which are specially constructed on the chronological sequence of Thackeray's narrative is much easier to define. When one number has been concluded with a dramatic, provocative scene, it is probable that the next number will provide an explanation-retrospect to fill in the background.[24] Examples could be drawn from any of the major novels that appeared in serial form. Most famous is perhaps the conclusion of No. IV (Ch. xiv) of *Vanity Fair,* where Becky receives old Sir Pitt Crawley's proposal of marriage, and is forced to reply, "O Sir Pitt! . . . O sir—I—I'm *married already.*" The first readers of *Vanity Fair* at this point had one month of suspense before them. Whom has Becky married? When? Why?

Critically, it is easy to find fault with this climactic scene. The reader has been led to believe that he knows Becky up to this point and has been in confidence with her motives and struggles up the social ladder. To be told suddenly that she has been married without our knowing it has about it some of the cheapness of Hollywood "double-take." [25] Yet when Thackeray constructed this culminating scene he had to choose whether to approach the episode in straight dramatic fashion or use the climax as a technical device to give his

---

[23] Nos. VII (Chs. xxi–xxiii), IX (Chs. xxvii–xxix), X (Chs. xxx–xxxii), and XVII (Chs. liii–lv)—chapter number given as in first edition. Thackeray's illness and the consequent lapse of several months in the publication of *Pendennis,* and his acknowledged weariness with the story (Lionel Stevenson, *The Showman of Vanity Fair,* New York, 1947, p. 154) may possibly have led him to plan the novel in larger sections, rather than in parts.

[24] There are many exceptions to this pattern, for example in the sequence of Nos. VI (Chs. xviii–xx) and VII (Chs. xxi-xxiii) of the first edition of *Pendennis.*

[25] Harry Warrington's proposal of marriage to Maria Castlewood is by-passed in the same way. *Virginians,* Chs. xviii and xxxvi.

narrative interest and impetus from one instalment to the next. That he chose the latter—and the explanation-retrospect which it entails—reveals something of Thackeray's whole attitude toward the dramatic scene, a matter to be considered in Section III of this survey.

(3) A final technical motive behind Thackeray's chronological redoublings lies in the nature of his subject-matter, in his desire to present a panoramic picture of society. He describes the problem openly in *Vanity Fair:* "Our history is destined in this chapter to go backwards and forwards in a very irresolute manner seemingly, and having conducted our story to tomorrow presently, we shall immediately again have occasion to step back to yesterday, so that the whole of the tale may get a hearing." [26] The doublings back to pick up different threads of the story, new scenes from the pageant of society, are by no means confined to *Vanity Fair.* More reversals in chronological sequence in the major novels can be attributed to this motive than to any other single cause.[27] These findings point to the truth of Lord David Cecil's view that in all Thackeray's novels the panorama of life is the real subject. "Only once did he paint openly a panorama of human life and call it *Vanity Fair.* But they are all really about Vanity Fair; Vanity Fair as seen in the life of a young man, Vanity Fair as seen in the life of a family, Vanity Fair as seen eternally the same in the life of the past." [28] Every Thackeray novel is in some degree a novel without a hero; in all of them the chief protagonist is society itself. Characters from his other novels enter and depart. They bring a sense that each story is selected from a large society which lives on outside the novels and independent of them. Thackeray is never happier than when in the midst of a large and varied number of characters, diverse incidents, and numerous

---

[26] Ch. xxv, p. 230. There are no grounds for Mr. Greig's implication (p. 116) that a chapter "chronologically misplaced" in Thackeray is therefore "probably an afterthought."

[27] Redoublings of this type are most numerous in *Vanity Fair,* but play a major part in the narrative technique of *Barry Lyndon, Pendennis,* and *Virginians.* They are least apparent in *Esmond* and *Philip.*

[28] "William Makepeace Thackeray," in *Early Victorian Novelists* (New York, 1935), p. 85. See also Dodds, p. 113.

interwoven plots, all clamering to be told and commented on. Even
in a novel so apparently confined to the biography of one hero as
*Philip,* Thackeray will double back and forth, following one aspect
of Philip's life, one group of his social relationships, and then another.[29]

The total of all the redoublings which can thus be ascribed to
motives of technique accounts for rather more than half of the redoublings in Thackeray's fiction. They can be counted as technical
devices, part of his strategy to keep the narrative alive and moving
on from one instalment to the next.


## B. *Motives of Temperament*

There remains a substantial number of redoublings in Thackeray's work where the motive is not primarily technical and where
the search for a cause leads us deeper into the mind and quality of
Thackeray as an artist.

(1) Thackeray is more interested in his characters' reactions to
events than he is in the events themselves. Many of his strongest
effects—and not a few of his weaknesses—can be traced directly to
this deep predisposition of his art. Around any dramatic incident
in his narrative Thackeray will search tirelessly to explore its reper-
cussions in the minds and sentiments of his characters: The action
as such may seem to get buried beneath the comments of Thackeray
and the characters upon it.

This produces many of the chronological redoublings in his narrative. He will leap far into the future and back again to get the
viewpoint of a particular personage. " 'I should like to have known
that Good Samaritan, sir,' our Colonel said, twirling his mustache,
when we saw him again, and his son told him that story." [30] Thirty
years are as nothing in Thackeray's sight as he sweeps forward to
pick up what Philip "yelled out, whilst describing the scene to his

[29] See e.g. *Philip,* Chs. iii (pp. 121–125), xviii, xxi (pp. 360–361), xxiii (pp. 384–389).
This type of redoubling to follow different scenes and characters is naturally encouraged when the characters are separated geographically, as when Dobbin is in India,
Philip Firmin is in France, or Harry Warrington, in his later years, is in America.
[30] *Newcomes,* Ch. xxxix, p. 408.

biographer in after days." [31] Needless to say, Thackeray has favorites among his characters, persons for whose comment and reactions he will pause at any time and double backward or forward without hesitation. Major Pendennis is one example,[32] the Baroness Bernstein, even more strikingly, is another. Viewed in the light of the swervings and redoublings she causes in the narrative, the Baroness appears as a magic mirror, in which all the events must be reflected as they pass. Clearly Thackeray found a special significance in her view of life; there are eleven redoublings in the narrative of *The Virginians* for her sake alone.

From Thackeray's work as a whole one may derive this generally valid formula: the more explosive and unexpected the scene, the more eager Thackeray is to explore different characters' reactions to it. That is to say, in terms of the present survey, the more explosive the scene, the more redoublings are set in motion as a result of it. Thus around the announcement that Harry Warrington "have been took by two bailiffs this evening" [33] there are clustered some ten redoublings, rounding up the reactions and sympathies of the Baroness, Parson Sampson, Maria Castlewood, Mrs. Lambert, and George Warrington himself, who is at this moment restored to life. In the same way the narrative will be found to weave around other stunning scenes in Thackeray—George Osborne's death at Waterloo, Lord Kew's duel with M. de Castillonnes, or Pendennis' sudden exclamation to Mirobolant, "By Jove, it's the cook!" Wherever a turn of the plot closely affects the hearts and ambitions of his characters, Thackeray will follow its ramifications wherever they lead.

(2) Every reader of Thackeray has noticed what may be called the retrospective vision in his work, the fondness for looking backward, the glowing effects of nostalgic memory which he can command. The sources of this mood of retrospect are subtle and deeply imbedded in Thackeray's temperament. I am confident that Lambert Ennis is close to the truth when he remarks that Thackeray

[31] *Philip*, Ch. xxv, p. 402. The long sweep ahead to "after days" occurs most markedly in the three late novels, *Virginians, Philip,* and *Denis Duval.*

[32] The Major is called on for further comments in *Newcomes* (Ch. xxiv, p. 240) and *Philip* (Ch. xiv, p. 259).

[33] *Virginians,* Ch. xliv, p. 377. Imprisonments in Thackery invariably bring on redoublings into the reactions of other characters; duels and threatened duels usually have the same effect.

loves the past because it is safe, whereas "the present and future are all so dangerous." [34] The springs of Thackeray's retrospective vision must lie in his innermost attitudes, in areas more accessible to psychological than to literary criticism.

The "reminiscential manner" [35] has direct effect on Thackeray's handling of chronological sequence in his narrative. Among his important novels, all but *Pendennis* are written to some degree as "memoirs" and told by a narrator in later years, after all the events of the narrative are past. This memoir pose gives Thackeray precisely the time relationship to his story which he desired to maintain —the view of all events spread out at once in a panorama before him. We see him in his first eager and extensive exploitation of this vantage-point in *Barry Lyndon,* where the recurring glances from present prosperity to future despair provide much of the delightful ironic self-revelation of the tale. In his last novel, *Denis Duval,* he acknowledges explicitly the technique which has served him so well: "Why do I make zigzag journeys? 'Tis the privilege of old age to be garrulous, and its happiness to remember early days. As I sink back in my arm-chair, safe and sheltered *post lot discrimina,* and happier than it has been the lot of most fellow-sinners to be, the past comes back to me—the stormy past, the strange unhappy yet happy past—and I look at it scared and astonished sometimes; as huntsmen look at the gaps and ditches over which they have leapt, and wonder how they are alive." [36] The writer of memoirs has freedom to move back and forth over the whole range of events, following any theme where it leads him.

Using this freedom, Thackeray gains new strength in his rôle as "social preacher." He sees human virtues and vanities in the long result of time. "I am speaking," he will say, "of simple old days, you understand. Of course there is *no* puffing, or jobbing, or false praise, or unfair censure now."[37] He can see events in the light of their consequences. At the height of Harry Warrington's bounty and

---

[34] *Thackeray: The Sentimental Cynic* (Evanston, Ill., 1950), p. 200. The quotation is from Thomas Carlyle.
[35] The phrase is Greig's, Ch. xvi.
[36] Ch. iv, pp. 490–491. Cf. *Newcomes,* Ch. xxiv, pp. 237–238.
[37] *Philip,* Ch. xxxi, p. 486. Cf. *Virginians,* Ch. liii, p. 445.

good fortune, Thackeray can glance forward for a moment to Harry's mother's reflection on his "prosperity—nay, . . . his extravagance and folly. How quickly his wealth has passed away!" [38]

With his memoir pose, Thackeray can view his characters now in the press of present action, now in the mature and deliberate retrospect of after life. To Boswell, who came to him plagued with worry, Dr. Johnson offered the advice, "Consider, Sir, how insignificant this will appear a twelvemonth hence." [39] The human truth of this remark is constantly woven into Thackeray's novels. Thus Samuel Titmarsh can be heard exclaiming to the cunning Mr. Smithers, "It's lucky, sir, that you are an old man, . . . and that the affair happened ten years ago; or, by the Lord, Mr. Smithers, I would have given you such a horse-whipping as you never heard of!" [40]

To gain any of these effects of perspective, and to accent the enduring significance of a scene, Thackeray will double forward and back through the chronology of his story. Clive Newcome, George Warrington, and Philip Firmin, in their days of struggle and poverty, were each happier than they realized at the time, and with each there is the flash far into the future to record the point unmistakably. " 'Oh,' says Clive . . ., 'it was a jolly time! I do not believe there was any young fellow in London so happy.' " [41] Becky Sharp is not allowed to enjoy her season in high society in full triumph. "Becky has often spoken in subsequent years of this season of her life, when she moved among the very greatest circles of the London fashion. Her success excited, elated, and then bored her." [42]

A survey of the chronological reversals in Thackeray's narrative, then, suggests three conclusions: (a) In constructing his narrative, Thackeray rarely feels bound to follow the chronological sequence of events "as they happened." He insists on his freedom to roam backwards and forwards through the events of his story. (b) In his redoublings, he is frequently motivated by considerations of technique. Such considerations, particularly those prompted by publi-

---

[38] *Virginians,* Ch. xliii, p. 363.
[39] Boswell's *Life of Johnson,* entry for 6 July 1763.
[40] *Great Hoggarty Diamond,* Ch. ix, p. 74.
[41] *Newcomes,* Ch. xvi, p. 170.
[42] *Vanity Fair,* Ch. li, p. 490.

cation in monthly parts, weigh much more heavily with him than his frequently announced disdain for the "artifice" of story-telling[43] has led us to believe. (c) His redoublings reveal a primary concern for the reactions of his characters to the events that pass, and a fondness for seeing those reactions in the light of time past, time present, and time to come. The first and third of these conclusions will concern us later, since they provide clues which bear directly on Thackeray's essential quality as a novelist.

# III

Coincident with Thackeray's doublings backward and forward in time as he tells the story is another characteristic narrative device —his variation between the method of telling the story personally, in his own words, and that of presenting it in dramatic scenes. It soon proves futile to survey simply these two poles of author-presentation and dramatic enactment. A Thackeray novel displays not only the two poles but every shade and variety of narrative presentation in between. The varieties of intermediate "semi-scenes" which he invents for his narrative shed new light on his purpose as a novelist.

It can be said to begin with that one's general impression in reading Thackeray is correct—he is reluctant to embark on a direct, dramatic scene. He makes little deliberate effort to prepare for a scene, and when one does arrive, he reserves at all times the liberty to intrude and interject comments of his own. [44] Percy Lubbock is again critically sound when he attributes to Thackeray a "constant tendency . . . to escape and evade the restrictions of a scenic method, and to present the story in a continuous flow of leisurely, contemplative reminiscence." [45]

---

[43] *Philip,* Ch. xxiii, p. 375.

[44] Here is the clearest critical distinction between Thackeray's work and Dickens'. Dickens' first advice to the would-be novelist was, ". . . the people should tell it and act it for themselves" (*Letters of Charles Dickens,* ed. by his sister-in-law and his eldest daughter, New York, 1879, II, 292).

[45] Page 94. Cf. Cecil, p. 98. The amount of narrative which receives some degree of scenic treatment is proportionately about equal in all of Thackeray's novels with the exception of *Barry Lyndon* and *Philip,* in both of which the proportion of the scenic is unusually high. The common assumption (e.g., Greig, p. 114) that the proportion of commentary to scene increased in Thackeray's later work is not borne out by the facts.

Many detailed observations of Thackeray's handling of the scene go to support this general conclusion. He very rarely gives us, for example, a scene which in its sheer drama or "theater" is felt to be presented for its own sake. His most memorable moments—of Beatrix descending the staircase, of Rawdon confronting Becky and Lord Steyne—are remembered not for the action that takes place, but for the vivid development and re-alignment of character which they suddenly announce. There are a few Thackeray scenes where the unfolding of dramatic action is the author's main concern: Major Pendennis' triumph over Morgan, Harry Warrington's combat with Will Castlewood, Denis Duval's encounter with Miss Rudge.[46] But usually Thackeray will circumvent the *scène à faire* entirely. Consider for example Laura Bell's quarrel with Blanche Amory.[47] We are told the quarrel is impending; we are told in a brief paragraph that "Laura fairly broke out into a loud and indignant invective." But the only *scenes* we are given are of Laura's telling Mrs. Pendennis about it afterwards, and (by virtue of a redoubling) of Blanche's goading Laura into jealousy some time before.

Thackeray's avoidance of violent, dramatic action is seen even more strikingly in his treatment of duels. With a novelist like Dumas, whom Thackeray so much admired, the duel is a climax of the story. With Thackeray, though more than a dozen duels are fought or threatened in his novels, they are almost never presented scenically. The build-up, the growing tension and animosity, is dwelt on; the duel when it comes is thwarted,[48] or touched on as if in passing, in a sentence or two[49]—or told about in retrospect.[50] Again we find the focus of Thackeray's vision turned on the reactions of his characters, rather than on the outbursts of dramatic action. "It is more with

[46] Such scenes grow perceptibly more numerous in the later novels. One suspects that it is in this increased appeal to melodramatic effect, rather than in his allegedly greater chattiness, that a falling off of Thackeray's creative power can be detected.

[47] *Pendennis,* Ch. xxv. Cf. the close of Ch. xli, where there is a scene of plans and anticipations of a dinner-party at Greenwich, but the party itself is passed over in a sentence.

[48] *Vanity Fair,* Ch. lv; *Virginians,* Ch. xi.

[49] *Esmond,* Bk. i, Ch. xiv; Bk. ii, Ch. xv; Bk. iii, Ch. vi; *Newcomes,* Ch. xxxiv.

[50] *Denis Duval,* Ch. iii. The most extensive duel-scenes in Thackeray appear in *A Shabby Genteel Story,* Ch. ix, and *Barry Lyndon,* Ch. ii; both duels turn out to have been faked.

characters than with astounding events that this little history deals," [51] he once wrote. "I own I think less of the engaged troops than of the people they leave behind." [52]

Another trait of Thackeray's narrative which reveals his lack of concern for the dramatic scene as such is his vagueness in locating scenes in time and place. Often as the first character speaks we do not know where or when the episode is taking place, or to whom the lines are spoken. Voices are heard first in a Thackerey scene; the fixing of the conversation in time and place, even the identification of the characters present, are left till later on, if indeed they are revealed at all. Philip suddenly is heard declaiming on love's magic: "Love, sir, flings a halo around the loved one." [53] It emerges that he is talking to Arthur Pendennis; then that Laura is present too, and the children. It is tea-time, at the Pendennises' home in London— which in turn reveals that this scene is taking place many months after the events of the rest of the chapter. In most of Thackeray's scenes traces of this vagueness can be found; they are scenes often without time or setting, conversations from that Fable-land from which Thackeray assures us his characters have come.[54]

Between the direct author-narration in Thackeray's novels and the rare dramatic scenes lies a host of varied and hybrid "semi-scenes." They are infinite in variety; they defy systematic description or classification. They have never been critically examined in Thackeray's fiction as a whole.[55] Yet however difficult it is to describe them, these subtle advances toward and retreats from dramatic presentation reflect an essential Thackerayan quality which must be considered. For the purposes of this consideration, they may be grouped into three main types.

(1) *The Habitual Scene.* The most common and revealing type of semi-scene in Thackeray presents scene and dialogue not as of a specific time and place, but as a sample of the habitual speech and action of the characters. The habitual scene is usually clearly

[51] *Ravenswing,* Ch. i, p. 373.
[52] *Virginians,* Ch. lxiv, p. 551.
[53] *Philip,* Ch. xvi, p. 298.
[54] *Newcomes,* Ch. lxxx, p. 804.
[55] Baucke (see n. 5), pp. 94–116, identifies some of the complex methods of scenic presentation used in *Vanity Fair.*

marked by the "Clive would say" or the "Captain Rawdon often said" which introduces it. The habitual verb may be simply a method of approaching the scene; from the "would say" of the introduction the scene moves quickly into sharper and more specific focus. A scene designed to illustrate Beatrix Esmond's worldliness, for example, is introduced "habitually." "If Esmond remonstrated, the little rebel would say: 'Who are you? I shall go my own way, sirrah, and that way is towards a husband; and I don't want *you* on the way.' " [56] Into this speech Beatrix's mother breaks suddenly: " 'At least you own to your worldliness, my poor 'Trix' ' "—and a specific scene is under way. At other times—much less frequently— the habitual scene maintains its generalized, habitual form throughout, placing the entire scene at a distinct remove from actuality.[57]

It is possible to locate the precise point at which the habitual scene is born in Thackeray's work—at the close of Chapter ii of *A Shabby Genteel Story* (1840).[58] It is a perplexing scene, torn between the habitual and the specific; it reflects perhaps Thackeray's own uncertainty as he evolved a new technique. Thereafter in Thackeray's work there is no hesitation on this score. In all his major novels the habitual scene is an established method of introducing or maintaining a semi-dramatic presentation of his narrative.

(2) *The Intermittent Scene.* Moving across the broad expanse of his imagined history, Thackeray developed an extraordinary art of "hedge-hopping," jumping from one incident to another yet somehow fusing the fragmentary intermittent impressions into a whole scenic sequence. The result can be a chaos of disjointed detail,[59] but it rarely is. By virtue of his peculiar detachment, the timeless wisdom of his comment on events and character, Thackeray can touch the intermittent scene with magic. It becomes a delicate balance of scene and summary, of the voices and actions of people plus an acceleration of tempo which reveals their meaning and consequence.

---

[56] *Esmond,* Bk. ii, Ch. iii, p. 309.

[57] See *Ravenswing,* Ch. vii, pp. 453–454; *Barry Lyndon,* Ch. xiii, p. 160; *Newcomes,* Ch. lxxiv, pp. 748–749.

[58] One habitual quotation occurs earlier, in *Catherine* (1839–40), Ch. iv, p. 569.

[59] The sequences at the openings of Chs. lxxi and lxxv of *The Newcomes* are peculiarly unsucessful.

Examples can be found in all the major novels. As an illustration we may select the sequence describing Colonel Newcome's reaction to the news that his brother-in-law, Charles Honeyman, has been imprisoned for debt.[60] Pendennis and Warrington speak first; they are for letting the law take its course with Honeyman. But the Colonel is resolved to secure Honeyman's release. He gives Pendennis funds and asks him to make a settlement with the creditors. We skip forward to follow briefly Pendennis' visit with each of them. His visits are completely successful, and the scene flashes forward again to the Colonel's moral observations to Clive, who himself has run up some minor debts. "My boy, . . . you see to what straits debt brings a man . . ." Clive departs, and Colonel Newcome turns to Pendennis: "In God's name, keep my boy out of debt when I am gone, Arthur. I shall return to India very soon." His funds are exhausted by this Honeyman affair, and he must cut short his leave.

All this in less than three pages! Here are the Colonel's magnanimity, the creditors' cold calculations, Clive's shame for his own debts, and the Colonel's sadness and concern at having to part from his son again—all presented in a running sequence of scenic glimpses. The intermittent scene sacrifices much of the actuality of the dramatic scene fully prepared for and performed, but it gains something which was apparently more important to Thackeray: a coalescence of characteristic speech and action with the long-range moral perspective of the social preacher.

(3) *The Interjected Quotation.* In all of Thackeray's novels there are scattered bits of speech and dialogue, flung out in the course of author-narration as being somehow typical of the accent and manner of a character being referred to. Only rarely is the interjected quote accompanied by any gesture or visualized action; hardly ever does it conjure up a sense of specific scene. Consider for example the celebrated Chapter xxxvi of *Vanity Fair,* "How to live well on nothing a year." It is as thoroughly a chapter of author-commentary as any Thackeray ever wrote. It is interrupted twice by interjected quotations. Becky fears for her future, and cautions her husband,

---

[60] *Newcomes,* Ch. xxvi, pp. 262–265. The intermittent scene is used more frequently in *The Newcomes* than in any of the other novels.

"Gambling, . . . dear, is good to help your income, but not as an income itself. Some day people may be tired of play, and then where are we?" Further on, we have the complaint of their Parisian landlord after the Crawleys have gone: *"Ah, Monsieur! . . . ils m'ont affreusement volé."*

The interjected quotation lends a vitality to Thackeray's long blocks of commentary; not the vitality of an actual dramatic scene, but of the spoken voice suddenly heard through the author's narration, clear, with its distinctive accent.[61] There are abundant examples of the interjected quotation in Thackeray's fiction, from first to last. It is admirably suited to his bent as a novelist, for it allows him freedom to reminisce over his narrative at will, yet always be able to call on his characters to speak their own words and confirm the point he is making.

The types of semi-scene which Thackeray resorts to could be enumerated almost indefinitely. There are purely allegorical scenes —of Darby and Joan, Jones and Brown, or what not—connected only by implication with the action of the story,[62] imagined scenes, where Thackeray confesses that he does not know precisely what took place, but he "fancies" it "must have been" something like this;[63] reported scenes, in which the characters' direct discourse is paradoxically rendered indirectly;[64] there are even times when Thackeray invites the reader to look to his own experience and compose his own scene as he pleases.[65] There is seemingly no end to Thackeray's invention of semidramatic scenes.

Faced with such a bewildering array of devices for avoiding dramatic enactment of the story, one is forced to seek the governing motive behind them. Thackeray's invention of scenes midway be-

---

[61] "I know the sound of their voices," Thackeray said of his characters when (in "De Finibus," *Roundabout Papers*) he wished to show that he knew them utterly. It has not been sufficiently remarked that Thackeray's scenes generally are *heard* rather than visualized. Frequently he is content to use straight line-by-line dramatic dialogue in his scenes, without benefit of stage-directions.

[62] See *Shabby Genteel Story,* Ch. iii, pp. 25–26; *Philip,* Ch. xxiii, p. 374; *Newcomes,* Ch. i, pp. 1–5.

[63] See *Newcomes,* Ch. lix, p. 619; Ch. lxi, pp. 642–643; *Virginians,* Ch. xlii, pp. 353–354; Ch. lxii, p. 519.

[64] See *Barry Lyndon,* Ch. iii, p. 43; *Newcomes,* Ch. lxxi, p. 726.

[65] See *Catherine,* Ch. iv, p. 568; *Pendennis,* Ch. xv, p. 136; *Philip,* Ch. xvii, p. 296.

tween author-narration and dramatic presentation is always re-
sourceful and usually effective. But what leads him to apply his
inventiveness in his direction in the first place?

From the evidence of the scenes alone we can derive a portion of
the answer. There is one quality which is shared in common by all
these types of semi-scene—they are all in some degree *illustrative*.
They are all offered as being significant because, beyond their artistic value as discriminated occasions, they illustrate a truth of character or human behavior which Thackeray means to convey. It goes
without saying that his allegorical scenes exist primarily to illustrate
a general moral truth. It is nearly as obvious that his habitual scenes
do the same; they convey enduring, recurrent traits of character
rather than momentary or chance reactions under the stress of an
actual scene. Again, the onset of a scene in Thackeray is very commonly heralded by a generalized comment: "Rebecca always knew
how to conjure away these moods of melancholy," [66] or, "Without
wishing to disparage the youth of other nations, I think a well-bred
English lad has this advantage over them that his bearing is commonly more modest than theirs." [67] The scene then follows to illustrate this general truth. In Thackeray's early work the illustrative
character of his scenes is occasionally explicit; certain scenes in
*Catherine, The Ravenswing,* and *Barry Lyndon* are introduced by a "for
example," or "for instance." In his mature fiction the illustrative
quality of the scene is less deliberately pointed, but it remains a
distinctive characteristic of his scenic method.[68] It reveals an essential quality of Thackeray's orientation to the craft of fiction.

From a close examination of Thackeray's scenes, then, three conclusions may be drawn: (a) As students of Thackeray have noticed
before, he usually avoids the visualized dramatic scene in his fiction
and resorts to other less directly representational methods of narration. (b) Between the method of dramatic presentation and that of
author-narration, Thackeray invents a full spectrum of semi-scenes,
each recording the spoken voice of his characters, but each distinctly

---

[66] *Vanity Fair,* Ch. xxx, p. 279.

[67] *Newcomes,* Ch. xxi, p. 203.

[68] The same conclusion is suggested if one asks what sort of material normally demands
scenic treatment in Thackeray's fiction. One finds that the majority of his scenes exist
to illustrate an accent of speech, trait of character, or recurrent note of human vanity.

removed from "actuality." (c) The many types of semi-scene have one feature in common, in that they exist not only for their intrinsic effect, but also to illustrate and convey general truths of character and behavior.

# IV

It remains to coordinate the facts of Thackeray's handling of chronological sequence and of the scene, and to suggest the bearing of this survey on our final description of his quality as a novelist. It is clear that fidelity to a particular moment in time, or to systematic chronological sequence, is not essential to his creative art. He is most at ease when he has ample freedom to roam backwards and forwards "timelessly." It is equally plain that his creative energy is most active when it is not confined to the time and setting of a specific scene to be acted out; he moves most freely when he can bob in and out of the action, select, synthesize, and comment.

We have evidence for one further delimitation of Thackeray's artistic range: he is not primarily interested in the portrayal of individualized, self-operative fictional characters. There is some familiar evidence which would seem to suggest such a conclusion— Thackeray's forgetfulness of the names of his characters,[69] his recurrent reference to them as puppets,[70] his selection of stereotype names for minor characters—Miss Grains, the brewer's daughter, and Mr. Pestler, the apothecary; but all of these may be accounted for by traits of mind and temper quite peripheral to Thackeray's creative genius.[71] More pertinent would be the evidence suggested

---

[69] There are examples of changes of names in *A Shabby Genteel Story* and *Philip*, and in *Vanity Fair;* in *Pendennis* and *Newcomes* characters die, only to be revived later on. For Thackeray's confession of such blunders, see his *Roundabout* essay, "De Finibus," and Ray, II, 500, 685.

[70] Notably, of course, in the last lines of *Vanity Fair* and in the Preface, "Before the Curtain," to the first book-form edition. See also *Philip*, Ch. xlii, p. 620, the last paragraphs of *Newcomes,* and many other places in Thackeray's work.

[71] The same can be said of a point advanced on the other side of this issue by Steveson (p. 154), who regards Thackeray's "habit of carrying characters over from one story to another" as "evidence of the strong reality that his creations had in his imagination." This does not necessarily follow; the carrying-over can be explained quite as satisfactorily in terms of Thackeray's often expressed loneliness and longing for companionship.

by Lord David Cecil [72] that there is patent inconsistency in some of Thackeray's major characterizations, though it is difficult to feel that such inconsistencies have been conclusively demonstrated.[73]

What is provided by a survey of Thackeray's narrative technique is a wealth of other evidence, woven deeply and consistently through all of Thackeray's fiction, which points in essentially the same direction. In Thackeray's doublings away from the specific time of an action, his lightning switches from a characterization now to a characterization "in after years," there is implied an urge to catch not the eccentricity or special vividness of the moment, but the enduring response which is remembered for a lifetime.[74] In his withdrawals from the actual to the habitual scene there is the same motive at work. What is true of characters at any one moment is not so important to Thackeray as what is true of them in the long run and in retrospect, when they are seen under the glance of eternity, and interpreted in the light of timeless moral comment. In the occasional scenes which are referred to the reader's own experience for confirmation there is the clearest evidence that it is the lasting truth of human nature, rather than the random truth of diverse individuals, that lies closest to the heart of Thackeray's creation. To embrace the enduring emotions and experience of his characters, the author's own chorus of comment is heard persistently, echoing the worldly wisdom of a lifetime: "Who does not know that face of pity? Whose dear relations have not so deplored him, not dead, but living? Not yours? Then, sir, if you have never been in scrapes; if you have never sowed a handful of wild oats or two; if you have always been fortunate, and good, and careful, and butter has never melted in your mouth, and an imprudent word has never come out of it; if you have never sinned and repented, and been a fool and been

---

[72] Pages 106–108. Lord David is thinking especially of Lady Castlewood in *Esmond.* Other characters deserving of such analysis are Morgan in *Pendennis,* Philip Firmin, and Lord Castlewood. Fanny Mountain, and the Baroness Bernstein in *Virginians.*

[73] Gordon N. Ray (*The Buried Life: A Study of the Relationship between Thackeray's Fiction and his Personal History,* Cambridge, Mass., 1952) provides valuable biographical evidence to account for inconsistencies in several of Thackeray's major characterizations.

[74] In this Thackeray is in clear contrast to Dickens, who (as Thackeray recognized and deplored—Ray, *Letters,* II, 772) rejoices in depicting eccentricities.

sorry—then, sir, you are a wiseacre who won't waste your time over an idle novel, and it is not *de te* that the fable is narrated." [75]

It is what his characters represent that is the sure and stable center in Thackeray's work. The timeless and enduring traits of human nature are what he seeks to evoke, and to this purpose his entire narrative technique has been shaped and modified. The Jamesian critic may object that Thackeray's scenes are blurred and muffled, and that the dramatic scene is an author's "best possible warrant" [76] that his fiction is valid. But Thackeray is not seeking for the Jamesian effect in fiction, but for something quite different. His concern is not so much with the scene vividly realized as with the worldly wisdom and truth that may be abstracted from it. He devoted all his craftsmanship to the task of sifting out that wisdom from the pageant that moved before him in his novels. He invented an entire range of narrative devices with which he could discriminate and reflect the essence of the characters and events he was portraying. To have evolved for this special purpose a distinctive style, an original management of time, and countless new shades of scenic presentation is more than to have developed a "Thackerayan manner"; it is the mark of genius.

---

[75] *Virginians,* Ch. lxi, p. 513.
[76] Lubbock, p. 101. That Thackeray was aware of the special power of the scene is evidenced by the fact that well over two-thirds of his chapters and monthly instalments conclude with a scene of some sort.

# 11

## *Determinism and Responsibility in the Works of George Eliot*

————◆————

### George Levine

EDITORIAL NOTE. *Silas Marner has long been considered an unexception-able "minor classic" of realistic fiction suitable for grade school students. One consequence is that generations of readers have refused to look at any of the other novels. The situation today is very different. Seminars on George Eliot are offered at important graduate schools; there are new editions of* Adam Bede *(1859),* The Mill on the Floss *(1860),* Felix Holt, The Radical *(1866),* Middlemarch *(1871–2),* Daniel Deronda *(1876), as well as* Silas Marner *(1861).* Middlemarch *is now become a classic of the college curriculum, almost as omnipresent as Freud's* Civilization and its Discontents. *Eliot occupies a key position in F. R. Leavis'* The Great Tradition *(1948), as the link between Jane Austen and Henry James. In the same year appeared Joan Bennett's* George Eliot: Her Mind and Art *which in turn was followed by four books in the 1950s—*The Victorian Sage *by John Holloway,* The Novels of George Eliot *by Barbara Hardy,* Movement and Vision in George Eliot's Novels *by Reva Stump, and a second* The Novels of George Eliot *by Jerome Thale.* The Art of George Eliot *by W. J. Harvey appeared in 1961 and David Dachies'* George Eliot: Middlemarch *two years later. A useful collection of critical essays and excerpts from Henry James through the 1950s is provided by Robert Stang's paperback* Discussions of George Eliot *(1960). The present essay is by a younger Victorian scholar who is particularly concerned with the way in which ideas find expression in works of art. George Eliot was an intellectual and a considerable scholar as well as a novelist. We admire her social insight, the masterful way in which she constructs and sets in motion a dense, particularized, and believable fictional world. George Levine's essay attempts to come to grips with the structural principles which helped mold the shape of this complex fictional creation.*

The nature and degree of George Eliot's commitment to a deterministic world view have been the source of considerable difficulty in the criticism of her work. Critics who concern themselves with the subject take, for the most part, the view either that her belief in determinism seriously marred her art or, on the other hand, that despite apearances she was not a consistent determinist.[1] In both cases, however, determinism evokes extraordinary intensity of feeling, almost everyone agreeing that a commitment to it tends to be detrimental to the artist because it forces a distortion of the facts of

---

[1] Most of the critics who discuss her determinism do so in order to criticize. See, especially Gerald Bullett, *George Eliot: Her Life and Books* (London, 1947): "Determinism is a form of death because it makes everything, including our own thinking, a mindless mechanism." More recently, William J. Hyde in "George Eliot and the Climate of Realism," *PMLA,* LXXII (March 1957), has written: "What matters is that George Eliot based her sequence of action not so much on direct observation and recording of life, as she did her characters, but on a preconceived moral theory of consequences that served to direct it toward an end" (p. 163). This is an argument similar to David Cecil's in his *The Early Victorian Novelists* (London, 1934). See especially p. 319. Again, Robert Preyer in a valuable article, "Beyond the Liberal Imagination: Vision and Unreality in 'Daniel Deronda'," *Victorian Studies,* IV (September 1960), argues that the Deronda half of the novel is important because in it for the first time George Eliot breaks through the restricting dogma of determinism. Implicitly Mr. Preyer assumes that determinism for George Eliot is equivalent to necessitarianism.

existence (or at least a depressing interpretation of them) and leads to an underestimation of man's capacity for action and of his potential dignity.

I shall argue, however, that in one important and widely acceptable use of the term, George Eliot was a consistent determinist, and that this sense is in no way incongruous with her continuous emphasis on moral responsibility and duty. Her novels, letters, and essays suggest that her position—never, so far as I know, fully articulated in print—was very close to John Stuart Mill's, and that if she was inconsistent she was no more so than Mill. Mill's views on determinism, moreover, though they have never pleased absolutists, have considerable philosophical support, belonging as they do to a tradition which stems back at least as far as Hume's *Inquiry* and extending forward to one of the most powerful contemporary schools of academic philosophy—that of linguistic analysis. With the philosophical tools at their disposal neither Mill nor George Eliot could have carried analysis as far as contemporary analysts do; but the position is not an easily discredited one, either philosophically or, as it is embodied in George Eliot's works, artistically: it does at least as much justice to the facts of existence as any indeterminist position or any less flexible determinist one.

The danger in a detailed discussion of this position, of course, is to treat George Eliot as a philosopher rather than an artist. For although she was widely read in philosophy and translated Spinoza's *Ethics,* Feuerbach's *Essence of Christianity,* and Strauss's *Life of Jesus,* the fact that she never felt impelled to set down her own thoroughly worked out system or to state finally her views on the problem of determinism should suggest that at best she was an amateur philosopher using her wide reading for purposes essentially unphilosophical. Her novels and essays are full of protests against the rigidity of systems,[2] but refusal to work out an all-embracing philosophical system is not necessarily incompatible with consistency. And her

---

[2] See especially her essay on the German philosopher Gruppe (*Leader,* 28 July 1855, pp. 723–724) in which she makes plain her distaste for German system-making and praises Gruppe for his refusal to indulge in it. One of her most famous comments on the dangers of dogma and general systems comes in *The Mill on the Floss:*

All people of broad, strong sense have an instinctive repugnance to the men of maxims; because such people early discern that the mysterious complexity of our

determinism was flexible enough, she thought, to be applicable without distortion to the life she tried to represent with scrupulous fidelity. Determinism informed her artistic vision; she not only believed in it as an abstract truth but saw it working even in the routine actions of ordinary life. To be sure, in her novels she does not use it as an abstract argument, but it is persistently there; and for this reason it is important that it be understood by her critics and, where necessary (though abstractions are regarded by critics with a kind of horror), even discussed in the abstract.

There are three basic stances taken by philosophers on the matter of determinism: 1) that the world is rigidly determined and that, in fact, there is no such thing as human responsibility;[3] 2) that though almost everything is determined, the relation of cause and effect is broken in matters of human choice: thus man is free and therefore responsible;[4] 3) that the world is rigidly determined, even in cases of human choice, but that man remains responsible for his actions. The last position of course causes most of the logical difficulties, and it is this position which, I believe, George Eliot shared with Mill.

---

life is not to be embraced by maxims, and that to lace ourselves up in formulas of that sort is to repress all the divine promptings and inspirations that spring from growing insight and sympathy. And the man of maxims is the popular representative of the minds that are guided in their moral judgment solely by general rules, thinking that these will lead them to justice by a ready-made patent method, without the trouble of exerting patience, discrimination, impartiality—without any care to assure themselves whether they have the insight that comes from a hardly-earned estimate of temptation, or from a life vivid and intense enough to have created a wide fellow-feeling with all that is human. (Bk. vii, ch. ii)

All quotations from George Eliot's works, unless otherwise noted, are from the Cabinet Edition, 24 vols. (London and Edinburgh, n.d.).

[3] See, for example, C. D. Broad, *Determinism, Indeterminism and Libertarianism* (Cambridge, England, 1934).

[4] George Eliot's contemporary, J. A. Froude, though not a philosopher himself, took this position. He wrote, "a conviction assures us that there is somewhere a point of freedom. What that point is, where other influences terminate and responsibility begins, will always be of intricate and often impossible solution. But if there is such a point at all, it is fatal to necessitarianism, and man is what he has been hitherto supposed to be—an exception in the order of nature, with a power not differing in degree but differing in kind from those of other creatures" ("Spinoza," *Westminster Review,* LXIV, July 1855, 20). To Sara Hennell George Eliot wrote about this article, "I don't at all agree with Froude's own views" (*The George Eliot Letters*, ed. Gordon S. Haight, 7 vols., New Haven, 1954–56, II, 211; henceforward *GEL*).

If one can accept it (as most contemporary analytic philosophers do), one not only avoids the underestimation of man's capacity to learn and to act with dignity and responsibility which many writers feel is an inevitable conjunct of determinism; one sees it also as it was for George Eliot, an indispensable means of rationally defending the possibility of just those qualities. She found, one might infer from available materials, that the only valid interpretation of her vision was deterministic, for it was the only one that could adequately account, among other things, for her sense of man's dependence on man, his ability to learn and grow, and his obligation always to follow the promptings of duty. The key to her determinism lies in her refusal to discount the human will. Thus, an investigation of what her deterministic position was and of why she made so full a commitment to it, may make it possible to move a little closer to understanding how determinism actually works in her novels and in what important ways it affected, whether to distort and darken or to enrich, her particular artistic perception of the world.

For George Eliot determinism was an entirely secular position— the belief that every event has its causal antecedents. Although in her early years she was a pious Calvinist, her mature belief in determinism was entirely divorced from the Calvinistic concept of pre-determinism, which suggests some supernatural power figuring beforehand the necessary course of things. Her novels, for example, are not fatalistic, whatever the appearances, since they always make it abundantly, sometimes terrifyingly, clear that her characters' fate is in large measure of their own making. Lydgate's "spots of commonness" are as much responsible for his failure as Rosamond's callous egoism. We may, it is true, be asked to feel sympathetic to Dolly Winthrop when she says, "We may strive and scrat and fend, but it's little we can do arter all—the big things come and go wi' no striving o' our'n— they do that they do." [5] But Mrs. Poyser is much more clearly George Eliot's spokesman when, perplexed by the conflicting theories of conflicting sects, she argues, "I see plain enough we shall never do it without a resolution, and that's enough

[5] *Silas Marner,* Ch. xiv.

for me." [6] In the end, this common sense position adequately sum-marizes George Eliot's most important views on freedom and respon-sibility (and the views of Mill and many other modern analysts as well).

But having turned from religion she still felt the pull of Calvinist determinism, and she looked to science and philosophy for an ex-planation. She saw that determinism was clearly implicit in New-ton's physics and in the theory of the association of ideas, and that utilitarians and positivists were committed to the view that there were fixed laws of nature and that man, a part of nature, was subject to those laws. Thus Comte argued: "all events what ever, the events of our own personal and social life included, are always subject to natural relations of sequence and similitude, which in all essential respects lie beyond the reach of our interference." [7] George Eliot had committed herself to such a view fairly early. To Charles Bray, author of *The Philosophy of Necessity* and the man who was probably the first to expose her to a systematic and scientific-seem-ing determinism, she wrote in 1857, "in the fundamental doctrine of your book—that mind presents itself under the same condition of invariableness of antecedent and consequent as all other phenomena (the only difference being that the true antecedent and consequent are proportionately difficult to discover as the phenomena are more complex)—I think you know I agree." [8] This is Comtean, even to the parenthetical qualification. [9]

---

[6] *Adam Bede*, Ch. XVII.

[7] Auguste Comte, *A General View of Positivism*, tr. J. H. Bridges, Academic Reprints (Stanford, n.d.), pp. 28–29.

[8] *GEL*, v, 403.

[9] It is important, however, to see that though George Eliot's thought seems pervaded by the details of positivistic and contemporary scientific philosophy, her position was probably not so much caused by them as refined by them. Her temperament and her own broad intellect shaped most of her major beliefs before she was exposed to the systematic philosophies of Mill, Spencer, and Comte. She wrote,

I never had any personal acquaintance with J. S. Mill . . . and though I have studied his books, especially his Logic and Political Economy, with much benefit, I have no consciousness of their having made any marked epoch in my life.

Of Mr. Herbert Spencer's friendship I have had the honour and advantage for twenty years, but I believe that every main bias of my mind had been taken before

The scientific bias of this view would seem to push in the direction of amorality (as, for instance, it did much more clearly though not yet finally with Pater as early as 1866 in his essay on "Coleridge"),[10] but as is obvious in most of the philosophical writings of this "age of ideology," almost every theory had a strong moral bias. As the universe tended to become for certain thinkers more materialistic and amoral, they struggled fearfully and vigorously to control the forces of irrationality and violence which would be unleashed with the destruction of traditional sanctions. Thus we find Comte, Mill, and Spencer outlining possible sciences of society (with various degrees of belief in the possibility of finally achieving such sciences) according to which men might live together in utopian harmony, and we find George Eliot, with what amounts at times almost to desperation, taking up a moral stance at every point.

## I

Despite her emphasis on the claims of duty and the power of the will, the world which George Eliot describes in her novels is meant to be consistently deterministic. And I should like here to look briefly at some of the most important philosophical and moral implications for her of the deterministic idea—simple at bottom but leading to enormous complications—that every event has its causal antecedents.

(1) George Eliot saw a deterministic universe as a marvelously complex unit in which all parts are intricately related to each other, where nothing is really isolable, and where past and future are both implicit in the present. Nothing in such a universe is explicable without reference to the time and place in which it occurs or exists.

I knew him. Like the rest of his readers, I am of course indebted to him for much enlargement and clarifying of thought. (*GEL,* vi, 163)

For more on this point, see Paul Bourl'honne, *George Eliot essaie de biographie intellectuelle et morale, 1819–1854* (Paris, 1933), p. 112, and Michael Wolff, "Marian Evans to George Eliot: The Moral and Intellectual Foundation of her Career," a microfilmed doctoral dissertation (Princeton, 1958), pp. 145–146. The latter is the most useful and thorough intellectual biography of George Eliot I have seen.

[10] Pater's ideas met with George Eliot's fairly strong disapproval, despite the similarity of their views on history and systems. See *GEL,* v, 455.

This suggested that one can never make a clear-cut break with the society in which one has been brought up, with one's friends and relations, with one's past. Any such break diminishes a man's wholeness and is the result of his failure to recognize his ultimate dependence on others, their claims on him, and the consequent need for human solidarity. For George Eliot, every man's life is at the center of a vast and complex web of causes,[11] a good many of which exert pressure on him from the outside and come into direct conflict with his own desires and motives.

It is obvious that George Eliot's extraordinary insight into the workings of society is closely related to this view, probably both as cause and effect. The full scale portrayals of small town society which we get in *The Mill on the Floss* and pre-eminently in *Middlemarch* depend on a rich and vital sense of the way in which every man's life impinges on many others. A refusal to accept responsibility for the claims that society puts upon one leads to destruction or dehumanization. So old Peter Featherstone dies a defeated, willful animal cut off from all normal human relationships. So Maggie, having cut herself off from society by her one yielding to impulse, has to die (however melodramatically) in her effort to reestablish normal human relationships. And any character who, like Tito or Bulstrode, attempts to blot out the past or cut himself off from old friends or relatives, fails inevitably; the result of his attempts is moral disintegration. The persistent theme of egoism which isolates man from his natural ties is also related to the notion of a complex deterministic universe. This theme is worked out almost in paradigm in the story of Hetty Sorrel in *Adam Bede*, but we see it again in the brief but brilliant portrait of Mrs. Transome in *Felix Holt* and in the story of Gwendolen Harleth in *Daniel Deronda*.

In her review of Riehl's *Natural History of German Life* George Eliot emphasizes the importance of continuity. Riehl, she notes approvingly, sees "in European society *incarnate history,* and any attempt to disengage it from its historical element must, he believes, be simply

---

[11] Several critics have called attention to the persistent web imagery in *Middlemarch*. Quentin Anderson, for instance, suggests that "the master image of the book . . . is the image of human relationships as a web" ("George Eliot in Middlemarch," *From Dickens to Hardy*, The Pelican Guide to English Literature, ed. Boris Ford (London, 1959), vi, 276–277).

destructive of social vitality. What has grown up historically can only die out historically, by the gradual operation of necessary laws." But what applies to society as a whole applies equally well to the individual. This view accounts in part for her insistence on the importance of early life in the formation of character in, for instance, the portraits of Maggie and Gwendolen. It accounts, moreover, for what seems her almost melodramatic concern with people cut off from their real parents (Hetty, Esther Lyon, Arthur Transome, Tito, Gwendolen, Deronda, and even the Spanish Gypsy). The view, moreover, confirmed George Eliot in what she regarded as a conservatism which, as a child, she breathed in with the Midland atmosphere.[12] Thus, we find her "radical" novel, *Felix Holt,* to be firmly antirevolutionary, and her radical hero actually forced to battle with the proletariat whose interests he in theory protects. Since real change can only come about through the slow increment of myriad causes working through history, revolution is doomed to failure.

The insistence on unity, harmony, duty, and slow growth, which we see in George Eliot's broad social analyses and in her minute psychological investigations of egoism and division within a single human soul, obviously has its roots in a moral bias. But the bias, for George Eliot, has its rational justification in determinism.

(2) A deterministic universe, as George Eliot understood it, is a democratic one. The emphasis rests not on the Byronic and extraordinary but on the ordinary; the occurrence of large heroic action is unlikely though not by any means impossible. Since, as John Holloway says, George Eliot believed that "Man is a part of Nature, and Nature is a vast and complex system of which the parts are subordinate to impersonal forces governing the whole," she felt as well that "the individuals that belong to such a system cannot be heroes."[13] Determinism, of course, need not necessarily be antiheroic: the Hegelian version, for instance, raises to almost godlike stature the world-historical figure who, acting from a vision which

[12] *Impressions of Theophrastus Such,* Ch. ii, "Looking Backward." This chapter in particular is useful to anyone interested in establishing the "non-intellectual" influences on the development of her mature views.
[13] *The Victorian Sage: Studies in Argument* (London, 1958), p. 127.

is far ahead of his time's, prepares the way for future changes which further reveal the working out of the mind of God in history. Marxism too, as an anti-metaphysical outgrowth of Hegelianism, has its world-historical heroes. But even in these systems, the hero is a rare figure behind whom the great masses of people struggle helplessly in the grip of historical processes.

The heroic, as we shall see, is not entirely excluded from George Eliot's novels, but even the strongest figures in the novels—with the possible exception of Savonarola, Deronda, and Mordecai—could be better described as ordinary than heroic. For the most part, George Eliot was concerned with ordinary life and felt it dangerous to emphasize the heroic. Her contempt for the Byronic hero echoes throughout her letters, *Felix Holt,* and *Daniel Deronda* precisely because she felt that a concentration on the heroic, out of reach of all but a handful of great men, tended to make one dissatisfied with life as it has to be lived. Moreover, the heroic—even the nobly heroic—is inevitably combined with egoism and a consequent tendency to disregard the necessary but ordinary ties which bind man to his friends, relatives, and society. No man is entitled to expect much personal gratification from so complex a universe running according to invariable laws which apply indifferently to all men. The external pressure of these laws (or, as they manifest themselves in the novels, the external pressure of society) is too great for any single man completely to overcome. "There is no creature," she warns, "whose inward being is so strong that it is not greatly determined by what lies outside it." [14] Thus, in all the novels but *Daniel Deronda,* heroism takes the shape of resignation exclusively, a willingness to renounce not only personal satisfactions but the possibility of great achievement for good causes. The brilliant hovering irony of the portrait of Dorothea in the early part of *Middlemarch* suggests how, even for the characters with whom she tended to sympathize excessively, George Eliot was aware of the important and debilitating role egoism plays in the shaping of heroic objectives.

The one significant exception to this tendency deserves more extended treatment than it can be given here. But in Daniel Deronda

[14] *Middlemarch,* "Finale."

and Mordecai, George Eliot creates characters who are meant to have heroic stature. Their activities are to help create a new nation. It is not surprising that they are two of the weakest (if still the most interesting) characters George Eliot ever created. Their kind of heroism was what she aspired to, but it was also incompatible with her particular vision; it suggested the possibility of great and rapid changes, of significant and conscious tampering with the course of history, where, as a determinist, she instinctively felt that such tampering had become almost impossible. To create such characters she had to go outside the limits of the ordinary life of England which her novels (except *Romola,* of course) had hitherto described, into a world which, however wide her reading, she did not really understand.

It is important to note, on the other hand, that George Eliot did not believe, as Holloway argues, that individuals, if they can't be heroic, must then be obscure and petty. Certainly they must remain obscure, but, she insisted, "there is nothing petty to the mind that has a large vision of relations, and to which every single object suggests a vast sum of conditions." [15] Since, that is, every act is related in some way to every other, the most apparently unimportant act may have important ramifications, and the most apparently unimportant person must be accorded considerable respect. "We insignificant people," she says in the famous "Finale" of *Middlemarch,* "with our daily words and acts are preparing the lives of many Dorotheas, some of which may present a far sadder sacrifice than that of the Dorothea whose story we know. . . . The growing good of the world is partly dependent on unhistoric acts."

(3) Deterministic theory translated into the practice of her fiction became grounds according to which one might abjure coincidence and condemn chance. Nothing, she argued, happens accidentally, and a belief in the possibility of some kind of occurrence not usually produced by the normal workings of the laws of nature became to her one of the positive signs of moral weakness. Since similar events have similar effects (unless other causes are secretly at work), George Eliot believed it morally reprehensible to rely on the unlikely

---

[15] *Mill on the Floss,* Bk. IV, Ch. i.

or unusual, even if there is a remote chance that it might happen. For example, Gwendolen expects triumph from her marriage with Grandcourt, Arthur expects nothing to come of his liaison with Hetty, Lydgate imagines he can break his vow of temporary celibacy without hurting his scientific work: in each case the more likely upshot helps destroy the character who would rather hope for the unlikely. When "chance" does occur, to be sure, George Eliot is not suggesting that it is outside the normal laws of nature, but only that the elaborate and complex system of causes has been working beyond the knowledge of her characters.

In *Daniel Deronda* and *Middlemarch* "chance" becomes a dominant motif: the vivid opening scene in *Deronda* in which Gwendolen plays passionately at the luridly lit gaming table introduces the theme and sets its moral tone; and this tone is close to that of *Middlemarch* when Lydgate succumbs to the vice he had previously despised in Mr. Farebrother and becomes feverishly absorbed in gambling at billiards. In less obvious ways it appears in all her novels and is always associated with evil. "Favourable Chance," she says in *Silas Marner,* "is the god of all men who follow their own devices instead of obeying a law they believe in. Let even a polished man of these days get into a position he is ashamed to avow, and his mind will be bent on all the possible issues that may deliver him from the calculable results of that position" (Ch. ix).

(4) Finally, and most important for George Eliot, a deterministic world such as she envisioned is one in which duty becomes primary (as it does, of course, in Comte's positivistic system). Since, as we have already remarked, every act, no matter how trivial, has a vast number of consequences, not all of them traceable, she felt that it behooves every human being to exercise the greatest care in his actions to avoid causing misery to others. To F. W. H. Myers she made a remark which has since become notorious: that although God was "inconceivable," and immortality "unbelievable," Duty was "peremptory and absolute." [16] In a letter written to Mrs. H. F. Ponsonby in 1874 she explained this severe and tough-minded view:

[16] F. W. H. Myers, *Essays Modern* (London, 1885), p. 207.

I suppose that there is not a single man, or woman, who has not
more or less need of that stoical resignation which is often a hidden heroism, or who, in considering his or her past history, is not
aware that it has been cruelly affected by the ignorant or selfish
action of some fellow-being in a more or less close relation of life.
And to my mind there can be no stronger motive, than this perception, to energetic effort that the lives nearest to us shall not
suffer in like manner from us.[17]

This idea is so fundamental to the novels that examples here would
be superfluous.

It would seem that at least a fifth implication should follow from
the belief that every event has its causal antecedents, and this, perhaps, the most important of all: that what man is, what he wills,
what he becomes, is necessarily determined in such a way that he is
incapable of anything but acquiescence in the pull of his unconscious
desires and the push of external forces. But this is precisely the view
that George Eliot despised as morally enervating and vicious, and
which she tended to call necessitarianism.[18] Along with John Stuart
Mill, she insisted that this position did not follow.[19] Both began their
attack on it from a position of common sense. Mill, as we shall see
more fully later, began with a perception that the word "Necessity"
was misleading, that it "carried with it a misleading association;
and that this association was the operative force in the depressing
and paralysing influence which I had experienced: I saw that
though our character is formed by circumstances; and that what
is really inspiriting and ennobling in the doctrine of free-will, is the

---

[17] *GEL,* vi, 99.
[18] She said she hated "the ugly word" (*GEL,* vi, 66).
[19] As I have already suggested, George Eliot's views on determinism and necessitarianism, as far as I can find them expressed explicitly in her writings, are strikingly
similar to (though not necessarily dependent on) those of Mill and, less completely,
of Comte. All three writers emphasize the moral implications of the views, and Mill,
with George Eliot, stresses the importance of the individual in a deterministic scheme
and the possibility of his altering in some measure the course of things. Anyone
wishing to find a more systematic and full exposition of the position would do well
to read the Sixth Book of Mill's *System of Logic,* "On the Logic of the Moral Sciences,"
especially Chapters ii, x, and xi. In the following discussion I shall be relying heavily
on Mill's exposition. All references are to the first edition, *A System of Logic; Ratiocinative
and Inductive* (London, 1843), 2 vols.

conviction that we have real power over the formation of our character; that our will, by influencing some of our circumstances, can modify our future habits or capacities of willing." [20]

Just as Mill began his analysis of the term "Necessity" out of a deep personal need to throw off the weight of depression that determinism had laid upon him, so George Eliot worked her way out of the dilemma of determinism because of her deep moral bias. Aware of the philosophical commonplace that no one can be obliged to do something unless he is capable of doing it, yet feeling with equal strength the call of duty, she, like Mrs. Poyser, asserted the common sense point that nothing will get done unless we make the effort and that experience tells us we can make it: "Every fresh morning is an opportunity that one can look forward to for exerting one's will. I shall not be satisfied with your philosophy till you have conciliated necessitarianism . . . with the practice of willing strongly, of willing to will strongly, and so on, that being what you certainly can do and have done about a great many things in life." [21] This is clearly not yet a sufficient justification of the position, but it is an important first step toward what might very well be the solution of the modern school of linguistic analysis (an immediate descendant of positivism). What it amounts to, however, is that in matters of choice determinism is "ethically irrelevant." [22]

It is important to see, however, on what grounds Mill and, one might safely infer, George Eliot were able satisfactorily for themselves to reconcile determinism with responsibility. The attempt has

---

[20] *Autobiography of John Stuart Mill* (New York, 1924), p. 119. Both Mill and George Eliot regard the problem of free-will in terms which would be unacceptable to contemporary philosophical analysts, although their manner of solution is similar. The central distinction lies in what the analysts might call their failure to perceive. that the "will" is not a faculty, acting, as it were, divorced from the whole person. Gilbert Ryle has been the most outspoken of contemporary philosophers on this point. He rejects, as Mill and George Eliot did not, the extension of the mechanical model of the universe from physical nature to moral and voluntary acts, and has therefore changed all the major terms of the discussion of "free-will." See especially his *The Concept of Mind* (London, 1949), Ch. iii. Ryle's essay on the subject, "It Was to Be," in *Dilemmas* (Cambridge, England, 1953), is a good example of his method.
[21] *GEL*, vi, 66.
[22] Stephen Pepper, *Ethics* (New York, 1960), p. 46.

been made by philosophers over many centuries, but no one not a partisan of a particular contemporary view can look back over the history of the problem and be wholly satisfied that the reconciliation has been accomplished. W. D. Ross, one of the most eminent of twentieth-century moral philosophers, after a long discussion of the problem, says: "This attempt to reconcile responsibility with Determinism can, then, hardly be deemed successful. . . . A philosophical genius may some day arise who will succeed in reconciling our natural thought about freedom and responsibility with acceptance of the law of causality; but I must admit that no existing discussion seems to be very successful in doing so." [23] And although there have been a good many brilliant assaults on the problem since Ross wrote these words,[24] it is apparent that neither side is going to make any important concessions. In the face of the confusion of professional philosophers I do not pretend here to offer a solution. What I wish to do is outline the way Mill and George Eliot made the reconciliation and to suggest that if their answer is not *the* answer, it is *an* answer which must be accorded respect; if this is the vision embodied in George Eliot's works, one cannot dismiss her determinism out of hand.

## II

The problem really begins with what Ross calls "our natural thought about freedom," that is, our instinctive feeling that somehow we are free to will whatever we wish within the limits of physical possibility, and that we are responsible for what we do. It is the point from which George Eliot seems to begin. To Mrs. Ponsonby she wrote:

> As to the necessary combinations through which life is manifested, and which seem to present themselves to you as a hideous fatalism which ought logically to petrify your volition—have they, *in fact,* any such influence on your ordinary course of action in the pri-

---

[23] *Foundation of Ethics* (Oxford, 1939), p. 230.
[24] See especially A. J. Ayer, *Philosophical Essays* (London, 1954), Ch. xii; P. H. Nowell-Smith, *Ethics,* Penguin Books (London, 1954), Chs. xix-xx, and, by the same author, "Freewill and Moral Responsibility," *Mind,* LVII (1948), 45–61; also Stuart Hampshire, *Thought and Action* (London, 1959), passim.

mary affairs of your existence as a human, stoical, domestic creature? And if they don't hinder you from taking a bath, without
which you know you cannot secure the delicate cleanliness which
is your second nature, why should they hinder you from a line of
resolve in a higher strain of duty to your ideal, both for yourself
and others? [25]

This certainly is typical of the way in which, for George Eliot, determinism reinforced a moral bias. She didn't allow philosophy to
alter her instinctive and most strongly felt impressions (rather, with
some analysts today, she used it to fortify them); what is essential is
that she *felt* she was free to will and responsible for her acts at the
same time that she believed in universal causality.

Before indicating in more theoretical terms how George Eliot
justified her sense of responsibility, it is important to repeat that she
was committed to universal causality. Certainly, there are occasions
when she appears to be taking a fuzzy, religio-metaphysical liber-
tarian position, but on these occasions she is usually talking meta-
phorically or attacking some of the cruder positions which determinism might produce.[26] In a letter to Bray, who ruled out the
possibility of free will altogether, and who was so infatuated with
his deterministic system that he minimized the importance of the
individual, she wrote of "our total inability to find in our natures a
key to the Divine Mystery." [27] And in her outraged rejection of the
view that "the relations of men to their neighbours may be settled
by algebraic equations," [28] she seemed to be rejecting the possibility
of a science of society based on the fixed laws of moral causation.
But in fact, in these and many other similar arguments she is not
rejecting the laws of causality. Rather, she is indicating that there
are severe limitations to man's knowledge and that the phenomena
of mind and of moral behavior are, as Comte argued before her, far
too complicated to be reducible to formulas. All of her objections
to ordering the phenomena of consciousness into precise formulas
seem to be little more than an outgrowth of her insistence on the

---

[25] *GEL,* vi, 98.
[26] See, for example, her argument against "men of maxims" in note 2, above.
[27] *GEL,* ii, 403.
[28] *Essays,* "The Natural History of German Life: Riehl."

importance of the individual. It is on this point that she differed from Bray, Comte, and the other philosophers whose systems tended to over-value Man at the expense of man.[29]

The three major aspects of George Eliot's reconciliation of determinism with responsibility seem to correspond to those of Mill: (1) her sense of the great and bewildering complexity of the causes which form human behavior; (2) her recognition of the difference between cause and compulsion; (3) her belief that each man's character plays an important role in determining what be becomes.

(1) *Complexity.* Her view of this point is similar to that of Comte and John Stuart Mill, although again, as in most cases, it is probably only the details which she borrowed from them. Here is Mill's statement:

> the agencies which determine human character are so numerous and diversified (nothing which has happened to the person throughout life being without its portion of influence), that in the aggregate they are never in any two cases exactly similar. Hence, even if our science of human nature were theoretically perfect, that is, if we could calculate any character as we can calculate the orbit of any planet, *from given data;* still as the data are never all given, nor ever precisely alike in different cases, we could neither make positive predictions, nor lay down universal propositions.[30]

As a philosopher George Eliot recognized this complexity,[31] but as an artist she emphasized it. She tried to show, as Bourl'honne remarks, that "l'homme n'est pas un, qu'il est un composé de tendances multiples et diverses, le plus souvent opposées entre elles, et

---

[29] Indeed, it is astonishing that there are so few records of her criticism of Comte. His assertion, that "the only real life is the collective life of the race; that individual life has no existence except as an abstraction" (*A General View,* p. 404), must certainly have infuriated her as did Young's poetry or Dr. Cumming's evangelical preaching.

[30] *System of Logic,* II, 494. Here is Comte's view on the subject: "invariability in all primary aspects is found compatible with modifications in points of secondary importance. These modifications become more numerous and extensive as the phenomena are more complex. The reason of this is that the causes from a combination of which the effects proceed being more varied and more accessible, offer greater facilities to our feeble power to interfere with advantage . . . the extensive modification of which society admits, go far to keep up the common mistake that social phenomena are not subject to any constant law" (*A General View,* pp. 31–32).

[31] See, for example, her essay on Riehl.

que, par consequent, suivant les rapports et l'équilibre qui s'établis-
sent entre ces tendances, l'homme devient ceci ou cela. Il y a donc
une certaine indetermination dans la destinée de l'individu; le
caractère n'est pas constitué des l'origine d'une manière absolue et
définitive." [32] But this proves that each individual is likely to be
different and, perhaps, that his fate is not determinable by man, not
that there is a certain indetermination in his development; it implies,
on the contrary, that were it possible to know every causal factor in
a character's life, one could, as Mill himself argues, accurately work
out what he would become.[33] Accordingly, the argument from complexity merely suggests that man is too ignorant to know *how* he is
determined, and that whatever laws apply to character, they are
more complex than physical laws. Complexity may account for the
"mystery" in human behavior and even for man's natural feeling
that he is a morally free agent, but it cannot logically justify that
feeling.

(2) *Cause and Compulsion.* On this point, George Eliot has very
little explicitly to say, but in her treatment of character the idea is
often implicit. Again, Mill's statement seems to me close enough to
her view to be useful:

> human actions . . . are never (except in some cases of mania)
> ruled by any one motive with such absolute sway, that there is
> no room for the influence of any other. The causes, therefore, on
> which action depends, are never uncontrollable; and any given
> effect is only necessary provided that the causes tending to pro-
> duce it are not controlled.[34]

That a person holding what is called the Necessitarian doctrine
should on that account *feel* that it would be unjust to punish him
for his wrong actions, seems to me the veriest of chimeras. Yes,
if he really "could not help" acting as he did, that is, if his *will*
could not have helped it; if he was under the action of such a

---

[32] *George Eliot,* p. 155.

[33] This, however, is to say little more than that if you know everything about a man
you know everything about him. Gilbert Ryle makes an important distinction between being able to predict what will happen and determining it, and he suggests
that there is nothing binding on a person whose actions have been predicted. In other
words, ability to predict does not imply necessitarianism (*Dilemmas*, Ch. ii).

[34] *System of Logic,* II, 484.

violent motive that no fear of punishment could have any effect; which, if capable of being ascertained, is a just ground of exemption, and is the reason why, by the laws of most countries, people are not punished for what they are compelled to do by the immediate danger of death.[35]

The point is that although every action is caused, few causes are uncontrollable in the sense that no effort to alter them can succeed.[36] As long as the cause is not a compulsion, that is, as long as it is not physically impossible or excessively dangerous to will differently and as long as one is not so mentally ill that one cannot will differently even if one wants to, one is responsible for his actions. To take an example: in *Adam Bede*, Arthur Donnithorne was free to avoid the circumstances which drew him into sexual relations with Hetty Sorrel. He was aware that he should have told Mr. Irwine about his feelings, but he chose not to. And even though he was helped in avoiding confession by Irwine's overly decorous refusal to make him talk, Arthur was under no compulsion to be silent. At one point in the conversation between Arthur and Irwine, Irwine figuratively and implicitly makes the distinction between cause and compulsion. Arthur says to him:

> "Well, but one may be betrayed into doing things by a combination of circumstances, which one might never have done otherwise."
> "Why, yes [Irwine replies], a man can't very well steal a bank-

---

[35] John Stuart Mill, *An Examination of Sir William Hamilton's Philosophy*, 2 vols. (New York, 1874), ii, 296–297.

[36] I recognize the circularity of this reasoning. To say that a cause is controllable by other causes is simply to push the question back, not to resolve it. The act of controlling a cause is itself caused, and one might go on infinitely asking what causes the cause which causes the cause, etc. This is precisely the kind of difficulty the analytic philosophers would object to. One must recognize, for example, the difference between robbing a bank because one wants the money and robbing it because one is forced at gunpoint to do so. Nowell-Smith makes explicit, it seems to me, the point of view that Mill is taking up here when he attacks the libertarians who, making the objection of circularity to an argument like Mill's, ask, "Can we justly blame a man if vicious actions are due to hereditary epilepsy or to the influence of a corrupt and vicious court?" Nowell-Smith replies, "To this the answer is that we can and do. So long as we persist in supposing that, to be moral, an action must be uncaused, we could only push the moral responsibility back in time; and this, so far from solving the problem, merely shows the impossibility of any solution on these lines" ("Freewill and Moral Responsibility," p. 50).

note unless the bank-note lies within convenient reach; but he
won't make us think him an honest man because he begins to
howl at the bank-note for falling in his way." (Ch. xvi)

The bank-note's presence, that is to say, is one of the causes of the
theft, but there is nothing in its presence serving as a compulsion
to make a man steal it. The thief could have avoided stealing it had
he wanted to strongly enough, and he was therefore responsible for
his action. Significantly, a bit earlier in the same chapter in which
Arthur and Irwine have the preceding conversation, Arthur says
to Adam, "I fancy you would master a wish that you had made up
your mind it was not quite right to indulge, as easily as you would
knock down a drunken fellow who was quarrelsome with you." And
a bit later: "You've got an iron will, as well as an iron arm. But
however strong a man's resolution may be, it costs him something
to carry it out, now and then. We may determine not to gather any
cherries, and keep our hands in our pockets, but we can't prevent
our mouths from watering" (Ch. xvi).

Of course, the point about Arthur is that once his mouth started
watering, an action truly compelled because he has no control over
his salivary glands, he would take his hands out of his pockets and
start picking cherries. The second action, however, is not compelled
by the loveliness of the cherries or the actions of his salivary glands;
it is merely caused by them and several other things—primarily by
a weakness of will. The mark of strong will, according to George
Eliot, is the ability to avoid being influenced by merely selfish causes.
Thus Adam Bede, watering mouth or not, would keep his hands in
his pockets. And in the novels there are no occasions I can think of
in which a character is *compelled* to make an important choice. Many
of the moments of choice do, however, give the impression that the
main character is coerced into the action by some internal compulsion. One thinks of Tito, suddenly confronted by the escaped
Baldassare at the Duomo in Florence. His rejection of his foster
father escapes from him almost instinctively. But what George Eliot
is suggesting in this incident and in many others in her novels is
that we frequently make our decisions long before we are required
to make them public. Thus Tito, through his elaborate course at

deceit about Baldassare before the encounter at the Duomo, had in fact already chosen to reject him. In less obvious ways, this is true of Gwendolen's decision, in the brilliant proposal scene in *Daniel Deronda*, to marry Grandcourt, and of Maggie's avoidance of a decision, as she is rowed down river by Stephen Guest. These characters are responsible for their decisions as fully as if they had, at the moment when the choice was necessary, balanced the alternatives carefully in their minds and hearts.

For the most part, it is true, George Eliot concerns herself in her novels with external pressures or internal desires which give the appearance at least at some point of being remediable. She does not press back to ask what were the causes which shaped the susceptibility or what were the causes which shaped the causes which shaped the susceptibility. Her concern is with the immediate and the practical (but this we see is true of Mill as well). The typical George Eliot story shows how a character (Lydgate, for example), under the influence of strong social pressures, reveals certain flaws in his character which, in combination with the social pressures, cause his moral failure. But it is important to see that George Eliot holds him responsible for his own character and his own motives.

Moreover, she doesn't suggest that Adam Bede, for example, because he is strong, is less fully determined in his actions by external and internal causes than Arthur, who is weak. For George Eliot strong will is a sign rather of a man who, aware of the power of causes to shape him (as Tito, for example, was not aware), is educated by this awareness. Felix Holt's self-justifying speech to Esther Lyon states the case plainly:

> It all depends on what a man gets into his consciousness—what life thrusts into his mind, so that [the desire to give up "worldly good"] becomes present to him as remorse is present to the guilty, or a mechanical problem to an inventive genius. There are two things I've got present in that way: one of them is the picture of what I should hate to be. I'm determined never to go about making my face simpering or solemn, and telling professional lies for profit; or to get tangled in affairs where I must wink at dishonesty and pocket the proceeds, and justify that knavery as part of a system that I can't alter. If I once went into that sort of struggle for success, I should want to win—I should defend the wrong that

I had once identified myself with. I should become everything that I see now beforehand to be detestable. (Ch. xxvii)

(3) *Character.* This brings us to what Mill regarded as the strongest argument against necessitarianism: a man is himself one of the causes of what he becomes. As we have already seen, in his *Autobiography* Mill indicates that this idea is what saved him from the overpowering depression belief in determinism had forced upon him. Here is his most systematic statement of the view:

> [Man] has, to a certain extent, a power to alter his character. Its being, in the ultimate resort, formed for him, is not inconsistent with its being, in part, formed *by* him as one of the intermediate agents. His character is formed by his circumstances (including among these his particular organization); but his own desire to mould it in a particular way, is one of those circumstances, and by no means one of the least influential. . . . We are exactly as capable of making our own character, *if we will,* as others are of making it for us.[37]

Man is on this account no longer a merely passive figure compelled by the power of innumerable causes, but an active force with some power to choose among a number of possible alternatives. According to this argument, it is true, a man's action can never be uncaused. If, however, we put the idea in different terminology—"He can never act without a motive, conscious or otherwise"—it loses its depressing effect.[38] And his character, shaped in the past by experience of right and wrong, pain and pleasure, can act on what the experience taught, if it will. George Eliot never puts the argument in such thoroughly Benthamite terms (although she does specifically recognize the usefulness of legal punishment), but the view, slightly modified, runs through all her works. When her characters come to a point at which they must make a crucial decision,

---

[37] *System of Logic,* II, 485.

[38] Hume in the eighteenth century and Nowell-Smith in the twentieth make the same point Hume says, "By liberty, then, we can only mean a *power of acting or not acting according to the determinations of the will*" (*An Inquiry Concerning the Human Understanding,* sec. 8); Nowell-Smith puts it a little differently, "To be 'free' in this sense is to be free to do what one wants to do, not to be able to act in spite of one's desires" (*Ethics,* p. 279).

she does not mean the decision to be a mere formality. Arthur really
has an opportunity to confess to Mr. Irwine, just as Romola has the
opportunity *not* to return to Tito at Savonarola's prompting, and
Gwendolen not to marry Grandcourt. The difference lies in the
characters' consciousness of their own motives. Arthur yields to the
habits of his nature without fully understanding them. Romola, on
the other hand, behaves in a way counter to her usual proud nature,
and humbles herself before Tito. A character, for George Eliot, becomes what he makes himself: he can, in some limited degree, move
counter to the push of external circumstance, and, by allowing himself to become aware of his own motives, can even at times overcome
them by changing them. In "Janet's Repentance," for example,
Janet Dempster, an alcoholic and therefore almost compelled,
not merely caused, to drink, is saved from moral destruction by
her own powerful desire to overcome her habit (and by Mr.
Tryan.

There is nevertheless no indication in George Eliot's writings that,
as Ernest Baker wishfully remarks, for her "Ultimately, the will is
free." [39] She did not believe that the will had to be "free" in the
sense of "uncaused" (the sense to which, unless specifically stated
otherwise, I am attempting to restrict it in this paper) in order that
every man be responsible for his actions. It is likely, rather, that she
accepted Mill's arguments, when, in combating the necessitarian
position, he wrote,

> to think that we have no power of altering our characters, and
> to think that we shall not use our power unless we have a motive,
> are very different things, and have a very different effect upon the
> mind. A person who does not wish to alter his character, cannot
> be the person who is supposed to feel discouraged or paralyzed
> by thinking himself unable to do it. The depressing effect of the
> fatalist doctrine can only be felt where there *is* a wish to do what
> that doctrine represents as impossible. It is of no consequence
> what we think forms our character when we have no desire of
> our own about forming it; but it is of great consequence that we
> should not be prevented from forming such a desire by thinking
> the attainment impracticable, and that if we have the desire, we

[39] *History of the English Novel*, 10 vols. (London, 1930), viii, 235.

should know that the work is not so irrevocably done as to be incapable of being altered.[40]

This is very similar to the argument which George Eliot used in the letter to Mrs. Ponsonby I have already quoted. Her insistence that every man should exercise his will did not commit her to the view that every man is capable of any choice. As Irwine says to Donnithorne, "A man can never do anything at variance with his own nature" (Ch. xvi). But within the limits of his nature, man is capable of altering his character by willing to alter it. Only people who surrender hopelessly to their impulses or to the pressures of external circumstances—people like the young Arthur Donnithorne —appear wholly determined in their actions by forces external to themselves. And even they, since they almost deliberately refuse to be more than passive and unaware of the forces that are driving them, are contributing to the external causes of their moral decline.

# III

It might seem that for a moralist, belief in a universe wholly governed by the laws of cause and effect is the starting point for little more than a series of subtle wranglings about the possibility of any moral act whatever. On the contrary, however, according to George Eliot and to most determinists moral philosophers, a deterministic universe is the *only* kind of universe in which moral acts are possible. In a wholly or even partially undetermined universe, every act would be capricious because it need not be the result of one's own past thinking and experience or of one's consciousness of its possible effects. It would, as W. D. Ross says, "have no moral value. . . . because it would not be the result of any thought about the nature of the act, and of any consequent impulsion to do it. It would be an unintelligent and unmotived leap in the dark." [41] Since in such a world there would be no necessary or consistent connection between

[40] *System of Logic*, ii, 486.
[41] *Foundation of Ethics*, p. 231.

the past and the present, between one's thinking and one's actions, between *any* two things, morality, as we presently conceive it, would be impossible. As I have already suggested, determinism was for George Eliot a theory which she used to support her moral biases; without determinism she could have found no rational justification for them.

It is therefore, George Eliot says, the presence of "undeviating law" which "alone can give value to experience and render education in the true sense possible." [42] Experience is valuable only in so far as it can teach, and it can teach only in so far as it is consistent. If, for instance, a certain act produces an undesirable effect, one will avoid doing it again unless one wants to produce that effect. But if the effect does not consistently follow from the action, one can have learned nothing (and may therefore, for example, put his hand on hot stoves frequently, only occasionally, if at all, to be burned). One will not know whether any act is worth doing, and whatever one chooses to do in the future cannot be rationally dependent on what one did in the past. The great moral teacher in the world, as George Eliot saw it, was experience, and at its best dogma—unquestioned rule inherited from the past—could only serve as a frequently misleading shortcut:

> The divine yea and nay, the seal of prohibition and of sanction, are effectually impressed on human deeds and aspirations, not by means of Greek and Hebrew, but by that inexorable law of consequences, whose evidence is confirmed instead of weakened as the ages advance; and human duty is comprised in the earnest study of this law and patient obedience to its teaching . . . every past phase of human development is part of that education of the race in which we are sharing; every mistake, every absurdity into which poor human nature has fallen, may be looked on as an experiment of which we may reap the benefit. A correct generalization gives singnificance to the smallest detail. [43]

But where no generalization is possible, she implies, nothing has significance.

[42] "Mackay's Progress of the Intellect," *The Writings of George Eliot*, Warwickshire Edition, 25 vols. (Boston, 1907), xxii, 279.
[43] Ibid.

Thus, for George Eliot morality and responsibility are wholly bound up in determinism, and they are not achievable, as libertarians would have it, by denying the universality of cause and effect. A man is only good in so far as he has trained himself to exercise his will for what past experience has taught him is the good. George Eliot believed that the only way one can transcend circumstance is by recognizing clearly that the "law of consequence" is irrevocable and invariable—"human duty is comprised in the earnest study of this law and patient obedience to its teaching"— that the past is a permanent part of one's character, and one's society is, and should be, a very powerful influence on one's actions. In other words, one overcomes the depressing effects of determinism by understanding it. This can be viewed, of course, as just another version of the vicious Hegelian-Marxist paradox that freedom is the recognition of necessity. But a theory has its value, in good part, in the context which it fills. For Hegel and Marx the paradox was intended to shift responsibility from the individual to the state and to make the individual a passive creature of the state. And it is to the cerdit of George Eliot that she indulges this paradox in its most acceptable form—not to diminish man's responsibility or to submit him to some higher power, but to increase it and to give meaning and direction to his activity for good.

Moreover, the determinist-freedom paradox, as George Eliot resolves it, is not paradoxical at all. The difficulty, according to her implicit analysis, is essentially linguistic. If we mean by free "uncaused," then our actions are never free and the paradox is meaningless. But if we are willing to shift the meaning of "free" to "capable of reasonable choice in accordance with our motives" (which is all the novels or letters allow), then there is no conflict between determinism and "freedom." This kind of semantic shift is unlikely to satisfy those who argue that man is wholly the master of his fate, and who mean something quite different by the word. But such "freedom" has its attractions: it is the condition of a man who knows why he does what he does, who knows the probable effects of his actions, who understands the forces of habit, emotion, and circumstance working upon him, and who is therefore able to avoid succumbing irrationally to their influence.

And this is the condition of George Eliot's heroes when they arrive at their moral maturity. They all share a sense of their littleness in the universe and a consequent willingness to renounce their own desires for "wider and nobler" ends. All of them come to understand that their lives are irrevocably dependent on the lives of others. On the other hand, the unhappy characters, the ones who strive blindly for romantically inaccessible ends, are unhappy precisely because they are not conscious of the invariable "law of consequence" and allow their egoistic desires to push them toward ruin by forcing them to demand too much of the world. In *Daniel Deronda,* the clearest sign of Gwendolen Harleth's regeneration is her recognition for the first time that "her horizon was but a dipping onward of an existence with which her own was revolving" (Ch. lxix). And in *The Mill on the Floss* even Maggie's wretchedness after her father's bankruptcy is blamed on her lack of "knowledge of the irreversible laws within and without her, which, governing the habits, becomes morality, and developing the feelings of submission and dependence, becomes religion" (Bk. IV, Ch. iii).

Determinism, then, manifests itself in George Eliot's works, not only in her analysis of how her weak characters degenerate, but equally in her description of the growth to maturity of her heroes and heroines. Determinism, for her, is at the root of education, and it therefore pervades her novels: in the constant interplay between the individual and society and the consequent elaborate portraits of, for example, the towns of St. Oggs, Florence, and Middlemarch; in the instinctive and traditional shrewdness of Mrs. Poyser in *Adam Bede,* the Dodsons in *The Mill on the Floss,* and the Garths in *Middlemarch;* in the ineluctable reactions of their deeds upon the virtuous and villainous alike, in the traditionalism and fundamental conservatism of the strong-willed, powerful Adam Bede and Felix Holt, in her anlysis of the debilitating effects of egoism and of the moral power of external goodness (as exemplified by Maggie's edition of *The Imitation of Christ* or the homiletic and tedious Daniel Deronda). And the insights and limitations of these specifically deterministic aspects of her work are linked whether as cause or effect is not clear —to her vivid sense of introspective psychology, and of social relations in a universe undirected (as any later naturalist would have seen it) to the problems of humanity.[44]

Whatever her philosophical conclusions might have been, George Eliot's handling of the problem was artistic rather than theoretical. Determinism was for her not a rigid and depressing system but an aspect of the world which she saw and dramatized. She was concerned with the practical rather than the philosophical consequences of her views. She knew that somehow evil was to be avoided and her interest was not in finding someone to blame for it—in discovering whether or not she had a philosophical right to blame anyone—but in averting it. For her, the man who excuses himself from responsibility because he was caused to do wrong is arguing beside the point. In *Adam Bede*, when Arthur Donnithorne suggests that a man is excusable if he succumbs to a severe temptation, Mr. Irwine replies with what must be George Eliot's own answer: "Our deeds carry their terrible consequences, quite apart from any fluctuation that went before—consequences that are hardly ever confined to ourselves. And it is best to fix our mind on that certainty, instead of considering what may be the elements of excuse for us" (Ch. xvi). And Mr. Poyser takes a similar common sense position: "I see plain enough we shall never do it without a resolution, and that's enough for me" (Ch. xvii).

[44] "For if it be true that Nature at certain moments seems charged with a presentiment of one individual lot, must it not also be true that she seems unmindful, unconscious of another?" (*Adam Bede,* Ch. xxvii).

# 12

## *Thomas Hardy*

———◆◆◆———

## Raymond Williams

EDITORIAL NOTE. *Hardy was born in rural Dorsetshire in 1840 and lived on until 1928. His father was a mason and carpenter and a local fiddler at church services, dances and weddings—where he was joined by young Tom and his brothers. At sixteen the future writer was apprenticed to an architect and began at about the same time, to educate himself in Greek and Latin. As Raymond Williams indicates, Hardy has been called—patronizingly—one of the great autodidacts of English literature. Certainly he was one of the most productive: fourteen novels (the last written in 1892) and over a thousand lyrics and narrative poems in addition to a two volume epic drama of the Napoleonic Wars,* The Dynasts. *Henry James and Robert Louis Stevenson could see no value in his novels and other critics admired or rejected them on rather irrelevant grounds, i.e., Hardy appeared to be a precursor of the "sexual revolution." The poetry was to become significant and a vital force only in the years after World War I. There are Hardy cults—pro and con—and there is a Hardy "problem." Raymond Williams approaches the matter as a socialist and a man who was also born into what he describes as a cultural tradition "much older and more central in this country than the comparatively modern and deliberately exclusive circuit of the 'public schools.'" Hardy is here pre-*

*sented as a representative figure in a period of drastic social disorganization,*
*an artist who registered the stress of many and complicated pressures. He*
*expresses what it is to hold with educated procedures but to be unable to*
*sympathize with the quality feeling of educated people.*

# I

Some years ago a critic described George Eliot, Thomas Hardy
and D. H. Lawrence as "our three great autodidacts." The description is interesting as an indication of what, in England, a recognized
education has been supposed to be. All three writers were actively
interested in learning, and read a good deal for themselves, but none
of them was without formal education. George Eliot was at school
till sixteen, and only left because her mother died. Hardy was at
Dorchester High School till the same age, and then completed his
professional training as an architect. Lawrence went into the sixth
form at Nottingham High School, and after a gap went on to Nottingham University College. By nineteenth-century standards, these
levels of formal education are high, and indeed they are still higher
than that granted to three out of four English children today. Moreover, each writer got an additional kind of education in what were
active centres of reading and discussion: George Eliot at Coventry
with the Brays and the Hennells; Hardy at Dorchester with William
Barnes and Horace Moule; Lawrence at Eastwood and Ilkeston,
with Hopkin and the Pagans. The flat patronage of "autodidact"
can be related to only one fact: that none of the three was in the
pattern of boarding school and Oxford or Cambridge which by the
end of the century was being regarded not simply as a kind of
education but as education itself: to have missed that circuit was
to have missed being "educated" at all.

To many of us now, George Eliot, Hardy and Lawrence are
important because they connect directly with our own kind of
upbringing and education. They belong to a cultural tradition much
older and more central in this country than the comparatively
modern and deliberately exclusive circuit of the "public schools."
The effects of this tradition are apparent everywhere in their writing,
for all their strong differences as individuals. It is difficult enough to
fight past the patronage of "autodidact," but it is perhaps even more

difficult to distinguish and reject the next stage of patronage, when "in spite of circumstances" and "because of circumstances" uneasily combine in a recognition of literary greatness. I am concerned here particularly with Hardy, and with that odd free association which would have us call him a peasant, or an educated peasant. Even sympathetic critics have accepted the coarse stereotype expressed in a characteristic tone of Somerset Maugham's:

> When the ladies retired to the drawing-room I found myself sitting next to Thomas Hardy. I remember a little man with an earthy face. In his evening clothes, with his boiled shirt and high collar, he had still a strange look of the soil.

This connects with Henry James's "the good little Thomas Hardy" and, perhaps, with F. R. Leavis's "in its clumsy way, *Jude the Obscure* . . . is impressive." The tone of patronage, supported by crude and direct presuppositions about class, connects disturbingly with a tone of literary patronage, and, more damagingly, with a strong unconscious presupposition about the substance of Hardy's fiction. If he was a countryman, a peasant, a man with the look of the soil, then this is the point of view, the essential literary standpoint, of the novels. That is to say, the fiction is not only about Wessex peasants, it is by one of them, who of course had managed to get a little (though hardly enough) education. Some discriminations of tone and fact have then to be made. First, we had better drop "peasant" altogether: where Hardy lived and worked, as in most other parts of England, there were virtually no peasants. There were landowners, tenant farmers, dealers, craftsmen and labourers, and that social structure—the actual material, in a social sense, of the novels—is radically different, in its variety, its shading, and many of its basic human attitudes, from the structure of a peasantry. Secondly, Hardy is none of these people. Outside his writing, he was one of the many professional men who worked within this structure, often with uncertainty about where they really belonged in it. Within his writing, his position is similar. He is none of these characters, but an observer and chronicler of them, often again with uncertainty about his relation. He was not writing for them, but about them, to a mainly metropolitan and unconnected literary public. The effect of these two points is to return attention to where it properly belongs, which is Hardy's attempt to describe and value a way of life with which he was closely yet ambiguously connected, and the literary methods which follow from the nature of this attempt. As so often, when the current social stereotypes are removed, the critical problem becomes clear in a new way. It is the critical problem of so much of English fiction, since the actual yet incomplete and ambiguous social mobility of the nineteenth century. And it is a question of substance as much as of method. It is common to reduce Hardy's fiction to the impact of an urban alien on the "timeless pattern" of English rural life. Yet, though this is sometimes there, the more common pattern is the relation between the changing nature of country living, determined as much by its own pressures as by pressures from "outside," and one or more characters who have become in some degree separated from it yet who remain, by some tie of family, inescapably involved. It is here that the social values are dramatised in a very complex way, and it is here that most of the problems of Hardy's actual writing seem to arise.

One small and one larger point may illustrate this argument, in a preliminary way. Everybody seems to treat Tess as simply the passionate peasant girl, seduced from outside, and it is then rather surprising to read, quite early in the novel, one of the clearest statements of what has become a classical experience of mobility:

> Mrs. Durbeyfield habitually spoke the dialect; her daughter, who had passed the Sixth Standard in the National School under a London-trained mistress, spoke two languages: the dialect at home, more or less; ordinary English abroad and to persons of quality.

Grace in *The Woodlanders,* Clym in *The Return of the Native,* represent this experience more completely, but it is in any case a continuing theme, at a level much more important than the trivialities of accent, and when we see this we need not be tempted, as so often and so significantly in recent criticism, to detach *Jude the Obscure* as a quite separate kind of novel. A more remarkable example of what this separation means and involves is a description of Clym, in *The Return of the Native,* which belongs in a quite central way to the argument I traced in *Culture and Society:*

Yeobright loved his kind. He had a conviction that the want of most men was knowledge of a sort which brings wisdom rather than affluence. He wished to raise the class at the expense of individuals rather than individuals at the expense of the class. What was more, he was ready at once to be the first unit sacrificed.

The idea of sacrifice relates, in the whole action, to the familiar theme of a vocation thwarted or damaged by a mistaken marriage, and we shall have to look again at this characteristic Hardy deadlock. But it relates also to the general action of change which is a persistent social theme. As in all major realist fiction, the quality and destiny of persons and the quality and destiny of a whole way of life are seen in the same dimension, and not as separable issues. It is Hardy the observer who sets this context for personal failure:

> In passing from the bucolic to the intellectual life the intermediate stages are usually two at least, frequently many more; and one of these stages is sure to be worldly advance. We can hardly imagine bucolic placidity quickening to intellectual aims without imagining social aims as the transitional phase. Yeobright's local peculiarity was that in striving at high thinking he still cleaved to plain living—nay, wild and meagre living in many respects, and brotherliness with clowns. He was a John the Baptist who took ennoblement rather than repentance for his text. Mentally he was in a provincial future, that is, he was in many points abreast with the central town thinkers of his date . . . In consequence of this relatively advanced position, Yeobright might have been called unfortunate. The rural world was not ripe for him. A man should be only partially before his time; to be completely to the vanward in aspirations is fatal to fame . . . A man who advocates aesthetic effort and deprecates social effort is only likely to be understood by a class to which social effort has become a stale matter. To argue upon the possibility of culture before luxury to the bucolic world may be to argue truly, but it is an attempt to disturb a sequence to which humanity has been long accustomed.

The subtlety and intelligence of this argument from the late 1870s come from a mind accustomed to relative and historical thinking, not merely in the abstract but in the process of observing a personal experience of mobility. This is not country against town, or custom against conscious intelligence. It is the more complicated and more urgent historical process, in which education is tied to social advancement, within a class society, so that it is difficult, except by a bizarre personal demonstration, to hold both to education and to social solidarity ("he wished to raise the class"). It is the process, also, in which culture and affluence come to be recognized as alternative aims, at whatever cost to both, and the wry recognition that the latter will always be the first choice, in any real history (as Morris also observed and indeed welcomed). The relation between the migrant and his former group is then exceptionally complicated: his loyalty drives him to actions which the group can see no sense in, its overt values supporting the association of education with personal advancement which his new group has already made but which, for that very reason, he cannot accept. Within these complex pressures, the return of the native has a certain inevitable nullity, and his only possible overt actions seem merely perverse. The need for social identification with the country labourers produces Yeobright's characteristic negative identification with them, by becoming a labourer himself and making his original enterprise that much more difficult: "the monotony of his occupation soothed him, and was in itself a pleasure." All this is understood and controlled by Hardy, but the pressure has further and less conscious effects. Levin's choice of physical labour, in *Anna Karenina,* includes some of the same motives but in the end is a choosing of people rather than a choosing of an abstract nature—a choice of men to work with rather than a natural force in which to get lost. This crucial point is obscured by the ordinary discussion of Hardy's attachment to country life, which would run together the "timeless" heath or woods and the men working on them. What seems actually to happen, however, is a separation between these, and a substantial choice of the former (as later, very clearly, in Lawrence). It is from this attachment to a nature beyond men, to be intuitively apprehended and merged with, as an alternative to social action, that Hardy can appear to solve a very particular crisis. The original humanist impulse—"he loved his kind"—becomes, in this sense, anti-human: men are creatures crawling on this timeless expanse, as the imagery of the heath and Yeobright's work on it so powerfully suggests. It is a very common transition in the literature of that period, but Hardy is never very comfortable with it,

and the original impulse, as in *Jude the Obsure,* keeps coming back,
and makes more precise identifications. But while the merging with
a nature beyond man lasts, there is an apparently profound basis for
the tone which has been there from the beginning: the observation,
for the benefit of others, of the crudity and limitations of "the bu-
colic." The complexity of Hardy's fiction shows in nothing more
than this: that he runs the whole gamut from the external observation of customs and quaintnesses, modulated by a distinctly patronising affection (as in *Under the Greenwood Tree*), through a very positive
identification of intuitions of nature and the values of shared work
with human depth and fidelity (as in *The Woodlanders*), to the much
more impressive but also much more difficult humane perception of
limitations, which cannot be resolved by a nostalgia or a practice of
charm or an approach to mysticism, but which are lived through by
all the characters, in the way of life to which all belong, the limitations of the educated and the affluent bearing an organic relation to
the limitations of the ignorant and the poor (as in parts of *Return of
the Native* and of *Tess* and *Jude*). But to make these distinctions, and
to see the variations of response with the necessary clarity, we have
to get beyond the stereotypes of the autodidact and the countryman,
and see Hardy in his real identity: both the educated observer and
the passionate participant, in a period of general and radical change.

## II

Hardy's writing, or what in abstraction can be called his style, is
obviously affected by the crisis we have sought to describe. We know
that he was worried about his prose, and was reduced by the ordinary educated assumptions of his period to studying Defoe, Fielding,
Addison, Scott and *The Times,* as if they could have helped him.
His complex position as an author, writing about country living to
people who almost inevitably saw the country as empty nature or as
the working-place of their inferiors, was in any case critical, in this
matter of language. What have been seen as his strengths—the bal-
lad form of narrative, the prolonged literary limitation of traditional
forms of speech—seem to me mainly weaknesses; this is what his
readers were ready for: a "tradition" rather than human beings.

These devices could not in any case serve his major fiction, where it was precisely disturbance rather than continuity which had to be communicated. It would be easy to relate Hardy's problem of style to the two languages of Tess: the consciously educated and the unconsciously customary. But this comparison, though suggestive, is inadequate, for the truth is that to communicate Hardy's experience neither language would serve, for neither in the end was sufficiently articulate: the former dumb in intensity and limited in humanity; the latter thwarted by ignorance and complacent in habit. The marks of a surrender to each mode are certainly present in Hardy, but the main body of his writing is a more difficult and complicated experiment. For example:

> The season developed and matured. Another year's instalment of flowers, leaves, nightingales, thrushes, finches, and such ephemeral creatures, took up their positions where only a year ago others had stood in their place when these were nothing more than germs and inorganic particles. Rays from the sunrise drew forth the buds and stretched them into long stalks, lifted up sap in noiseless streams, opened petals, and, sucked out scents in invisible jets and breathings.
>
> Dairyman Crick's household of maids and men lived on comfortably, placidly, even merrily. Their position was perhaps the happiest of all positions in the social scale, being above the line at which neediness ends, and below the line at which the *convenances* begin to cramp natural feeling, and the stress of threadbare modishness makes too little of enough.
>
> Thus passed the leafy time when arborescence seems to be the one thing aimed at out of doors. Tess and Clare unconsciously studied each other, ever balanced on the edge of a passion yet apparently keeping out of it. All the while they were converging, under an irresistible law, as surely as two streams in one vale.

This passage is neither the best nor the worst of Hardy. Rather, it shows the many complicated pressures working within what had to seem a single intention. "The leafy time when arborescence" is an example of mere inflation to an "educated" style but the use of *"convenances,"* which might appear merely fashionable, carries a precise feeling. "Installment" and "ephemeral" are also uses of a precise kind, within a sentence which shows mainly the strength of what could be called an educated point of view: the consciousness of the natural process, in "germs and inorganic particles," is a necessary accompaniment, for Hardy's purpose, of the more direct and more enjoyed sights and scents of spring. It is loss, not gain, when Hardy reverts to the simpler and cruder abstraction of "Dairyman Crick's household of maids and men," which might be superficially supposed to be the countryman speaking, but is actually the voice of the detached observer at a low level of interest. The more fully Hardy uses the resources of the whole language, as a precise observer, the more adequate the writing is. There is more strength in "unconsciously studied each other," which is at once educated and engaged, than in the "two streams in one vale," which shares with the gesture of "irresistible law" a synthetic quality, here as of a man playing the countryman novelist. Hardy's mature style is threatened in one direction by a willed "Latinism" of diction or construction, of which very many particular instances can be collected, but in the other direction by this much less noticed element of artifice, which is too easily accepted, within the patronage we have discussed, as the countryman speaking (sometimes, indeed, it is literally the countryman speaking, in a contrived picturesqueness which is now the novelist's patronage of his rural characters). The mature style itself is unambiguously an educated style, in which the extension of vocabulary and the complication of construction are necessary to the intensity and precision of the observation which is Hardy's essential position and attribute.

> The gray tones of daybreak are not the gray half-tones of the day's close, though the degree of their shade may be the same. In the twilight of the morning, light seems active, darkness passive; in the twilight of evening, it is the darkness which is active and crescent, and the light which is the drowsy reverse.

This is the educated observer, still deeply involved with the world he is watching, and the local quality of this writing is the decisive tone of the major fiction. The complication is that, socially, this is a very difficult and exposed position for Hardy to maintain. Without the insights of consciously learned history, and of the educated understanding of nature and behaviour, he cannot really observe at all, at a level of extended human respect. But the ordinary social model which includes these capacities is, very clearly, in Hardy's time, one

which includes, in its attachment to class feelings and class separa-
tions, a decisive alienation.

> If these two noticed Angel's growing social ineptness, he noticed
> their growing mental limitations. Felix seemed to him all Church;
> Cuthbert all College. His Diocesan Synod and Visitations were the
> mainsprings of the world to the one; Cambridge to the other. Each
> brother candidly recognized that there were a few unimportant
> scores of millions of outsiders in civilized society, persons who were
> neither University men nor Churchmen; but they were to be
> tolerated rather than reckoned with and respected.

This is what is sometimes called Hardy's bitterness, but which in
fact is only sober and just observation. What Hardy sees and feels
about the educated world of his day, locked in its deep social prejudices and in its consequent human alienation, is so clearly true that
the only surprise is why critics now should still feel sufficiently identified with that world—the world which coarsely and brutally dismissed Jude and millions of other men—to perform the literary
equivalent of that stalest of political tactics: the transfer of bitterness,
of a merely class way of thinking, from those who exclude to those
who protest. We did not, after all, have to wait for Lawrence to be
shown the human nullity of that apparently articulate world. Hardy
shows it, convincingly, again and again. But the isolation which
then follows, while the observer holds to educated procedures but
is unable to feel with the existing educated class, is severe. It is not
the countryman awkward in his town clothes, but the more significant tension—of course with its awkwardnesses, its clumsinesses, its
spurts of bitterness and nostalgia—of the man caught by his personal
history in the general structure and crisis of the relations between
education and class, relations which in practice are between intelligence and fellow-feeling. Hardy could not take the James way out,
telling his story in a "spirit of intellectual superiority" to the "ele-
mentary passions." As he observes, again, of the Clare brothers:

> Perhaps, as with many men, their opportunities of observation
> were not so good as their opportunities of expression.

That, after all, was the nullity, in a time in which education was
used to train members of a class and to divide them from other men

as surely as from their own passions (for the two processes are deeply connected). And yet there could be no simple going back.

> They had planted together, and together they had felled; together they had, with the run of the years, mentally collected those remoter signs and symbols which seen in few are of runic obscurity, but all together made an alphabet. From the light lashing of the twigs upon their faces when brushing through them in the dark, they could pronounce upon the species of tree whence they stretched; from the quality of the wind's murmur through a bough, they could in like manner name its sort afar off.

This is the language of the immediate apprehension of "nature," for in that form, always, Hardy could retain a directness of communication. But it is also, more specifically, the language of shared work, in "the run of the years," and while it is available as a memory, the world which made it possible is, for Hardy, at a distance which is already enough to detach him: a closeness, paradoxically, that he is still involved with but must also observe and "pronounce upon." It is in this sense, finally, that we must consider Hardy's fundamental attitudes to the country world he was writing about. The tension is not between rural and urban, in the ordinary senses, nor between an abstracted intuition and an abstracted intelligence. The tension, rather, is in his own position, his own lived history, within a general process of change which could come clear and alive in him because it was not only general but, in every detail of his feeling, observation, and writing, immediate and particular.

# III

Every attempt has been made to reduce the social crisis in which Hardy lived to the more negotiable and detachable forms of the disturbance of a "timeless order." There was of course nothing timeless about nineteenth-century rural England. Its characteristic methods and relationships were specifically modern: a rural civilization, if that is the term, created in the shadow of the successful bourgeois and industrial revolutions. What happened to agriculture in the second half of the nineteenth century was part of the process begun in the sixteenth century, and immensely quickened in the late eighteenth century, by which a commercial society was created. This is where the concept of "the peasant" is most absurdly misleading; the actual social relationships, of the rural England Hardy describes, are those of rent and trade. The class system is not something that comes from outside, into an otherwise unchanging rural scene. The rural scene, rather, is a class system, of a kind determined by the development of the society as a whole. We miss most of what Hardy has to show us if we impose, on the actual relationships he describes, a pastoral convention of the countryman as an age-old figure, or a vision of a prospering countryside being disintegrated by Corn Law repeal or the railways or agricultural machinery. It is true that there are continuities, beyond a dominant social situation, in the lives of a particular community (though two or three generations, in a still partly oral culture, can often sustain an illusion of timelessness). It is also obvious that, in most rural landscapes, there are very old and often unaltered physical features, which sustain a quite different time-scale. Hardy gives great importance to these, and this is not really surprising, when we consider his whole structure of feeling. But all these elements are overridden, as for a novelist they must be, by the immediate and actual relationships between people, which occur within existing contemporary pressures and are at most modulated and interpreted by the available continuities.

The pressures to which Hardy's characters are subjected are then pressures from within the system of living, not from outside it. It is not urbanism, but the hazard of small-capital farming, that changes Gabriel Oak from an independent farmer to a hired labourer and then a bailiff. Henchard is not destroyed by a new and alien kind of dealing, but by a development of his own trade which he has himself invited. Grace Melbury is not a country girl "lured" by the fashionable world, but the daughter of a successful timber merchant whose own social expectations, at this point of his success, include a fashionable education for his daughter. The Lady Day migrations, the hiring fairs, the intellectually arrogant parson, the casual gentleman farmer, the landowner spending her substance elsewhere: all these are as much parts of the country "way of life" as the dedicated craftsman, the group of labourers, and the dances on the green. It is not

only that Hardy sees the realities of labouring work, as in Marty
South's hands on the spars and Tess in the swede field. It is also that
he sees the harshness of economic processes, in inheritance, capital,
rent and trade, within the continuity of the natural processes and
persistently cutting across them. The social process, created in this
interaction, is one of class and separation, as well as of chronic in-
security, as this capitalist farming and dealing takes its course. The
general depression of agriculture made the margins of security
smaller, but it did not introduce the disturbance, which had precise
social causes within the rural structure. The depopulation of the
countryside, of which so much has been made, was itself partly determined by the eighteenth-century reorganisation of agriculture,
which had preceded the industrial revolution. Again it was not
some general way of life that was being abandoned. If we study rural
depopulation in detail, we find that few of the farmers, the actual
occupiers of land, left the countryside. The people who went were,
overwhelmingly, the landless labourers, who had been enlarged as
a class by the enclosures. Once the industrial revolution was under
way, it had further effects on country living: the introduction of
new transport and machinery, the replacement of local craftsmen,
who were the other main class to migrate. But the rural economy on
which these effects fell was already changing, in just these directions,
from its own internal pressures, within the general social emphases
of a commercial society. The profound disturbances that Hardy
records cannot then be seen in the sentimental terms of a pastoral:
the contrast between country and town. The exposed and separated
individuals, whom Hardy puts at the centre of his fiction, are only
the most developed cases of a general exposure and separation. Yet
they are never merely illustrations of this change in a way of life.
Each has a dominant personal history, which in psychological
terms bears a direct relation to the social character of the change.
One of the most immediate effects of mobility, within a structure
itself changing, is the difficult nature of the marriage choice. This
situation keeps recurring, in terms which are at once personal and
social: Bathsheba choosing between Bolwood and Oak; Grace between Giles and Fitzpiers; Jude between Arabella and Sue. The
specific class element, and the effects upon this of an insecure econ-

omy, are parts of the personal choice, which is, after all, a choice primarily of a way to live, of an identity in the identification with this or that other person. And here, significantly, the false marriage (with which Hardy is so regularly and deeply concerned) can take place either way: to the educated coldness of Fitzpiers, or the coarseness of Arabella. Here, most dramatically, the condition of the internal migrant is profoundly known: the social alienation enters the personality and destroys its capacity for any loving fulfilment. The marriage of Oak and Bathsheba is a case of eventual stability, after so much disturbance, but even that has an air of inevitable resignation and lateness. I do not doubt that Hardy, under pressure, came to generalise and project these very specific failures into a fatalism for which, in the decadent thought of his time, the phrases were all too ready. In the same way, seeing the closeness of man and the land being broken, by the problems of working the land, he projected his insistence on closeness and continuity into the finally negative images of an empty nature and the tribal past of Stonehenge and the barrows, where the single observer, at least, could feel a direct flow of knowledge. Even these, however, in their deliberate hardness—the uncultivable heath, the bare stone relics—confirm the human negatives, in what looks like a deliberate reversal of the pastoral. In them the general alienation has its characteristic monuments, though very distant in time and space from the controlling immediate disturbance.

## IV

If we see the development of the English novel through Jane Austen and George Eliot to Henry James and Conrad, we shall find no room for Hardy, except in a patronising aside. But, if we look, in detail, at the radically altered England of the nineteenth century, we can see a more central tradition, through Dickens and George Eliot to Hardy and Lawrence. These are novelists all separated, in different degrees, from what was becoming and formally still stands as the dominant social and literary culture. Half a century later, we can perhaps more clearly recognise the disturbance through which they lived and of which they wrote, a disturbance which is still quite central. What others have seen as their awkwardness, their failures of tone, their persistent and now apologised-for concern with social history and ideas, can be seen, from where we are living, as their original, disturbing and yet finally convincing substance. Thomas Hardy, we have to say, is our flesh and our grass.

# 13

## Instress and Devotion in the Poetry of Gerard Manley Hopkins

### Bell Gale Chevigny

EDITORIAL NOTE. *Gerard Manley Hopkins was born in 1844 and died in 1889 at the tragically early age of forty-five, his works unpublished and unread except by a few close friends. He was four years younger than Hardy, who had the luck to live on thirty-nine years longer and find a responsive new audience for his poetry in the 1920s. The audience for Hopkins emerged in the 1930s. In this sense we may speak of him as the latest, if not the last, of the Victorians. In his lifetime his work was seen only by a few friends—Robert Bridges, Canon Dixon, and Coventry Patmore. There were at least two reasons which explain this lack of an audience. He knew, to begin with, that his poems would be almost incomprehensible to an audience which acclaimed Tennyson. His originality struck even his good friends as an indulgence in eccentricity; there appeared to be no one who could understand the nature of his poetic endeavor. To further complicate matters, he was a Catholic convert who became a Jesuit priest in 1877, a man who believed it was his duty to renounce all hope of literary renown.*

Too little is known about how Hopkins the priest made his peace with Hopkins the poet, how the struggle between the exercise of art and the demands of devotion was resolved. There is plentiful evidence of the struggle—Hopkins's silence in the seminary and during his Tertianship, his hesitation before "heaven's baffling ban" described in "To seem the stranger lies my lot," and his expressed notion that it is presumptuous to publish without a providential sign. But there is also, without apology, the poetry, which is evidence that the struggle was sometimes resolved. Indeed, Hopkins's characteristic poems are most meaningfully considered as acts or occasions of devotion. They represent Hopkins's counterpart to St. Ignatius Loyola's spiritual exercises which he so much admired.

Critics have amply demonstrated that Hopkins's poetry coincides with traditional Catholic thought and with Ignatian meditative method.[1] It is not my purpose to elaborate on these studies, but rather to suggest that the poems on their own terms fulfilled an urgent need in Hopkins's spiritual life. Hopkins's notion of "instress" may be considered the single key to his aesthetics and his spiritual growth, and a nearly constant controlling factor in his developing poetry. It embraced Hopkins's special desire for poetry and for belief not only at the instant when each was first richly conceived, but also and repeatedly during the later years when the changed nature of experience created a need for new modes of understanding. Given this unity of inspiration, a chronological study of the poems is indicated: in such a study one may observe the way in which the uses of instress grow and accumulate as Hopkins's sense of experience and the themes of the poems change. Such an approach offers the further advantage of more fully unifying Hopkins's work than is generally done. One need not, as many critics are inclined to do, concentrate on the poems of nature or of spiritual isolation at the expense of the

[1] The most thorough of such studies are John Pick, *Gerard Manley Hopkins: Priest and Poet* (Oxford, 1942), and David A. Downes, *Gerard Manley Hopkins: A Study of His Ignatian Spirit* (New York, 1959).

poems of priesthood. Finally, this approach reveals that Hopkins adapts certain Romantic, specifically Coleridgean, tenets to a powerful, orthodox faith. From this vantage point, we can see Hopkins providing a poetry which at once sustains Romantic tradition and belongs to the Victorian resurgence of orthodoxy.

"Inscape" and "instress" are the deliberately idiosyncratic terms with which Hopkins chooses to describe what he considers his distinctive aims in poetry. Neither term has a sharply delineated significance. Inscape, or distinctive, unique form, is used by Hopkins in senses that apply either to natural objects themselves or to the making of a poem, or both. Since I am concerned with states of mind and belief, and shades of feeling which make a poem possible, instress is the more telling term for my purposes. Like inscape, instress has a double sense: it applies to both the object itself and the observer. Objectively, it is an energy determining and sustaining unique form, or inscape: "all things are upheld by instress and are meaningless without it."[2] Ultimately, in this sense, instress is God. Subjectively, it is that power which actualizes the inscape in the mind of the beholder.[3] According to J. Hillis Miller, in his definitive analysis of these terms, subject and object share "their possession of the inward energy of instress." Further, "in the moment of perception a 'stem of stress' is created between subject and object to which the subject contributes as much as does the object: 'What you look at hard seems to look hard at you'."[4] A demonstration, or revelation, of such a fused gaze is perhaps a poem. That is, a poem in which instress operates most fully will capture the meeting of objective and subjective energies in a form.

Such an idea is, of course, essentially Romantic. In Victorian literature the analogies to it are only partial. On the one hand, we see identification between subject and object, but the primacy of energy disappears. Thus Newman, in the *Apologia pro vita sua,* coolly

[2] "Parmenides," *Journals and Papers of Gerard Manley Hopkins,* ed. Humphry House and Graham Storey (London, 1959), p. 126.

[3] W. H. Gardner, *Gerard Manley Hopkins: A Selection of his Poems and Prose* (Baltimore, 1953), pp. xx–xxi.

[4] "The Creation of the Self in Gerard Manley Hopkins," *ELH,* XXII (1955), 304. The quotation from Hopkins may be found in *Journals and Papers,* p. 204.

characterizes his conversion as the enduring "thought of two and two only absolute and luminously self-evident beings, myself and my Creator" (ch. i). And he prefaces the last section of his book thus: "so now I will proceed . . . identifying myself with the Church and vindicating it" (ch. v). He offers identity as lucid, accomplished fact, and is thus utterly alien to Hopkins's dynamic reciprocity. On the other hand, we find subjective energy, but now God retreats, and there is no vision of a meeting of energies. Browning offers a version of subjective instress in "the play, the insight and the stretch" which Andrea del Sarto enviously attributes to Raphael. The humanistic value of a reach that exceeds its grasp is essentially its own reward. Perhaps, in "The Everlasting Yea" of *Sartor Resartus*, Carlyle comes closest to the idea Hopkins represents by discovering that Nature is the "Living Garment of God" and by reading in this discovery a command for personal productivity. But Carlyle's complex parodic manner makes this virtually the only point of comparison.

To find relations for Hopkins's poetry, a longer backward leap is needed. The analogy to Coleridge's aesthetics is plain. For Coleridge, poetry is above all organic, an act of fusion. Moreover, Coleridge's definition in Chapter XIII of *Biographia Literaria* of "primary imagination" as "the living power and prime agent of all human perception" is analogous to Hopkins's objective instress, original energy. And Coleridge's "secondary imagination," which is "an echo" of the primary, "co-existing with the conscious will," suggests Hopkins's subjective instress or responsive energy. Coleridge and Hopkins alike would hold that both powers are greatest when the distinctions between them vanish. Coleridge tells the Lady in "Dejection: An Ode," "we receive but what we give." Wordsworth knows likewise, in "Tintern Abbey," that the world is what the eye and ear "half create / And what perceive." Coleridge and Wordsworth also know—as does Keats in his "Sonnet on Visiting the Tomb of Burns"—the sad consequences for vision when personal creative energies flag. Hopkins freshly suffers this pain also. Hopkins differs from the Romantics only in his description of what gives him pleasure. For the Romantics, fusion is sought with unity, life, or beauty. Hopkins cherishes these values too, but the name he gives them is Christ. For the Romantics, the emphasis is on the poet's creative imagination. Hopkins rarely emphasizes the role of imagination so explicitly. Rather, the imagination goes in priestly garb: it takes the form of Christian discipline and Christian passion and its spring is the will. Poetry for Hopkins is always analogous to devotion. Just as a poem is the meeting of objective and subjective energies in a form, devotion is the meeting of the object of faith and a will to believe in an act of apprehension.

In this connection, it is interesting to look at two poems written within the year before Hopkins was converted to Catholicism. "Nondum" is about the frustrations a man feels when he practices a belief without seeing God:

> We see the glories of the earth
> But not the hand that wrought them all:
> Night to a myriad worlds gives birth,
> Yet like a lighted empty hall
> Where stands no host at door or hearth
> Vacant creation's lamps appal.

This is impressive poetry, but it does not bear Hopkins's distinctive mark. In manner and sentiment, it more readily suggests Tennyson and Arnold. Since instress does not operate in any sense, the description cannot properly be called an inscape. What is seen is empty matter, its inner conformation not yet revealed because the necessary energy is absent. "Creation" is "vacant" of both the Creator and the creative spirit who goes out to meet Him in His works. Both faith and Hopkins's special sort of verse are remote for the same reasons: the poet has not yet willed to see the world as God's energy. In "The Half-way House," which is about the idea of conversion, Hopkins recognizes the crucial function of will:

> Hear yet my paradox: Love, when all is given,
> To see thee I must see thee, to love, love;
> I must o'ertake thee at once and under heaven
> If I shall overtake thee at last above.

Faith is necessarily tautological; it may be obtained only when a man believes. Love may be apprehended only by the lover; seek and ye shall find. This is not to say that Hopkins is in this poem giving up the longing for vision expressed in "Nondum," but that he knows he can see only by seeing. Here is where his poetry can serve him. We have already remarked that his concept of instress involves a double movement analogous to that of faith, but poetry is also valuable in a more urgent way. Writing poetry is an act of overtaking at once and under heaven; it is a mode of seeing in time in order to see eternally. Energetically to conceive something itself informed with divine energy is to believe. As Hopkins says of God in his first mature poem, "The Wreck of the Deutschland" (which anticipates in germ the major discoveries of Hopkins's later poetic career): "tho' he is under the world's splendour and wonder, / His mystery must be instressed, stressed." Poetry of instress is devotion.


In tracing the contours of instress in Hopkins's verse, we will not necessarily be exposing only his finest poetry, although his best poems generally call for such interpretation. The presence of instress in his poems is not a mark of poetic value, but of a style of intensity which is peculiar to Hopkins. The quest for climactic meetings of energies or wills is for Hopkins a recurrent passion and a major theme in his aspirations.

In the three phases of Hopkins's mature poetry—composed at the times of his ordination, his priesthood in England, and his sojourn in Ireland—he is concerned with different matters, with uncovering different sorts of inscape. Generally speaking, in the early period the inscapes, or particular forms sought, are in the natural world, God's handiwork; in the middle period they are human beings with whom Hopkins has to deal as a priest; in the late period they are versions of his own soul. We will see that the relationship between the two functions of instress varies with the inscape which serves as their meeting-ground.

"God's Grandeur," "Spring," "The Windhover," and "Hurrahing in Harvest," all written in 1877, the year of Hopkins's ordination, describe a dramatic line of emergence. Hopkins's sense of the dynamics of faith increases in direct relation to his realization of the dynamics of his sort of poetry. (Again, we are not concerned with measuring his growth by any standard but his own; we can, I think, decide which poems best fulfill the implications of his idea of instress.) In the opening lines of "God's Grandeur" we see how far we have come from "Nondum"—"The world is charged with the grandeur of God." The word "charged" is borrowed from the idiom of energy, as are the phrases "it will flame out" and "it gathers to a greatness." The opening of the poem reveals creation as an inscape supported by instress in the objective sense. It goes on, however, to lament the treading of generations, whose heavy shoes at once dull men's contact with the true earth and mutilate the form which would reveal God to them. In the sestet, however, we learn that man's brutal insensitivity cannot damage original energy. Night falls, but dawn springs:

> Because the Holy Ghost over the bent
> World broods with warm breast and with ah! bright wings.

These last lines—especially the abrupt "ah!" that appears to escape involuntarily at the last moment—reveal what has been implicit in the poem all along—that Hopkins has been meeting the creation with an energy of his own, a quietly persistent instress.

It remains for that meeting of energies to be dramatized explicitly. "Spring" does not do this (although the exact conveying of visual and aural effects in the octave implies Hopkins's active eye and ear) because no personal force develops. It is written in May, two or three months after "God's Graudeur," when that grandeur has indeed flamed out, gathered to a greatness. But Hopkins's concern is not now for the insensitivity of generations throughout time, but rather for the misdirected sensitivity of individuals in a rich moment. Girl and boy, he fears, may "sour with sinning" through an urgent physical response to the natural wealth of spring. Such a response he sees as limited because, in its simple animality, it is blind and disobedient to the divine energy which made spring itself. God's creation is now ambivalent; its beauty may be the source of faith or of sin. The poet realizes that the mere perception of God's grandeur and the brooding of the Holy Ghost is not enough. Christ, who was man, must "Have, get . . . Innocent mind and Mayday in girl and boy." There must be an immediate meeting in time. Thus, although in "Spring" and "God's Grandeur," Hopkins has left behind the impasse of "Nondum," these poems still say "not yet."

They are preparative exercises, they point to what is needed. Only "The Windhover: To Christ our Lord," written in the end of May, can say "now."

I will not attempt to sort out the extraordinarily numerous interpretations of "The Windhover." The reading of Herbert Marshall McLuhan in "The Analogical Mirrors" remains the most satisfactory because it emphasizes neither a commitment to limitation, which W. H. Gardner's reading suggests, nor a preparation to grapple, which Raymond V. Schoder describes.[5] Rather, McLuhan's reading suggests both that the poem has the excitement of fulfillment and that in the moment of the poem's existence, personal transformation occurs, without struggle. It is significant that in this poem God's grandeur is expressed in an individual bird, generations of men in the individual "I." The poem is thus prepared to express a mirroring of what is Christlike in nature by what is Christlike in man; or, to adopt my terminology, to describe the meeting of objective and subjective energies. The octave presents us with the bird's mastery, a version of divine instress, from the point of view of the poet who is still relatively unreleased; his heart is in hiding. In the opening lines of the sestet, however, the heart comes out of hiding, demands that all that the bird's glory represents be caught and brought down, that it enter and be made fast to his hidden heart. Such a union with Christ as this "buckling" makes possible releases the hidden heart in a glory that is more impressive than even the bird's flight: "AND the fire that breaks from thee then, a billion / Times told lovelier, more dangerous, O my chevalier." The identification of Christ's spirit with man is lovelier and more dangerous than the identification of Christ's spirit with the bird's flight alone because Christ was a man. In the moment of identification the two divine and conscious energies meet. In the last three lines Hopkins sustains this idea, but with the added realization that Christlike though he is, he is also a man, one of the treading generations. But though he too, earth-bound, plods, he is a man plodding with Christ, and the earth he treads is

---

[5] "The Analogical Mirrors" appears in the Kenyon Critics volume, *Gerard Manley Hopkins* (New York, 1945); Schroder's article, "What does 'The Windhover' Mean?," in Norman Weyand, S. J., ed., *Immortal Diamond*. (New York, 1949), and Gardner's analysis in *Gerard Manley Hopkins,* I (New Haven, 1944).

no longer "bleared, smeared with toil," but shines as does a furrow that has met the contact of the plow. The blue-bleak embers that "Fall, gall themselves, and gash gold-vermilion" speak both for Christ and for man. God descended into man as Christ, suffered and illuminated the world. Man is fallen, but may suffer in identity with Christ, and hence cast forth glorious light.

If "The Windhover" dramatizes the reciprocal confrontation of the two aspects of instress, "Hurrahing in Harvest," written in the month Hopkins was ordained, is a sort of coda, a description, after this experience, of the transfigured world. In contrast to his method in "God's Grandeur" and "Spring," he now looks at the world in his own person, aware that the self must be out of hiding to see God and be godlike. Hopkins lifts up his heart to the world's glory and receives from the Saviour who is in the world "Rapturous love's greeting." Beauties have always been present in the bright wings of the Holy Ghost or the wings of the windhover, but his self is now so emancipated that he can freely perceive them and in fact become them, gaining wings too:

These things, these things were here and but the beholder
   Wanting; which two when they once meet,
The heart rears wings bold and bolder
   And hurls for him, O half hurls earth for him off under his feet.

Because he is instinct with Christ and the earth is instinct with Christ, the dramatic paradox is that to meet the earth is almost to leave the earth. Time so shows eternity that it almost loses itself. It is a radical moment for Hopkins's poetry: the inscape, the autumnal scene is so dominated by the union of reciprocal energies that it "half " disappears altogether. The "half " is crucial. No instress can be realized without the actual form that expresses it. In "The Half-way House" Hopkins has told us that to see God he must indeed see. A poem, the quest for and the show of vision, is vitally necessary to his belief; it is at once a jumping-off place and a focus of faith.

The second period, the period of Hopkins's priesthood, is heralded by "Binsey Poplars." The poem is at once an epitaph for some of his favorite poplars which are felled, and a taking leave of natural inscapes. (Such poems as "Ribblesdale" are rare reversions.) A metaphor at the poem's center has far-reaching implications for his poetry:

> Since country is so tender
> To touch, her being só slender,
> That, like this sleek and seeing ball
> But a prick will make no eye at all.

Nature, as we have seen, provides a sort of eye on God for Hopkins. When it is destroyed, it is as if he were suddenly deprived of vision. But since he knows the necessity of finding an exact form for seeing God, and since he is now occupied with priestly duties, he turns to his fellow man and makes him his inscape.

He turns first to other selves, like Duns Scotus and Henry Purcell, who have by their own active perceptions met divine energy. The poems about these men are analogous to "God's Grandeur" and "Spring" in the first period because the aspect of the poet's subjective instress is hidden, only implicit. But in later poems he turns to living men with whom he has some relation and sees them as forms of divine energy through his own dynamic relation to them. The analogy between Hopkins's inscaping of man and his earlier inscaping of nature breaks down, of course, when we consider that he is a priest. Men, no matter how beautiful they are physically, become full expressions of divine energy only when they have been helped to do so by Hopkins's own agency. His urgent anxieties at the end of "The Bugler's First Communion" and "The Handsome Heart" are based on his knowledge that divinity's residence in men is precarious. In "Felix Randal" this awareness is transformed, as was his disparagement of his own mere flesh in "The Windhover," and for some of the same reasons. In both poems his own person is fully engaged, his heart comes out of hiding. The octave laments the death of the beautiful lad whose sickness first caused him to curse and then, with the help of the priest, bred in him a "heavenlier heart." The first three lines of the sestet enact syntactically the interplay between the energies of the two men, the reciprocal energies of sympathy:

This seeing the sick endears them to us, us too it endears.
My tongue had taught thee comfort, touch had quenched thy tears,
Thy tears that touched my heart, child, Felix, poor Felix Randal.

The meeting of the two aspects of instress is caught in the pun on
"touch": Felix's tears touched the priest; his responsive touch removed the tears, dried the tears by quenching them. The poem's
special brilliance lies in its conclusion, in the restrospective vision of
Felix's still unconverted strength:

How far from then forethought of, all thy more boisterous years,
When thou at the random grim forge, powerful amidst peers,
Didst fettle for the great grey drayhorse his bright and battering
    sandal!

Ostensibly this is a praise of mere physical beauty. But we know
from the Sermon for Sunday evening, 23 November 1879, at Bedford
Leigh that the manly beauty of Christ was a subject of long medita-
tion for Hopkins.[6] And the vision of Felix making the shoe is shot
through with the realization that he would become Christlike. The
bright and battering sandal holds in balance its maker's brute beauty
and his potentiality to gash gold-vermilion. As an object it may even
be said to stand for the tough realization that "shéer plód makes
plough down sillion / Shine." In short, the last lines stand for Hopkins's ability to carry the strength of wisdom he gained from his mutual sympathy with Felix back into the world where that experience
is not yet realized. Felix Randal is dead, but the poem and the in-
scaped reality of the sandal give form to the reciprocal instress
Hopkins experienced.

"The Candle Indoors" was written a little earlier in the same period, but points, I think, to the sort of problem Hopkins will be
dealing with in the third period. Hopkins is here concerned with
human beings to whom he bears no real relation. They are "Jessy
or Jack," two people sitting by a candle seen through a window.
Light has ever represented for Hopkins the presence of God in

[6] Christopher, S. J., ed., *The Sermons and Devotional Writings of Gerard Manley Hopkins*
(London, 1959), pp. 35–36.

nature or Christ in man. He looks at the man and woman, searching for some evidence in them of divine energy. But the scene is
characterized by a vagueness unusual in Hopkins ("Some candle
clear burns somewhere," "what task what fingers ply") and Hopkins
is unable to inscape it. The light then is like the light of "vacant
creation's lamps"; it too appals. His reaction is by now characteristic;
he realizes that he has been looking simply for objective energy
without sending it out from himself. He cannot find form because
he is cut off from the light. He resolves, therefore, to retreat within
himself:

> Come you indoors, come home; your fading fire
> Mend first and vital candle in close heart's vault:
> You there are master, do your own desire.

He knows he must crowd closer to his inner light, "have, get" more
Christ in himself to be able to see Christ outside again. And light,
since it is Christ's truth, will make him master of himself; love will be
so self-evident that to mend his heart will be simply to fulfill his desire. For lack of answer outdoors he has gone indoors to himself, but
he does not find final answers there. The poem ends with a series of
accusing questions:

> What hinders? Are you beam-blind, yet to a fault
> In a neighbour deft-handed? Are you that liar
> And, cast by conscience out, spendsavour salt?

In the last period Hopkins retrenches, goes home to himself to
face these questions. Paradoxically, the metaphorical attempt to go
home coexists with Hopkins's actual exile, his period of teaching in
Ireland. Hopkins's unhappiness there partly accounts for the difficulties he had in accepting himself "at home." In the sonnet, "To
seem the stranger lies my lot," he says he is "at a thírd / Remove." In
England he had alienated his family by his conversion; now his isolation is complicated by his geographical separation from England
itself, which he calls "wife / To my creating thought." England, as
we saw, provided first natural beauty, then men, as matter to inscape. In Ireland, Hopkins's chariness with his own freedom to
explore and his reluctance to cultivate acquaintance deprived his
thought of wives. He was thrown upon himself and that self was rid-

den by illness, overwork, and depression. We cannot look then to find in his inscaping of himself a meeting of powerful energies. Rather, one of the greatest sources of torments in the "terrible sonnets" is Hopkins's painful awareness that such a meeting is withheld. The value of confrontation and union is expressed nowhere more forcefully than here when they are beyond attainment. The frustration described comes from the denial of full religious experience, but in "Thou art indeed just, Lord," Hopkins openly laments too his artistic sterility:

> birds build—but not I build; no, but strain,
> Time's eunuch, and not breed one work that wakes.
> Mine, O thou lord of life, send my roots rain.

It is possible that the force of anguish in the other sonnets derives from Hopkins's sense that writing is threatened when union with God is frustrated.

Thus although the terrible sonnets set up a sort of dialogue by splitting the self into two warring persons, the parts of the self do not inform one another; they are isolated from all outside and from each other. The situation of the early nature poems, in which Hopkins did not bring enough of himself to experience, is drastically reversed. Now Hopkins is all self, and does not allow external energies to affect him. In "I wake and feel the fell of dark, not day," the hopelessness of his predicament is clear. In "The Candle Indoors" he could not find meaning in the candle-light, but there was no question of the light's existence. Now, in "Thou are indeed just, Lord," even the reality of daylight is unavailable because his inner light is quenched. Prayer then is hopeless, moving from dark to dark.

> And my lament
> Is cries countless, cries like dead letters sent
> To dearest him that lives alas! away.

The doctrine that self-definition is always meaningful ("the rehearsal Of own, of abrúpt sélf " so praised in "Henry Purcell") now recoils on itself with a vengeance. "God's most deep decree / Bitter would have me taste: my taste was me." (Is there perhaps a play on "taste," as preference, here?) Left to himself, man can only produce a parody of instress, a meeting of corrupting energies: "Selfyeast of spirit a dull dough sours."

In the same spirit of self-flagellation, Hopkins, in the next sonnet, "Patience, hard thing! the hard thing but to pray," mocks the idea of relief: "Patience who asks / Wants war, wants wounds." The sweating self is incapable of granting to his own heart what he asks of God. Again the prayer is empty. But by the next sonnet the tone is changed. He begins by adopting a Christlike tone towards himself:

> My own heart let me more have pity on; let
> Me live to my sad self hereafter kind,
> Charitable; not live this tormented mind
> With this tormented mind tormenting yet.

The way out of the hopeless defeating humility of self-hatred is the way of kindness to oneself, a way that is only at first glance less humble. As the conclusion of the poem shows, the minimal gesture of kindness allows for a real humility:

> Soul, self; come, poor Jackself, I do advise
> You, jaded, let be; call off thoughts awhile
> Elsewhere; leave comfort root-room; let joy size
> At God knows when to God knows what.

We now see that the inscaping of the mere self failed because it precluded the possibility of external energy, of mercy; the humility of hatred was in fact pride.

It is by the granting of this minimal kindness to himself, by refusing the luxury of despair, that "Carrion Comfort" becomes a great poem in Hopkins's own terms. Here Hopkins's racked self is the meeting-place of the two aspects of instress—the energy of a terrible God and the energy of Hopkins's tortured mind which will not yield to the despair which shuts out God. Even in the agony there is release not unlike that of "Hurrahing in Harvest" for he is purged of chaff and can lap strength. And his prayers, or questions, unlike those in the other terrible sonnets, get answers. Tortured, he asks why and he is answered, that he may be purged. Even in its agony, the poem involves a joining of identities not unlike that in "The Windhover," for in the wrestling he is not able to tell whose is the joy, his or God's. His heart "would laugh, chéer":

> Cheer whom though? the hero whose heaven-handling flung
>    me, fóot tród
> Me? or me that fought him? O which one? is it each one?
>    That night, that year
> Of now done darkness I wretch lay wrestling with (my God!)
>    my God.

In the terrible repetition of the last line, in the cry of man and the deeply accepted vision of God, are joined at last, and sealed in words, divine original energy and the energy of response.

Three years later, Hopkins performs his last great devotion in "That Nature is a Heraclitean Fire and of the comfort of the Resurrection." The furthest ranging of his poems, it is held together by the mature insight gleaned in "Carrion Comfort" that purgation is the condition of union with God. The "dead" Christian in Hopkins has been brought to life again through that poem's discovery that union may be wrung from man. Now the poet enables the priest to relive at once the great phases of his life, inscaping for him nature, man, and self in a massive but fresh unity. The variegated face nature shows is not unlike that it showed in many of the poems in the early period, but its variegation is no beautiful evidence of the creator, and there is no one masterful natural form. The sense of change is dazzling, frantic, finally terrifying in its universality, born of all elements. And it is significant that man emerges first, not with a beautiful body, as in the poems of the middle period, but as part of the primordial slime, notable only for the temporary physical impression he makes in the total fluctuation: "stanches, starches / Squadroned masks and manmarks | treadmire toil there / Footfretted in it." All nature is a bonfire in which the individual sparks of mankind are darkly drowned (the imagery is deliberately paradoxical as we shall see). Hopkins cries out, "O pity and indig | nation! Manshape, that shone / Sheer off, disseveral, a star | death blots black out." It is at this point that the thought of the Resurrection cancels his despairing cry. Here is the triumphant realization that although nature is all fire, it is not the ultimate fire: although it is continuous in man's experience, it cannot rival the beacon, the "eternal beam" of Resurrection. Nature consumes man, but only in the illusory way that a big fire appears to drown a smaller one, for fire cannot drown fire. One can resign the flesh to the worm, the world to ash, because of the recognition that as Christ is immortal so is the core of the self:

> In a flash, at a trumpet crash,
> I am all at once what Christ is, | since he was what I am, and
> This Jack, joke, poor potsherd, | patch, matchwood, immortal
>     diamond,
> Is immortal diamond.

Although this poem differs from those in the first two periods by allowing neither a sacramental nature to express God, nor a beautiful being to express Christ, it works in an analogous way. The inscape is different, presenting a ruthless nature and a puny man, but it serves the purpose of devotion in the same ways. It demonstrates that the energies of destruction meet the energies of indestructibility in the fact that Christ lived as a man in this flaming world.

# Sources and Acknowledgments

G. S. FRASER, "Macaulay's Style as an Essayist," *Review of English Literature* (October 1960) 9–19, republished by permission of the author and of the editors of *REL,* published by Longmans. Mr. Fraser is the author of many essays and several volumes, among them *The Modern Writer and His World, Yeats, Ezra Pound.*

WALTER E. HOUGHTON, "The Issue Between Kingsley and Newman," *Theology Today* (April, 1947) 80–101, reprinted by permission of the editors of *Theology Today.* Professor Houghton is at Wellesley College. Among his most important works are *The Victorian Frame of Mind, The Poetry of Clough, Victorian Poetry and Poetics* (with Robert Stange). Mr. and Mrs. Houghton are largely responsible for the forthcoming *Wellesley Index to Victorian Periodicals, 1824–1900,* an important research tool for all scholars of the period.

ASA BRIGGS, "Trollope, Bagehot, and the English Constitution," *The Cambridge Journal* (1952) 327–338, reprinted by permission of Bowes and Bowes Publishers Ltd., London. Professor Briggs is Pro-Vice-Chancellor (Planning) at the University of Sussex. He is the author of *Victorian People, Victorian Cities, The Age of Improvement, Chartist Studies,* and other works.

JOHN PETTIGREW, "Tennyson's *Ulysses:* A Reconciliation of Opposites," *Victorian Poetry* (January, 1963) 27–45. Reprinted by permission of the editors of *Victorian Poetry.* Mr. Pettigrew teaches at Trinity College, University of Toronto in Canada.

ROBERT O. PREYER, "Two Styles in the Verse of Robert Browning," *English Literary History* (March, 1965) 62–84. Professor Preyer is Chairman of the Department of English and American Literature at Brandeis University, author of *Bentham, Coleridge, and The Science of History* and a number of essays and studies.

KENNETH ALLOTT, "The Introduction" to *Matthew Arnold: A Selection of His Poems,* edited with an introduction by Kenneth Allott, The Penguin Poets series, 1954. Reprinted by permission of the publishers, Penguin Books Ltd. Dr. Allott is A. C. Bradley Professor of English Literature, University of Liverpool, and editor of *The Poems of Matthew Arnold* and co-author, with his wife, of *The Art of Graham Greene.*

C. B. COX, "A Dickens Landscape," *The Critical Quarterly* (Spring, 1960) 58–60. Reprinted by permission of the editors of *The Critical Quarterly.* Professor Cox is at The University, Hull, and is an editor of *The Critical Quarterly* as well as a critic, editor of *Dylan Thomas: A Collection of Critical Essays* and other writings.

JULIAN MOYNAHAN, "The Hero's Guilt: The Case of *Great Expectations,*" *Essays in Criticism* (January, 1960) 60–79 reprinted by permission of the editors of *Essays in Criticism,* Oxford. Julian Moynahan is a Professor at Rutgers University and the author of a novel, *Brother and Sister,* and a well known volume on D. H. Lawrence, among other writings.

GABRIEL PEARSON, "Dickens and His Readers," *Universities and Left Review* (now *New Left Review*) (Spring, 1957) 52–60, reprinted by permission of the publisher, *New Left Review,* London. Mr. Pearson has recently edited a collection of critical essays on Dickens.

JOHN A. LESTER, JR., "Thackeray's Narrative Technique," reprinted by permission of the Modern Language Association from *PMLA* (June, 1954) 392–409. Dr. Lester is a Professor at Haverford College.

GEORGE LEVINE, "Determinism and Responsibility in the Works of George Eliot," reprinted by permission of the Modern Language

Association from  *PMLA* (June, 1962) 268–279. Mr. Levine teaches at Indiana University and is an editor of *Victorian Studies*.

RAYMOND WILLIAMS, "Thomas Hardy," *Critical Quarterly* (Winter, 1964) 341–351, reprinted by permission of the author and his publisher, Chatto and Windus Ltd., London. Raymond Williams is best known for *Culture and Society 1780–1950, The Long Revolution,* and *Drama From Ibsen to Eliot.* He is at Jesus College, Cambridge.

BELL GALE CHEVIGNY, "Instress and Devotion in the Poetry of Gerard Manley Hopkins," *Victorian Studies* (December, 1965) 141–153, reprinted by permission of the author and the editors of *Victorian Studies*. Mrs. Chevigny teaches at Queens College, The City University of New York.

# harper ✦ torchbooks

W. A. DUNNING: Reconstruction, Political and Economic: 1865-1877    TB/1073
HAROLD U. FAULKNER: Politics, Reform and Expansion: 1890-1900. † Illus.    TB/3020
ROBERT GREEN MC CLOSKEY: American Conservatism in the Age of Enterprise: 1865-1910    TB/1137
ARTHUR MANN: Yankee Reformers in the Urban Age: Social Reform in Boston, 1880-1900    TB/1247
CHARLES H. SHINN: Mining Camps: A Study in American Frontier Government. ‡ Ed. by R. W. Paul    TB/3062
VERNON LANE WHARTON: The Negro in Mississippi: 1865-1890    TB/1178

## American Studies: 1900 to the Present

A. RUSSELL BUCHANAN: The United States and World War II. † Illus.    Vol. I TB/3044; Vol. II TB/3045
FOSTER RHEA DULLES: America's Rise to World Power: 1898-1954. † Illus.    TB/3021
JOHN D. HICKS: Republican Ascendancy: 1921-1933. † Illus.    TB/3041
SIDNEY HOOK: Reason, Social Myths, and Democracy    TB/1237
WILLIAM E. LEUCHTENBURG: Franklin D. Roosevelt and the New Deal: 1932-1940. † Illus.    TB/3025
ARTHUR S. LINK: Woodrow Wilson and the Progressive Era: 1910-1917. † Illus.    TB/3023
GEORGE E. MOWRY: The Era of Theodore Roosevelt and the Birth of Modern America: 1900-1912. † Illus.    TB/3022
RUSSEL B. NYE: Midwestern Progressive Politics: 1870-1958    TB/1202
JACOB RIIS: The Making of an American. ‡ Edited by Roy Lubove    TB/3070
PHILIP SELZNICK: TVA and the Grass Roots: A Study in the Sociology of Formal Organization    TB/1230
IDA M. TARBELL: The History of the Standard Oil Company: Briefer Version. ‡ Edited by David M. Chalmers    TB/3071
GEORGE B. TINDALL, Ed.: A Populist Reader ‡    TB/3069

## Anthropology

JACQUES BARZUN: Race: A Study in Superstition. Revised Edition    TB/1172
JOSEPH B. CASAGRANDE, Ed.: In the Company of Man: Portraits of Anthropological Informants    TB/3047
W. E. LE GROS CLARK: The Antecedents of Man: Intro. to Evolution of the Primates. ° △ Illus.    TB/559
CORA DU BOIS: The People of Alor. New Preface by the author. Illus.    Vol. I TB/1042; Vol. II TB/1043
DAVID LANDY: Tropical Childhood: Cultural Transmission and Learning in a Puerto Rican Village TB/1235
L. S. B. LEAKEY: Adam's Ancestors: The Evolution of Man and His Culture. △ Illus.    TB/1019
ROBERT H. LOWIE: Primitive Society. Introduction by Fred Eggan    TB/1056
EDWARD BURNETT TYLOR: The Origins of Culture. Part I of "Primitive Culture." § Intro. by Paul Radin    TB/33
EDWARD BURNETT TYLOR: Religion in Primitive Culture. Part II of "Primitive Culture." § Intro. by Paul Radin    TB/34
W. LLOYD WARNER: A Black Civilization: A Study of an Australian Tribe. ¶ Illus.    TB/3056

## Art and Art History

WALTER LOWRIE: Art in the Early Church. Revised Edition. 452 illus.    TB/124
EMILE MÂLE: The Gothic Image: Religious Art in France of the Thirteenth Century. § △ 190 illus.    TB/44
MILLARD MEISS: Painting in Florence and Siena after the Black Death. 169 illus.    TB/1148
ERICH NEUMANN: The Archetypal World of Henry Moore. △ 107 illus.    TB/2020
DORA & ERWIN PANOFSKY: Pandora's Box: The Changing Aspects of a Mythical Symbol    TB/2021
ERWIN PANOFSKY: Studies in Iconology: Humanistic Themes in the Art of the Renaissance △    TB/1077

ALEXANDRE PIANKOFF: The Shrines of Tut-Ankh-Amon. Edited by N. Rambova. 117 illus.    TB/2011
JEAN SEZNEC: The Survival of the Pagan Gods △ TB/2004
OTTO VON SIMSON: The Gothic Cathedral △    TB/2018
HEINRICH ZIMMER: Myths and Symbols in Indian Art and Civilization. 70 illus.    TB/2005

## Business, Economics & Economic History

REINHARD BENDIX: Work and Authority in Industry    TB/3035
GILBERT BURCK & EDITORS OF FORTUNE: The Computer Age: And Its Potential for Management    TB/1179
ROBERT DAHL & CHARLES E. LINDBLOM: Politics, Economics, and Welfare    TB/3037
PETER F. DRUCKER: The New Society: The Anatomy of Industrial Order △    TB/1082
EDITORS OF FORTUNE: America in the Sixties: The Economy and the Society    TB/1015
ROBERT L. HEILBRONER: The Great Ascent: The Struggle for Economic Development in Our Time    TB/3030
ROBERT L. HEILBRONER: The Limits of American Capitalism    TB/1305
FRANK H. KNIGHT: The Economic Organization TB/1214
FRANK H. KNIGHT: Risk, Uncertainty and Profit    TB/1215
ABBA P. LERNER: Everybody's Business    TB/3051
PAUL MANTOUX: The Industrial Revolution in the Eighteenth Century ° △    TB/1079
HERBERT SIMON: The Shape of Automation: For Men and Management    TB/1245
PERRIN STRYKER: The Character of the Executive: Eleven Studies in Managerial Qualities    TB/1041

## Contemporary Culture

JACQUES BARZUN: The House of Intellect △    TB/1051
CLARK KERR: The Uses of the University    TB/1264
JOHN U. NEF: Cultural Foundations of Industrial Civilization △    TB/1024
NATHAN M. PUSEY: The Age of the Scholar: Observations on Education in a Troubled Decade    TB/1157
PAUL VALÉRY: The Outlook for Intelligence △.    TB/2016

## Historiography & Philosophy of History

JACOB BURCKHARDT: On History and Historians. △ Intro. by H. R. Trevor-Roper    TB/1216
J. H. HEXTER: Reappraisals in History: New Views on History & Society in Early Modern Europe △ TB/1100
H. STUART HUGHES: History as Art and as Science: Twin Vistas on the Past    TB/1207
ARNALDO MOMIGLIANO: Studies in Historiography ° △    TB/1288
GEORGE H. NADEL, Ed.: Studies in the Philosophy of History: Essays from History and Theory    TB/1208
KARL P. POPPER: The Open Society and Its Enemies △ Vol. I: The Spell of Plato TB/1101; Vol. II: The High Tide of Prophecy: Hegel, Marx and the Aftermath TB/1102
KARL R. POPPER: The Poverty of Historicism ° △ TB/1126
G. J. RENIER: History: Its Purpose and Method △ TB/1209
W. H. WALSH: Philosophy of History △    TB/1020

## History: General

L. CARRINGTON GOODRICH: A Short History of the Chinese People. △ Illus.    TB/3015
DAN N. JACOBS & HANS H. BAERWALD: Chinese Communism: Selected Documents    TB/3031
BERNARD LEWIS: The Arabs in History △    TB/1029
BERNARD LEWIS: The Middle East and the West ° △    TB/1274

## History: Ancient

A. ANDREWES: The Greek Tyrants △    TB/1103
ADOLF ERMAN, Ed.: The Ancient Egyptians    TB/1233
MICHAEL GRANT: Ancient History ° △    TB/1190
SAMUEL NOAH KRAMER: Sumerian Mythology    TB/1055
NAPHTALI LEWIS & MEYER REINHOLD, Eds.: Roman Civilization. Sourcebook I: The Republic TB/1231; Sourcebook II: The Empire TB/1232

2

3

CARL J. FRIEDRICH: The Age of the Baroque, 1610-1660. *
Illus.                                                TB/3004
RENÉ FUELOP-MLILER: The Mind and Face of Bolshe-
vism                                                  TB/1188
M. DOROTHY GEORGE: London Life in the Eighteenth
Century △                                             TB/1182
C. C. GILLISPIE: Genesis and Geology: The Decades
before Darwin §                                       TB/51
ALBERT GOODWIN: The French Revolution △               TB/1064
ALBERT GUÉRARD: France in the Classical Age △  TB/1183
CARLTON J. H. HAYES: A Generation of Materialism, 1871-
1900. * Illus.                                        TB/3039
J. H. HEXTER: Reappraisals in History △               TB/1100
STANLEY HOFFMANN et al.: In Search of France   TB/1219
A. R. HUMPHREYS: The Augustan World: Society and
and Letters in 18th Century England ° △        TB/1105
DAN N. JACOBS, Ed.: The New Communist Manifesto
& Related Documents. Third edition, revised   TB/1078
LIONEL KOCHAN: The Struggle for Germany: 1914-45
                                                      TB/1304
HANS KOHN: The Mind of Germany △                      TB/1204
HANS KOHN, Ed.: The Mind of Modern Russia: Historical
and Political Thought of Russia's Great Age  TB/1065
WALTER LAQUEUR & GEORGE L MOSSE, Eds.: International
Fascism, 1920-1945 ° △                                TB/1276
WALTER LAQUEUR & GEORGE L. MOSSE, Eds.: Left-Wing
Intellectuals Between the Wars, 1919-1939 ° △ TB/1286
WALTER LAQUEUR & GEORGE L. MOSSE, Eds.: 1914: The
Coming of the First World War ° △                     TB/1306
FRANK E. MANUEL: The Prophets of Paris: Turgot, Con-
dorcet, Saint-Simon, Fourier, and Comte       TB/1218
KINGSLEY MARTIN: French Liberal Thought in the
Eighteenth Century                                    TB/1114
L. B. NAMIER: Facing East: Essays on Germany, the Bal-
kans, and Russia △                                    TB/1280
L. B. NAMIER: Personalities and Powers △              TB/1186
L. B. NAMIER: Vanished Supremacies: Essays on Euro-
pean History, 1812-1918 ° △                           TB/1088
JOHN U. NEF: Western Civilization Since the Renais-
sance: Peace, War, Industry, and the Arts     TB/1113
FRANZ NEUMANN: Behemoth: National Socialism, 1933-
1944 △                                                TB/1289
FREDERICK L. NUSSBAUM: The Triumph of Science and
Reason, 1660-1685. * Illus.                           TB/3009
DAVID OGG: Europe of the Ancien Régime, 1715-
1783 ** ° △                                           TB/1271
JOHN PLAMENATZ. German Marxism and Russian Com-
munism ° △                                            TB/1189
RAYMOND W. POSTGATE, Ed.: Revolution from 1789 to
1906: Selected Documents                              TB/1063
WILLIAM PRESTON, JR.: Aliens and Dissenters: Federal
Suppression of Radicals, 1903-1933            TB/1287
PENFIELD ROBERTS: The Quest for Security, 1715-1740. *
Illus.                                                TB/3016
PRISCILLA ROBERTSON: Revolutions of 1848: A Social
History                                               TB/1025
GEORGE RUDÉ: Revolutionary Europe, 1783-1815 ** ° △
                                                      TB/1272
LOUIS, DUC DE SAINT-SIMON: Versailles, The Court, and
Louis XIV △                                           TB/1250
A. J. P. TAYLOR: From Napoleon to Lenin: Historical
Essays ° △                                            TB/1268
A. J. P. TAYLOR: The Habsburg Monarchy, 1809-1918 ° △
                                                      TB/1187
G. M. TREVELYAN: British History in the Nineteenth Cen-
tury and After: 1782-1919 ° △                         TB/1251
H. R. TREVOR-ROPER: Historical Essays ° △             TB/1269
ELIZABETH WISKEMANN: Europe of the Dictators, 1919-
1945 ** ° △                                           TB/1273
JOHN B. WOLF: The Emergence of the Great Powers,
1685-1715. * Illus.                                   TB/3010
JOHN B. WOLF: France: 1814-1919: The Rise of a Liberal-
Democratic Society                                    TB/3019

## Intellectual History & History of Ideas

HERSCHEL BAKER: The Image of Man                       TB/1047
R. R. BOLGAR: The Classical Heritage and Its Benefici-
aries △                                               TB/1125
J. BRONOWSKI & BRUCE MAZLISH: The Western Intellectual
Tradition: From Leonardo to Hegel △            TB/3001
NORMAN COHN: Pursuit of the Millennium △              TB/1037
C. C. GILLISPIE: Genesis and Geology: The Decades be-
fore Darwin §                                         TB/51
ARTHUR O. LOVEJOY: The Great Chain of Being: A Study
of the History of an Idea                             TB/1009
FRANK E. MANUEL: The Prophets of Paris: Turgot, Con-
dorcet, Saint-Simon, Fourier, and Comte       TB/1218
RALPH BARTON PERRY: The Thought and Character of
William James: Briefer Version                        TB/1156
BRUNO SNELL: The Discovery of the Mind: The Greek
Origins of European Thought △                         TB/1018
PAUL VALÉRY: The Outlook for Intelligence △    TB/2016
W. WARREN WAGAR, Ed.: European Intellectual History
since Darwin and Marx                                 TB/1297
PHILIP P. WIENER: Evolution and the Founders of Prag-
matism. △ Foreword by John Dewey              TB/1212

## Literature, Poetry, The Novel & Criticism

JACQUES BARZUN: The House of Intellect △              TB/1051
W. J. BATE: From Classic to Romantic: Premises of Taste
in Eighteenth Century England                         TB/1036
JAMES BOSWELL: The Life of Dr. Johnson & The Journal
of a Tour to the Hebrides with Samuel Johnson
LL.D.: Selections ° △                                 TB/1254
ERNST R. CURTIUS: European Literature and the Latin
Middle Ages △                                         TB/2015
ALFRED HARBAGE: As They Liked It: A Study of Shakes-
peare's Moral Artistry                                TB/1035
A. R. HUMPHREYS: The Augustan World: Society in 18th
Century England ° △                                   TB/1105
ALDOUS HUXLEY: Antic Hay & The Giaconda Smile. ° △
Introduction by Martin Green                          TB/3503
ALDOUS HUXLEY: Brave New World & Brave New World
Revisited. ° △ Introduction by Martin Green   TB/3501
HENRY JAMES: The Tragic Muse                          TB/1017
ARNOLD KETTLE: An Introduction to the English Novel. △
Volume I: Defoe to George Eliot                       TB/1011
Volume II: Henry James to the Present         TB/1012
RICHMOND LATTIMORE: The Poetry of Greek Tragedy △
                                                      TB/1257
J. B. LEISHMAN: The Monarch of Wit: An Analytical and
Comparative Study of the Poetry of John Donne ° △
                                                      TB/1258
J. B. LEISHMAN: Themes and Variations in Shakespeare's
Sonnets ° △                                           TB/1259
SAMUEL PEPYS: The Diary of Samuel Pepys. ° Edited by
O. F. Morshead. Illus. by Ernest Shepard      TB/1007
ST.-JOHN PERSE: Seamarks                              TB/2002
V. DE S. PINTO: Crisis in English Poetry, 1880-1940 ° △
                                                      TB/1260
ROBERT PREYER, Ed.: Victorian Literature             TB/1302
GEORGE SANTAYANA: Interpretations of Poetry and Re-
ligion §                                              TB/9
C. K. STEAD: The New Poetic ° △                       TB/1263
HEINRICH STRAUMANN: American Literature in the
Twentieth Century. △ Third Edition, Revised  TB/1168
PAGET TOYNBEE: Dante Alighieri: His Life and Works.
Edited with Intro. by Charles S. Singleton   TB/1206
DOROTHY VAN GHENT: The English Novel                  TB/1050
E. B. WHITE: One Man's Meat.                          TB/3505
BASIL WILLEY: Nineteenth Century Studies: Coleridge to
Matthew Arnold ° △                                    TB/1261
BASIL WILLEY: More Nineteenth Century Studies: A
Group of Honest Doubters ° △                          TB/1262
RAYMOND WILLIAMS: Culture and Society, 1780-1950 ° △
                                                      TB/1252
RAYMOND WILLIAMS: The Long Revolution ° △             TB/1253
MORTON DAUWEN ZABEL, Editor: Literary Opinion in
America          Vol. I  TB/3013; Vol. II  TB/3014

RALPH BARTON PERRY: Puritanism and Democracy
TB/1138
WALTER RAUSCHENBUSCH: Christianity and the Social
Crisis. ‡ Edited by Robert D. Cross        TB/3059
TIMOTHY L. SMITH: Revivalism and Social Reform: Amer-
ican Protestantism on the Eve of the Civil War △
TB/1229
ERNST TROELTSCH: The Social Teaching of the Christian
Churches ᵒ △          Vol. I  TB/71;  Vol. II  TB/72

# NATURAL SCIENCES
# AND MATHEMATICS

## Biological Sciences

CHARLOTTE AUERBACH: The Science of Genetics Σ △
TB/568
MARSTON BATES: The Natural History of Mosquitoes.
Illus.                                        TB/578
A. BELLAIRS: Reptiles: Life History, Evolution, and
Structure. △ Illus.                           TB/520
LUDWIG VON BERTALANFFY: Modern Theories of Develop-
ment: An Introduction to Theoretical Biology  TB/554
LUDWIG VON BERTALANFFY: Problems of Life △    TB/521
HAROLD F. BLUM: Time's Arrow and Evolution   TB/555
JOHN TYLER BONNER: The Ideas of Biology Σ △  TB/570
A. J. CAIN: Animal Species and Their Evolution △ TB/519
WALTER B. CANNON: Bodily Changes in Pain, Hunger,
Fear and Rage. Illus.                         TB/562
W. E. LE GROS CLARK: The Antecedents of Man ᵒ △
TB/559
W. H. DOWDESWELL: Animal Ecology. △ Illus.   TB/543
W. H. DOWDESWELL: The Mechanism of Evolution △
TB/527
R. W. GERARD: Unresting Cells. Illus.         TB/541
DAVID LACK: Darwin's Finches. △ Illus.        TB/544
ADOLF PORTMANN: Animals as Social Beings ᵒ △ TB/572
O. W. RICHARDS: The Social Insects. △ Illus.  TB/542
P. M. SHEPPARD: Natural Selection and Heredity △ TB/528
EDMUND W. SINNOTT: Cell and Psyche: The Biology of
Purpose                                        TB/546
C. H. WADDINGTON: How Animals Develop. △ Illus.
TB/553
C. H. WADDINGTON: The Nature of Life △        TB/580

## Chemistry

J. R. PARTINGTON: A Short History of Chemistry △ TB/522

## Communication Theory

J. R. PIERCE: Symbols, Signals and Noise: The Nature
and Process of Communication △                TB/574

## Geography

R. E. COKER: This Great and Wide Sea: An Introduction
to Oceanography and Marine Biology. Illus.  TB/551
F. K. HARE: The Restless Atmosphere △         TB/560

## History of Science

MARIE BOAS: The Scientific Renaissance, 1450-1630 ᵒ △
TB/583
W. DAMPIER, Ed.: Readings in the Literature of Science.
Illus.                                        TB/512
A. HUNTER DUPREE: Science in the Federal Government:
A History of Policies and Activities to 1940 △ TB/573
ALEXANDRE KOYRÉ: From the Closed World to the Infinite
Universe: Copernicus, Kepler, Galileo, Newton, etc. △
TB/31
A. G. VAN MELSEN: From Atomos to Atom: A History of
the Concept Atom                              TB/517

O. NEUGEBAUER: The Exact Sciences in Antiquity  TB/552
HANS THIRRING: Energy for Man △               TB/556
STEPHEN TOULMIN & JUNE GOODFIELD: The Architecture
of Matter: Physics, Chemistry & Physiology of Mat-
ter, Since the Beginning of Science ᵒ △       TB/584
STEPHEN TOULMIN & JUNE GOODFIELD: The Discovery of
Time ᵒ △                                      TB/585
LANCELOT LAW WHYTE: Essay on Atomism △        TB/565

## Mathematics

E. W. BETH: The Foundations of Mathematics △  TB/581
H. DAVENPORT: The Higher Arithmetic △         TB/526
H. G. FORDER: Geometry: An Introduction △     TB/548
S. KÖRNER: The Philosophy of Mathematics △    TB/547
D. E. LITTLEWOOD: Skeleton Key of Mathematics: A
Simple Account of Complex Algebraic Problems △
TB/525
GEORGE E. OWEN: Fundamentals of Scientific Mathe-
matics                                         TB/569
WILLARD VAN ORMAN QUINE: Mathematical Logic  TB/558
O. G. SUTTON: Mathematics in Action. ᵒ △ Illus.  TB/518
FREDERICK WAISMANN: Introduction to Mathematical
Thinking. Foreword by Karl Menger             TB/511

## Philosophy of Science

R. B. BRAITHWAITE: Scientific Explanation     TB/515
J. BRONOWSKI: Science and Human Values. Revised and
Enlarged Edition △                            TB/505
ALBERT EINSTEIN et al.: Albert Einstein: Philosopher-
Scientist. Edited by Paul A. Schilpp  Vol. I  TB/502
                                       Vol. II  TB/503
WERNER HEISENBERG: Physics and Philosophy: The Revo-
lution in Modern Science △                    TB/549
JOHN MAYNARD KEYNES: A Treatise on Probability. ᵒ △
Introduction by N. R. Hanson                  TB/557
KARL R. POPPER: The Logic of Scientific Discovery △
TB/576
STEPHEN TOULMIN: Foresight and Understanding: An
Enquiry into the Aims of Science. △ Foreword by
Jacques Barzun                                TB/564
STEPHEN TOULMIN: The Philosophy of Science △  TB/513
G. J. WHITROW: The Natural Philosophy of Time ᵒ △
TB/563

## Physics and Cosmology

JOHN E. ALLEN: Aerodynamics: A Space Age Survey △
TB/582
STEPHEN TOULMIN & JUNE GOODFIELD: The Fabric of the
Heavens: The Development of Astronomy and Dy-
namics. △ Illus.                              TB/579
DAVID BOHM: Causality and Chance in Modern Physics. △
Foreword by Louis de Broglie                  TB/536
P. W. BRIDGMAN: The Nature of Thermodynamics
TB/537
P. W. BRIDGMAN: A Sophisticate's Primer of Relativity △
TB/575
A. C. CROMBIE, Ed.: Turning Point in Physics  TB/535
C. V. DURELL: Readable Relativity △           TB/530
ARTHUR EDDINGTON: Space, Time and Gravitation: An
Outline of the General Relativity Theory      TB/510
GEORGE GAMOW: Biography of Physics Σ △        TB/567
MAX JAMMER: Concepts of Force: A Study in the Founda-
tion of Dynamics                              TB/550
MAX JAMMER: Concepts of Mass in Classical and Modern
Physics                                        TB/571
MAX JAMMER: Concepts of Space: The History of
Theories of Space in Physics. Foreword by Albert
Einstein                                       TB/533
G. J. WHITROW: The Structure and Evolution of the Uni-
verse: An Introduction to Cosmology. △ Illus. TB/504

8